swipe right

A FORBIDDEN ROMANCE

EMERALD BAY
BOOK 1

THEA LAWRENCE

EDITED BY
BEN BROWNING

For those of us who have always lived in someone else's shadow. Shine bright, and shine on.

And for my fellow neurodivergent babes who need a little "academic validation", aka getting dicked down by a hot professor.

also by thea lawrence

THE REVOLVER DUET

Babydoll: A Rockstar Romance

Dollhouse: A Rockstar Romance

PARANORMAL

Heathens: A Vampire Mafia Romance

author's note

A NOTE ON CONTENT:

Imogen has ADHD. I have AuDHD (autism and ADHD). Her experiences are similar to mine and how I navigated academia when I was entrenched in it.

I am still learning so much about my disabilities and how they affect my emotions, my thinking patterns, my reactions, and how I perceive the world around me. Writing has helped with that and even though my experiences may differ from others in terms of how I navigate the world and tell my story, my goal is to write neurodivergent characters who are layered and complex.

There are parts of Roman's past that are left unresolved, and this is based on my own experiences with suicidal ideation as well as losing a friend to suicide. Sometimes, there are no answers and Roman's story is about how we grapple with those questions and the pain that comes along with them.

The very brief discussions on substance abuse are based on my own experiences as a recovering addict as well as my family history.

CONTENT WARNINGS:

This book contains the following explicit content: Explorations of kink, praise kink, impact play, bondage, dom/sub dynamics, rimming/anal play, degradation kink (both the FMC and MMC use it), choking, public sex, voyeurism, exhibitionism, impact play, spit kink, and breeding kink (no pregnancy).

This book also contains topics such as: Open and frank discussions of medically assisted dying, discussions of suicide and its aftermath, light drug use, discussions of mental health issues and addictions of loved ones, explorations of grief, discussions of cancer, the loss of a parent (off page), and the suicide of a spouse (off page).

Your mental health is extremely important. If you or someone you know is experiencing suicidal thoughts or ideation, help is available.

Please go to https://blog.opencounseling.com/suicide-hotlines/ to find resources for your country.

There are reasons to stay.
You are loved, and you are never *ever* alone.

swipe right playlist

If you're reading this on your phone/tablet, clicking the image will take you to the playlist. Happy reading!

The Kinks - A Well Respected Man
Lana Del Rey - West Coast
Taylor Swift - Illicit Affairs
Noah Kahan - Everywhere Everything
Kings of Leon - I Want You
Gordon Lightfoot - Sundown
Taylor Swift - Down Bad
Fleetwood Mac - Silver Springs
Hozier - Shrike
Bush - Comedown
The Goo Goo Dolls - Iris
Taylor Swift - Cowboy Like Me
Glen Campbell - Southern Nights
Passenger - Losing My Religion

Taylor Swift - Lover
Joan Jett & The Blackhearts - Crimson and Clover
Noah Kahan - She Calls Me Back
Hozier - Unknown / Nth
Girl in Red - We Fell in Love in October
Harry Styles - Adore You
Taylor Swift - Labyrinth
Tracy Chapman - Fast Car
Coldplay - Sparks
The Ronettes - Be My Baby

character playlists

IMOGEN FLYNN

ROMAN BURKE

If you're reading this on your phone/tablet, clicking the image will take you to the playlists. Happy reading!

dicktionary

For readers who want to skip the spice, or run right into it, here's a handy dandy (pun absolutely intended) guide!

**Please note that these are all the chapters that feature on-page sexual content

academic glossary

Durkheim: Emile Durkheim was a French sociologist who is considered to be the father of modern sociology, along with Karl Marx and Max Weber. Durkheim's contributions to sociology include: the sociological method, the collective consciousness, organic solidarity, anomie, functionalism, and the causes of suicide.

Goffman: Erving Goffman was a Canadian sociologist most known for his study of symbolic interactionism. He also wrote about stigma, total institutions, and the social construction of the self. One of his most famous contributions to sociology is his theory of dramaturgy. You can find this in a separate definition below.

Bourdieu: Pierre Bourdieu was a French sociologist most famous for his theory of habitus, which is the way we view and respond to the social world by way of skills, character, and social class.

Foucault: Michel Foucault is probably one of the most famous academics. He was a historian, literary critic, political activist, and philosopher. Foucault wrote about power and control and his theoretical frameworks have been used in many disciplines from criminology to literary theory. His most famous work is *Discipline and Punish: The Birth of the Prison*, which is still widely cited by prison scholars today.

Jeremy Bentham: Jeremy Bentham is considered one of the fathers of modern criminology. He was a jurist, philosopher, and legal reformer. He is part of the "classical school" of criminology and invented concepts like the Panopticon.

Panopticon: The panopticon is a concept developed by Jeremy Bentham. It consisted of a multi-level circular building with individual cells and a singular guard tower in the center. The idea of the panopticon was that prisoners would never know if and when they were being watched. The idea was to monitor inmates with *one* singular guard and the inmates would regulate their own behavior and behave as though they're being monitored at all times. Foucault would later go on to use this concept in his book *Discipline and Punish* as a metaphor for modern disciplinary society.

Dramaturgy: Dramaturgy is a sociological concept that was developed by Erving Goffman (please note that it differs from the dramaturgy discussed in theater studies!). Dramaturgy states that all social interaction is dependent on the following factors: time, place, and the audience that we are "performing" for. Goffman proposes the idea of "backstage" and "front stage" selves and argues that we shift how we present ourselves based on the time, place, and our audience. For example, you are a different person with your co-workers than you are with your friends. You present one way on social media and another way in real life.

Identity Management: Identity Management Theory developed by William R. Cupach and Tadasu Todd Imahori and was based on Erving Goffman's 1967 book, *Interaction Ritual: Essays on Face to Face Behavior*. Identity management theory explores how people manage their identities in various cultures and social contexts. It argues that our self-image is never static and is influenced by a variety of factors, including social interaction and influence.

Teaching Assistant: A teaching assistant provides support to a professor during the semester. They grade papers, field questions, hold office hours, run tutorial/writing groups, and can even lead lectures depending on their relationship with their professor.

APA formatting: APA stands for American Psychological Association. It's a formatting style that's generally standard in sociology, criminology, psychology, and behavioral sciences.

"It is not in the stars to hold our destiny but in ourselves."

CHAPTER ONE

motion sickness

IMOGEN

NEW YORK CITY
TWO WEEKS BEFORE FALL SEMESTER

My ass is numb.

My back is killing me.

Even though I'm sitting still, there's sweat pouring off my face.

I fucking hate New York in the summer, and I'll be happy to leave it behind for the west coast. I'm almost ready to make the move across the country. I just need to pack the kitchen and find a place to live. In two weeks. No pressure. I'm great under pressure. I thrive under pressure.

My thumb is working overtime, scrolling through rentals in Emerald Bay, Washington as I sit, hunched over my phone on the orange & teal checkerboard floor. I'm surrounded by plates, old Tupperware containers, and appliances I didn't even know we had. We're supposed to have the kitchen packed and be ready to go in 90 minutes, but all the anxiety of trying to lock down a place to live has me rooted to the floor.

A notification pops up on my phone.

> LOGAN: Did you need me to pick you up from the airport?

Dr. Logan Flynn: 36 years old, the Wunderkind of the Flynn family, and my brother. Graduated high school at 15, finished his bachelor's at 19, and had his PhD by the time he was where I'm at now. I've always trailed behind him, and now we're continuing that tradition: he's teaching at the same school I'll be attending as a student.

Logan had nothing to do with me getting into Emerald Bay University, and we won't have any academic contact while I'm there. I still had to clear my application with the head of the department, I can't TA for him, and he can't teach any of the courses I'm in, and yet I'm still having trouble grappling with the whole thing.

Emerald Bay was actually my last resort. I wanted to stay at NYU, or get into Dartmouth, Princeton, or Harvard to differentiate myself from my brother, but I guess even stellar references from my professors and a good pitch wasn't good enough for any of their programs. That said, there aren't a lot of people who would be able to effectively take me on, given my topic. 'Kink and stigma among working professionals' is a fairly niche area of expertise, and so being accepted to EBU's sociology program under one of the leading researchers in the field may have been a blessing in disguise.

Kink gave me a space of refuge and a place to work through my grief. My dad died four years ago and for a year afterward, I couldn't feel much of anything. I was simply existing, moving forward on autopilot until I found it. Combined with journaling and grief counseling, it helped me find my way back to myself. I could weep openly as a submissive and have a play partner who could help me through it. I felt reborn in a way, and that change fascinated me.

I had a stumbling start to academia. I almost failed a couple of the required courses during my bachelor's degree because I could barely juggle my responsibilities. Poor time management, handing in the wrong assignments, rushing to complete papers at the eleventh hour... the list was endless. It wasn't until I was faced with the possibility of being the only Flynn to flunk out that I went out and got a formal diagnosis for ADHD. Since then, I've understood more about myself and my brain.

I sigh, returning to the task I've been hyper-fixated on for the past three days: finding a goddamn apartment.

The only thing all my introspection hasn't helped is my tendency to procrastinate.

"Just fit in the box, you bitch— ow! I am not above throwing a Chanel bag out the window!"

I can hear my roommate Piper in the other room, swearing and grunting.

"Is that the fake one?" I call out to her.

She pokes her head into the room, scowling at me, her dark brows knit together. Her inky black hair is a mess of wild and frizzy waves, and it makes for a striking image.

"First of all, yes. Second, you don't have to tell the whole neighbor-hood—" Her eyes dart around the kitchen and she does a double take. "Iggy! What the fuck?! You said you were packing!"

"I am!"

She's already storming toward me, clutching the fake Chanel bag like she's going to beat me with it, before I can even pretend to have been working.

"You've barely even started packing the kitchen!"

I grab a fork, keeping her at arms-length.

"Put the weapon down, Pipes."

"You first!"

I grab the bag, tugging hard on it. Piper lets out a yelp of surprise, stumbling forward before regaining her composure.

"Let go of it or I *will* beat your ass!" She laughs.

I release the bag and Piper grunts, tossing it somewhere among the pile of boxes in the living room.

"Fine, you win," I sigh. "I'm not about to get my face busted by some knock-off Chanel."

"Alright, so outside of getting in fights, what the hell have you been doing out here for 2 hours?" Piper asks.

"I'm packing *and* finding an apartment! It's called multitasking!"

"Very impressive," she replies, resting her hands on her hips.

Piper is that knock-the-wind-out-of-you kind of gorgeous, with intense green eyes, plump lips, and dewy skin that practically makes her glow. I don't think I've seen a pimple on her face in the three years since we've known each other.

"Remind me why you didn't opt for the campus dorms?" Piper asks.

"Because the idea of living with a bunch of freshmen while they're constantly blasting loud music and having sad sex isn't exactly my idea of paradise," I say flatly, glancing back down at my phone.

This deep into the search I'm scrolling through places that are not only outside of the town, but outside of my budget as well.

Fuck my fucking life, right?

Piper sighs, looking around at the complete disaster I've made of the space.

"Come on, Iggy, Jay's going to be here soon. We wanted to arrive right when the doors open, remember? 10:00 PM sharp."

Jay's Piper's boyfriend, and he's kind of the reason why my house hunting is getting so difficult. They're moving into a cute little one bedroom apartment together, one they annoyingly found almost immediately, which left me fending for myself. The plan was to go out to our local kink club for one last hurrah before the three of us leave New York behind for the next big chunk of our lives.

"Yeah," I sigh. "I guess I can apartment hunt tomorrow."

"You know, you can always stay with Jay and I—"

"Pipes? No offense, I love you guys, but that place is for you. I don't want to be crashing on your couch for a semester."

"We could all sleep in the same bed like Charlie and the Chocolate Factory," she suggests, pulling me to my feet and plunking a box down in front of me.

"Hard pass," I laugh as I scroll through the listings again, growing more and more hopeless.

No apartment, no job prospects, and on top of all of that, the university is taking its sweet fucking time processing their TA applications. Apparently, there aren't enough positions to go around and it's competitive. So, I'll be moving to Emerald Bay potentially homeless *and* broke.

"I should drop out."

"Nope!" Piper replies. "Why are you making this such a big deal, just stay with us!"

"I need a space to work and shit, and you're in a one-bedroom apartment. You know how crowded that's gonna be?"

Her eyes twinkle, and I already know what she's going to say before she says it.

"Well, maybe it's time you call your brother."

"Or, instead…" I grab a wine glass, holding it up in front of her. "I could break off the stem, and shove this right through my eye. Sounds about equal to me."

"Iggy, he's teaching at EBU, he's gonna find out you don't have a place. You could be living in a van down by the river and he'd still manage to drag you off to that house of his."

I shake my head.

I haven't told Logan about my living situation, or lack thereof. I'm just trying to avoid him jumping in to save the day like he always does.

"Hell no. I'm not living with my brother. He's got his own life—"

"And a big ol' house near the woods with two extra bedrooms."

I know she's right, and all I would have to do is text him, but I want a space of my own, somewhere where I don't have to compromise and don't have to worry about anyone else's rules. Besides, it's embarrassing to have to rent a room from my big brother. I'm 26 years old. I should have my shit together.

Just as I'm crafting the perfect comeback, I hear the lock click and the sound of Jay whistling as he walks through the door. Every time I see them together, I get reminded just how fucking lonely I am. I say I don't need anyone, but you'd think there'd be one decent fucking guy in New York who could change my mind about this whole commitment thing. Like Richard Gere does for Julia Roberts in Runaway Bride.

It would help if he was just as hot, too.

"Iggyyyy!" Jay calls out, dressed in a pair of leather pants and a black shirt, the sleeves rolled up to expose his tattooed forearms. "What's cookin' good lookin'?"

His brown eyes sparkle with mischief, his black hair pushed back and out of his chiseled face. He's got a long nose, a square jaw, and broad shoulders that look like they're practically bursting out of his dress shirt.

"I guess not much with the kitchen like this," he chuckles.

"Well, we were waiting for *you*," I fire back. "Someone's gotta grab things off the top shelves."

"Aren't you 5'10'?" He asks with a grin.

Piper rolls her eyes, patting him on the chest.

"Help her toss this shit into boxes. Then, we can get ready and head out."

She scurries off to the bathroom while Jay stares me down, folding his massive arms over his chest.

"You're still coming out tonight, right? There's a bondage workshop. You love those, no way you're skipping out."

"I don't know," I sigh as we get to work. "I still have to find a place."

"You don't have time to go out for like three hours?"

"Oh, please, it's more like six," I laugh. "I don't have much time left to find something before we move."

I'm restless, the kind of restless that makes me want to get things done. I'm fixated on finding a place to live, and it feels like I can't move forward until that feat is accomplished. Probably helps that I *literally* can't, either.

"You can stay with—"

"She said she hates us and doesn't want to!" Piper shouts from the bathroom.

"That's not true, and close the door when you pee, *please!*" I yell back.

"How long have you been looking today?" Jay asks.

"All day, dude. In between packing my bedroom and doing the readings for my first class."

"Well, there are still gonna be the same amount of zero apartments for the rest of the night, so take a break. It's not like you're watching the stock market."

"How can you be so cavalier about this?"

"I'm not being *cavalier*," he snickers. "I'm saying you need to give that big brain a rest. Besides, can't you just live with your brother?"

"Ha!" Piper cackles from the bathroom.

"Can you take her batteries out?" I ask him.

"I tried once," Jay replies. "Got a book to the face. Her life's mission is to drive us both crazy."

He grabs a handful of cutlery and tosses it in without a care in the world. Piper's going to flip when she sees what a shitty job we did, but at this point I just want it all to be over.

"We're saying goodbye to New York, Iggy! Normally, I'd let you make your own decisions, but you've been torturing yourself all week. We gotta go out with a bang— literally."

I hear the sink run from the other room as Jay gives that 'don't bullshit me' look he's so good at. I can't keep eating, sleeping, and breathing apartment listings.

"Fine, I'll go," I mutter.

"Yes! Hey Pipes, I got her!"

"What was that?!" Piper asks as she walks back into the room, pulling a leather skirt up past her hips.

"I'm coming with you guys."

"Yay!" She rushes for Jay and high fives him. "Teamwork!"

I walk into my fully packed bedroom, ripping open a box of fetish gear to pull out a little pastel pink latex dress and a pair of matching heels. I watch myself in the mirror as I tug my long lavender hair into a ponytail, smearing some glitter around my brown eyes before swiping on some bubblegum-pink gloss. The entire time, what Piper said about my brother and his giant empty house rattles around my head.

I need a place to live, and as much as I want my independence, I'm so stressed about finding an apartment that I can't even enjoy the excitement of moving to a brand new place.

I've lived in New York my whole life, but Logan moved to Emerald Bay after his PhD and never left, content to settle down and start fresh in a quiet little town.

Now, against my better judgment, I'm about to interrupt all of that.

I draft up a text, my thumb hovering over the send button. I feel so fucking childish, but it's my fault for waiting until the last minute to start apartment hunting.

"Uber's here!" Piper calls.

"Coming!"

Fuck it. I hit send, toss the phone in my bag, and rush out the door.

> IMOGEN: Hey, Logan. This is kind of awkward, but I need a place to live in Emerald Bay. Can I stay with you until I'm back on my feet?

CHAPTER TWO

a well respected man

ROMAN

EMERALD BAY
TWO WEEKS BEFORE FALL SEMESTER

I take a sip of my coffee, scowling a little at the bitterness as the dying August sun beats down on my back, a combination that feels more like a punishment than anything else. I'm almost finished with this last syllabus. All I have to do is send it to my TA and I'm free for a whole week's vacation.

For years I was a starving researcher, voraciously tearing through all manner of academia for something unique to be a part of. I was desperate to contribute, provide some meaningful social change through my work, and maybe I did. But from here, fifteen years in, all that I feel is exhaustion.

I sigh, pushing the cup lazily across my desk as the heat radiates through the tightly sealed windows. People keep asking me if I have plans, and the truth is I do, but telling your co-workers you're going to be sitting in your shitty, barely furnished apartment and drinking whiskey all week doesn't usually fill them with a lot of confidence.

Frankie's the worst, always calling me out as some sort of sad, lonely 40-something, but I *like* my solitude. It took a while after Christa's death, a few months, perhaps a little longer, but now I'm used to being alone. More than used to it.

It keeps me stable; balanced.

Or maybe comfortable would be the better word.

Grief steals so much. I think I must have read hundreds of papers on it, and even dozens more books, but two years on, I still couldn't say I have a full grasp on it.

All I know is I've been fighting like hell to dig my way out.

"Knock knock!"

Frankie Hughes' voice pierces through the door, followed only moments later by his surprisingly commanding 6'3" frame. His eyes are bright and sparkling, a vibrant green that never fails to catch a glance, but today it's his nervous smile that's doing the heavy lifting.

I lean back in my chair and take off my reading glasses with another deep sigh, lazily rubbing them off on my shirt.

"Here to ruin my day?"

Frankie straightens with a huff, stopping in the middle of my office as he pushes his shaggy golden hair out of his eyes. Even at 34 he's still got all those boyish features you expect in someone much younger, all except for the slightly crooked nose he got from a motorcycle accident back during his PhD. He walked away with his life, two metal rods in his legs, and a hell of a lot of trauma that he hides behind bad jokes.

"Why do you always say that? You think that's all I'm good for, ruining your day?"

"Frankie, you're the head of the department," I chuckle. "If you're not here to give me a raise, there really isn't any other option, is there?"

He rolls his eyes and slips into one of the chairs in front of my desk.

"Cut me some slack, okay? You know I hate being this kinda guy."

"So quit," I fire back, the slightest smirk on my face. It's a conversation we've had many times, and it always ends the same way.

"Are you nuts? Think of the perks! Like my office, you know, the one with the big window you wish you could look through every day of your life?" He heaves his own dramatic sigh. "God, look at your shitty window. I could never."

"Don't forget the pay, you've gotta be making the big bucks by now."

Frankie snorts and I watch the disillusionment sink in, the same way it has every other time we've done this little song and dance.

"Woah, woah, don't go crazy on me. This is academia, remember?"

"Right, of course, I almost forgot for a second."

Frankie spins around in my chair, extending his arms out to the side like some sort of oversized kid.

"And of course, I'm sure they'll make *me* organize the inevitable pizza lunch for the faculty to make up for the fact that they don't pay us enough. Just think, they might even give us a glass of wine to drink. Each!"

"I like pepperoni and mushroom," I mutter. "Red wine too, if you don't mind."

Frankie shakes his head.

"Alright, look, you know I hate to admit when you're right, but I do have *some* shitty news to go along with my wonderful presence. Tracy? Your TA? She's left the program."

"Goddammit."

Tracy had been my TA almost every semester since she started the program three years ago, and she was perfect. She knew how to grade papers, how to run tutorial groups, but mostly she knew how to keep my inbox empty. It's not that I don't like communicating with my students exactly, but when you've been doing this as long as I have, you get sick of answering the same questions over and over again.

"Yep, finally burned out." He shrugs, as if it was the most natural conclusion in the world. "She submitted her paperwork this morning."

I huff, staring at my syllabus and already thinking about all the editing I'll have to do.

"Who's going to keep me from getting emails at 3:30 in the morning?" I ask.

"Wow, that's compassionate," Frankie mumbles. "*What about me?* You're a real prick sometimes, you know that, right?"

"I'm a prick most of the time," I mutter. "Look, I feel terrible that Tracy had to leave, but she was the TA for *this class*. You know, the one I have to teach in two weeks?"

Emerald Bay is a prestigious university in a quiet town. It attracts a lot of eager young minds. The issue is getting them to stay beyond their bachelor's degree. While we offer competitive scholarships for graduate students, a lot of them just want to do their four years and start living their lives.

I don't blame them. Academia is a crumbling tower in a lot of ways. Low pay, long hours, and bundles of stress. Even the conferences, which seem like fun little vacations at first, quickly become an extra expense unless you've got someone like Frankie backing you up with extra funds. I've seen it dissolve friendships, and even marriages; it takes a certain kind of personality to survive it, and lately, I don't know if that's me anymore.

I rub my face with my palms, pressing the heels of my hands into my cheekbones to try and melt away the tension that's growing in my jaw.

"Calm down," Frankie chuckles. "I'm gonna get you a replacement soon."

I frown, narrowing my eyes at him.

"How soon?"

"What, soon isn't good enough for you now? You don't think I've got your back anymore?"

"Some HR person you are," I snort. "Isn't hiring part of your job?"

His eyes widen and he puts his hand over his chest with all the drama of a high school production.

"How *dare* you refer to me as HR."

Frankie likes the idea of responsibility, always has, but he's never been great at pivoting quickly to adapt when change suddenly hits. Sometimes I think he just wanted the title and the email signature, but even with all that in mind, he's done a pretty good job for the department.

"Well, there goes the t-shirt I was going to get you for your birthday," I grumble, sipping my coffee. "It said World's Best HR Rep. Got a picture of your face and everything."

"You're so fucking funny," he snipes.

"Thank you, nobody ever says that about me."

Frankie reaches across my desk, holding my gaze as he rips one of my post-it notes off of the stack, balls it up, and tosses it straight in my face.

"Alright, new topic. Are you coming out tonight?"

I shift in my chair, trying to avoid his gaze, but he doubles down with a more pointed look.

"What's that face for?" He tilts his head. "You don't even know what I invited you to, do you?"

I wince.

"Come on, man, Abi's birthday? I texted you and everything. Like a dozen times."

"No, you didn't."

Frankie looks overwhelmingly unimpressed, crossing his arms as he leans back in the chair.

"How about you check your phone, champ."

I sigh, pulling out my phone from the desk drawer and powering it up. I've hated these things and their incessant vibrations and beeps for as long as I've had one. I hate having it on when I'm trying to focus, hate how it goes off at the worst possible times. Worst of all, the idea of being constantly accessible makes me extremely uncomfortable.

I watch the thing boot up, doing my best to ignore Frankie's burning stare as I look down at the screen, hoping beyond hope that there won't be any messages.

But, of course...

> FRANKIE: Abi's party. Tomorrow night at Hi-Dive. This is your final warning! NO BAILING!!!

"Frankie, look, It's nothing personal but I'm just too old for—"

"For company? For joy? For camaraderie?!"

We've had this conversation many times before: Christa died two years ago, and I need to start picking up the pieces. Start to move on. But the thing is I tried, I really did. I sold the house and moved into the little apartment I've got now. I tried to dive headlong into my passions, my work, anything to get myself away from the same old thoughts, but I couldn't escape my grief. The opposite, even. It pounded at the door louder and louder, no matter where I holed up, always demanding my full attention.

And so, of course, I let it in.

"Look, correct me if I'm wrong, but you do the same thing every night, right? You go home, eat the same thing, drink the same thing, and maybe, *just maybe*, watch the Food Network if you're feeling spicy."

"What do you have against the Food Network?"

Frankie rolls his eyes, and I already know that he's not going to take no for an answer.

I used to be so different. I was jovial, funny, social, but that joy for life was sucked out of me when I watched Christa's casket being lowered into the ground, and the self-loathing only got worse when I started unearthing her secrets.

I wasn't enough to keep her demons away.

"Look, drinks are on me. It'll just be four of us. Completely relaxed, chill even. Besides, Abi asked for you specifically. You gonna turn down the birthday girl?"

"I don't believe that for a second," I scoff.

"Okay, so maybe *Logan* told me to bring you, but does that make a difference? Just do us all a favor and show that gorgeous face in public for once."

Logan's been one of my closest friends for at least three years. We've spent a lot of time sitting around a bottle of whiskey talking about what it means to lose someone.

But I even shut *him* out eventually.

I do it to everyone.

I've tried to find my old self, tried to breathe new life into the man I used to be, but I think he's gone, and I don't know if he'll ever make it back.

"Come on, Roman," Frankie urges, his eyes pleading. "The party's already started."

The pressure's on, and even though all I want to do is go home and fall onto the couch, I know Frankie well enough to be certain he'd show up and kick down my door.

And I have to admit, sometimes I love him for it.

I slide my laptop into my bag, slinging it over my shoulder as I follow Frankie into the hall.

"So, what does Roman Burke do on a full week's vacation?"

"Why are you so curious?"

He chuckles, shaking his head.

"Because I'm your friend? And I'm naturally curious?"

"Nothing," I sigh as we step inside the elevator and I hit the button for the lobby. "I'm doing absolutely *nothing*, Frankie. No plans, no work–"

"I don't believe that for a second," he laughs, staring up at the numbers as they flick on and off.

"I'm serious. I guess I'm going to cook, take Mitzy to the beach, sleep in–"

"Get laid..." Frankie wiggles his eyebrows and I roll my eyes. "Oh, come on, dude! If I looked like you, I'd be *swimming* in pu–"

Carol Barton's tight bun and stern expression greet us as the elevator doors slide open, and I can practically feel Frankie bite into his tongue as she steps in to join us.

"Dr. Burke... Dr. Hughes."

"Dr. Barton," I murmur. "Nice to see you."

She gives Frankie the stink-eye, but he's already staring up at the ceiling like his life depends on it, and then it's all silence until we hit the lobby. The swift click of Carol's heels against marble tile finally brings Frankie back to earth as we wait for the doors to close one final time.

"Do you... do you think she heard me?"

"Well, there's a chance she didn't figure it out, but there's only so many p-words someone would be excited to be swimming in," I laugh as the elevator dings for our floor, and we stumble out between the parked cars. "She's probably adding it to your file."

"You know what's crazy? That's not even the worst thing in there," Frankie chuckles, playfully punching me on the shoulder.

And there, for a just brief moment, I feel the old me start to emerge.

I wonder how long he'll manage to stick around this time.

CHAPTER THREE

no sugar tonight

ROMAN

The Hi-Dive is our spot, and has been for long a while. The lights are low and the place is relatively empty save for a few of the regular drunks crowding the bar like a watering hole. It smells like stale beer and cigarette smoke that's seeped into the walls and foundation. Logan said it reminded him of a Stephen King book, so naturally, it's been his favorite place to go on campus for years.

I spot Logan and Abi almost immediately as Frankie and I walk in. Logan's slightly disheveled sandy hair falls in his face and he pushes it back just before his hand shoots up to wave at me.

Beside him is Dr. Abigail King, with her long, jet black hair, and bright green eyes. Abi has always reminded me of someone ripped straight from a Gothic novel: a sort of put-together elegance without having to try very hard. Tonight is no different, lounging casually in a beautiful blood-red blouse, her crimson lips contrasting her pale skin as she grins.

"Oh my god, he showed up!" Abi digs through her bag with a sudden fevered excitement, dragging out her phone. "Hang on, I absolutely need to get a picture of this, it's a momentous occasion!"

I shake my head, rolling my eyes as she snaps a picture.

"That's beautiful, Roman. It really captures your winning personality."

I used to feel really comfortable going out, but I've been dodging plans for so long with this group that now, everyone looks sort of alien in this setting. I've gotten used to passing them in the hallways, or declining when Logan stops by my office to ask me if I want to grab lunch. And then I pack up for the day, go home, stare at the ceiling, and pass out for six hours.

I have a very specific routine, and this is cutting into my ceiling-staring time.

Logan flashes me that big, beaming smile and slides out of the booth to pull me in for a hug.

"It's good to see you somewhere besides your office, man."

"What kind of magic brought you out tonight?" Abi asks with a smirk.

"Less magic, and more of a bribe," I laugh.

"It was not a bribe!" Frankie shouts. "This guy and his fuckin' dramatics. I'm gonna go get drinks. Shots? Yes? Everyone's on board? Great."

"No!" I shout.

"I said great, Roman! It's too late!" Frankie calls as he makes a mad dash to the bar.

I walk over to Abi to give her a tight hug.

"Happy birthday, Abi. Sorry, I don't have a present for you."

"You being here is enough." She slips back and winks at me. "And if you let me use your Keurig while you're on vacation, you're in my good books."

"Sounds great. I'll give you my spare key. Just keep Logan out of there."

"Jokes on you dude," Logan replies as we all settle down at the booth. "I already got my own key cut."

Frankie saunters back to the table with a whole tray of drinks, including two pints of beer, one of which he sets down in front of me, along with a shot of god knows what. Abi leans in and sniffs it.

"Tequila?"

"Yup!" Frankie chirps.

"Where's the salt? And the lime?" She asks in disbelief.

"They were out of limes."

She raises a brow and Frankie smirks.

"Fine, if you don't want it—"

"Whoa, whoa!" She grabs her shot glass and protects it with her hand. "Let's not do anything crazy, okay?"

Frankie raises his glass and looks around the table.

"To Abi, congratulations on 26 years around the sun!"

Abi puts a hand on her chest, beaming at all of us.

"Thank you. You know, simply existing is such a feat. I'm surprised I made it."

I snicker and sip my beer as Frankie turns to me.

"And to Roman, for finally getting out of the office— and his apartment! This is a big day for you, man."

"Fuck you, Hughes."

"You'll have to buy me dinner first."

"So, you want it in a paper bag, or..."

Logan and Abi descend into giggles.

"The disrespect. Somewhere nice, at least! Like Arby's. Are you writing this down, man?"

"I'm taking mental notes," I mutter.

"Are we gonna toast or not?!" Abi shouts. "We gotta stop letting Frankie make speeches!"

Frankie raises his glass.

"Alright then: cheers, happy birthday, and fuck you, Abi!"

I almost choke watching Frankie toss his drink back before slamming it on the counter. He grimaces and starts to cough, along with Logan, who's already smacking the table. I'm starting to seriously consider tossing mine onto the ground and hoping no one notices.

"Son of a bitch that burns!" Frankie chokes.

"Yeah, see, the lime and salt would've felt real good right about now, huh, tough guy?" Abi teases as she pours her shot into her margarita.

"Cheater!" Logan bellows.

"I am not! There's already tequila in this! And lime juice, and salt, and I'm the birthday girl, so shut up!"

She shoves her hand in his face and Logan pretends to swat her away, but I can see the adoration in his eyes. Logan is head over heels for Abigail King, but we can't date people in our department. So far, it's hard to tell if there's anything going on between them aside from the odd nickname and the fact that they're always having lunch together. Relationships between colleagues aren't nearly as frowned upon as relationships between students and teachers. That's where the power dynamic gets really fucked up.

"Don't be a wuss, King," Frankie chuckles, pushing another shot toward her.

"Hey, don't talk to my date like that!" Logan teases.

"Your date?" Frankie asks with a raised brow.

It looks like Logan's testing his limits tonight, but Abi doesn't say anything, merely sipping her margarita as her cheeks turn pink.

"I'm paying for her drinks," Logan replies. "Therefore, she's my date."

"Only because you took my credit card," she fires back. "He said I wasn't allowed to pay for anything."

"Speaking of dates," Frankie cuts in, sliding back into his seat with his eyes fixed on me. "That's the next thing we've gotta do for this guy."

"What? I go out one time and all of a sudden I'm the group project?" I ask. "I haven't even been here for fifteen minutes."

"I don't think you should be in charge of this project," Logan pipes in. "I'm the best friend, and—"

"Why not?" Frankie retorts. "What's wrong with me being in charge?"

Christ, here they go. You get one shot of tequila into each of them and they'll snipe at each other all night.

"Because you haven't been in a relationship for years, dude! Unless you count that dominatrix you see."

"Nah, none of you are allowed to give me shit for that. It's stigmatizing! Also, don't knock it till you try it."

Years back, after his accident, Frankie got interested in the BDSM scene— academically at first, but he quickly dove right in, blending research and practice. He says it's as important to him as meditation is to some people.

I admit, I'm curious about it. He says it's a release, a way for him to be fully present in his body and feel everything all at once.

"Look, I don't need a relationship, but some people, who I just so happen to be looking directly in the eye, might enjoy some companionship. Or at least someone to watch Chopped with."

"Or maybe I should follow your lead and just hire someone to get freaky with," I snort.

Frankie's eyes light up.

"Now, there's an idea."

The last dregs of summer float through the air, along with the smell of french fries from the kitchen. I can hear car tires grinding against pavement as they pass by out front. Emerald Bay is so quiet sometimes, it's almost maddening.

The back door opens, Logan and Frankie coming stumbling out with cigarettes stuffed between their lips. We each look a slightly different shade of exhausted; the curse of academia. Late nights, early mornings, and way too much shit rattling around in our heads. Even while I'm doing other things, I'm thinking about all the work I have to catch up on, and I'm never really present. Turns out, once you form an obsessive relationship with your job, the habit becomes harder and harder to break. The work is always there for me when I need to consume myself with it.

I gesture to Frankie's cigarette.

"That shit'll kill ya, you know."

"Thanks, doc." He fires it up before passing the lighter off to Logan. "How's it hangin'?"

"Not bad," I murmur.

"God, I thought you were gonna tell that shitty joke— *long and a little to the left*," Logan sighs.

"Well, I didn't wanna make you feel inadequate," I snicker.

Logan grins and exhales a large cloud of smoke, flipping me off.

"You hate it in there, don't you?"

Frankie's eyes volley between us. I think he's always liked it when the two of us get into it like this. It's better than Monday Night Football for him.

"No!" I exclaim. "It's fine, it's just... you know, I've been such a..."

"Shut in?" Logan teases.

"I mean... I leave the house."

Frankie snorts.

"Really? I practically had to drag you out here by your hair."

"Anyway, work and the grocery store don't count, dude," Logan continues. "And we miss you, man"

I'll admit, I don't come out to these things often because I don't want to be that sad old bastard nursing a pint of beer, still stuck inside of his own head, but I don't think my friends give me enough credit.

"I'm not a *total* shut-in. I've tried to date, and I'm here, aren't I?"

Logan puts a hand on my shoulder, the two of us sharing a moment. I've been there for him, or at least tried as hard as I could to be, after his dad passed. Phone calls, lunches, and driving around the bay for hours... but Christa's suicide changed me profoundly. Since then I haven't been able to be there for him.

For anyone.

I pulled away from everything. I didn't have any answers, and no great reason why. I searched through every single thing she owned for a note or an explanation. What I found were hidden bottles of liquor and antidepressants that I didn't even know she was taking. It just left me with more questions and more guilt. I clearly wasn't there when I should have been.

I didn't ask the right questions; didn't say the right things.

Now I'm left swallowing my grief like poison.

"You know, Roman, if you really want to jazz up your vacation, I have a proposition for you," Frankie chimes in.

"What? The dominatrix thing? We already share a wall at work, I'm not sharing a dominatrix with you, too."

Frankie rolls his eyes.

"I don't mean the same person, dumbass. I mean I could show you how to find someone to have a kinky hookup with. You know, whatever you want."

"A professional?" I ask. "With this job? You know I don't have the money for that."

Frankie shakes his head.

"No, no. There's no money involved. It's usually people I meet on an app who are all in the scene. There's something for everyone on there."

Frankie's work on kink is written with compassion, empathy, and understanding. It's so richly detailed and illuminating that I have to admit, it's made me rethink my relationship with sex. It's also made me curious enough to start looking into some of the stuff he writes about myself, but I've never gotten farther than the suggested tab on PornHub.

"What's the app?" I ask, immediately regretting the apparent enthusiasm in my voice when Frankie's eyes light up.

He pulls out his phone and hands it to me, Logan looking over my shoulder with interest.

"KinkFinder," I mutter. "Is this like... Tinder for a dominatrix?"

"Well, yeah. You write a bio, list the kinky shit you're into, and swipe through until you find a match. Doms connect with subs and vice versa. Anything you want, really."

Just as Frankie begins to dive into the details the door flies open and Abi appears, her eyes bloodshot from too many margaritas. She glares at us, cocking her head to the side with irritation.

"You're leaving the birthday girl alone?!" She yelps. "What the hell, guys? We were supposed to do karaoke!"

Logan chuckles and crushes his cigarette before gently guiding her back inside.

"Come on. We'll duet on *Wanted Dead or Alive*. Roman and Frankie'll join us later, right fellas?"

We both wave and the door slams shut behind them, with a brief moment of silence between us before Frankie's face curls into a grin.

"Look, all I'm saying is that it's an option. It's helped me a lot, and I mean that beyond exploring my kinks and shit, man."

"What do you mean?"

"I see my body differently. I can stand to look at myself without any clothes on, directly at my legs. I couldn't manage that before, had to cover the mirror in the bedroom." Frankie lets out a sigh. "This whole thing has been healing for me. I'm writing a book about it."

Frankie's usually jovial, but guarded, whereas Logan is an open book about his pain. You wanna know something, Logan will give you the play-by-play but Frankie will just leave the room. This feels different though.

"Look, I'm not pressuring you, but don't think I don't remember those late night talks we had at your apartment after too much whiskey."

Maybe he's right. I feel like I've been lost in grief for so long that I've forgotten how to connect with anyone who's outside of it. When I socialize, it's in the halls at EBU, at conferences, and it's mostly about work.

"I'll think about it, okay?"

Frankie slings his arm around my shoulder.

"That's all I ask."

My head is swimming from what Frankie said, about how finding kink has helped to heal his wounds. Maybe he's right, maybe it could help me too. God knows I'm sick of doing the same thing over and over again like it's Groundhog Day.

We head back inside, finding Logan and Abi up onstage, already singing their hearts out to Bon Jovi, and Frankie buys us all another round. I envy how much fun they're having. Two years ago, I would have been right up on that stage with them.

I pull my phone out and quickly look up the app. It's a purple square with a white K. Pretty innocuous. Before I can think better of it, it's already downloaded and I'm scrolling through the front page blurb.

Find kinky singles near you, no matter if you're experienced or want to try something new!

I'm definitely new, not to mention curious.

"I'm really glad you came out tonight, Roman," Frankie says, startling me just as I hit the join button.

"Yeah." I quickly lock my phone and slide it back into my pocket. "Me too."

He snorts into his drink as he flashes me a big smile.

"No, you're not. You can't wait to go home and watch cooking shows or porn or whatever it is you do."

"Actually, I'm usually in bed with Mitzy reading a book by now," I murmur.

Mitzy was a bait dog until someone rescued her. I got her when she was still fairly young. Skinny as hell, and covered in bite marks and sores. She didn't trust me at all in the beginning. In fact, she spent the first few nights growling at me any time I tried to go near her. But I was patient, and determined to win her over. I'd sit with her for hours, reading to her or playing music on my phone to calm her down. I like to think we saved each other, but these days she's helping me more than the other way around.

"Well, we miss you, you know," Frankie says softly. "I know things have been tough for you, and—"

I cut him off with a wave of my hand before he can finish his sentence. The worst part about grieving is having to listen to everyone else tell you how sorry they are and how hard things have been for you, especially after so long.

"It's fine. Thanks, Frank."

He pats me on the shoulder, but the moment is undercut a little as Logan points at us aggressively from the stage, him and Abi preparing to launch into another song.

"We're going to get the whole gang up here for the next one!"

"No!" I shout.

Frankie boos and Abi frowns, crossing her arms over her chest.

"Come on, it's my birthday!"

"Yeah, it's her birthday!" Logan shouts, his voice booming through the mic as the introduction to Uptown Girl by Billy Joel pours through the speakers. "I know you can't resist this!"

Logan begins to dance, but he looks more like one of those inflatable tube things outside of a car sales lot while Abi is snapping her fingers and moving her shoulders from side to side. Neither of them have a rhythmic bone in their body, but it's still kind of adorable watching them try to coax us onto the stage.

Frankie lets out a deep sigh, draining his drink.

"You know as well as I do that there's only one way to stop him from dancing. You in?"

"I gotta take a leak," I lie.

I want to finish signing up for that app, but I can't just stay at the table or they'll keep harassing me until I join in.

"When you're back, then." Frankie pats my shoulder. "If I have to suffer through this, you do too."

"Sounds good," I chuckle.

I slip into the bathroom as Frankie heads for the stage, quickly picking a stall and locking it. The first thing I do is take my phone out of my pocket and open the app back up.

"Name..."

I don't want students finding me. That would be... well, a disaster.

I go with Henry, my middle name, and I use an old picture of myself from when I got some new tattoos added to my chest piece a few years back, cropping out most of my face.

I don't lie about anything else in my profile, even my inexperience with kink. From what I've read, some of this gets pretty intense, and I want someone who can ease me into all of it.

Then I get to the hardest part.

Kinks.

Do I have any?

I think I like the idea of being dominated, so I type it in. But there are four other boxes. Should I fill them all out?

God, I already hate this app. And yet, I'm still desperate to create a profile.

"Fuck it," I mutter.

I type *man being dominated* into Google, going straight for the images. Women in fetish gear, all leather and latex, holding whips. Men tied to chairs with ball gags in their mouths. It's surprising how quickly I'm responding to all of this, and I find myself reaching down to squeeze my cock through my jeans, but I stop myself.

I am not going to jerk off in a public bathroom.

But then I find the one image that sends shivers down my spine.

It's a stunning photograph of a woman wearing thigh high leather boots and nothing else. She's sitting on a man's face, one hand pressed into his chest. His ankles are bound, and his cock looks like it's in some kind of steel cage. The light's hitting her in all the right places to make her glow a gorgeous gold, almost like the sun is pouring in through an unseen window.

The look of ecstasy on her face, the total submission of her partner... it's like he's just a tool for her to use for her own pleasure. It's been a while since I've been *this* turned on. Even watching porn, it takes time for me to really get into it, but this?

This is different.

If the app can give me even a fraction of this, then I'm all in.

Without thinking, I find myself popping the button open on my jeans. It won't take me long to get off. Maybe a few minutes, especially if I can find more pictures like this.

Just as I'm reaching in to stroke my cock, the bathroom door slams open and I almost drop my phone straight into the toilet.

"Roman!" Logan bellows. "Are you in here?"

Jesus.

My heart pounds as I quickly button my pants up and grab my phone. I love the guy, but he has the worst goddamn timing.

"You know you could text me," I growl, opening the stall door and stepping outside.

Logan's at the urinal, glancing over his shoulder as I go to wash my hands.

"And what are the chances you'd answer?" He laughs.

I grunt, grabbing some paper towel and heading for the door.

"We're doing Prince next," Logan tells me, finishing up and heading for the sink. "And you, my friend, have yet to embarrass yourself."

I want to tell him I have to leave, that this isn't my scene anymore. I could make up an excuse easily, but I couldn't stand to see the hurt look on his face. I hate that guilt is the thing that keeps me here sometimes, but maybe it's important.

"Fine," I reply with a small smile. "But only if it's *When Doves Cry*."

Logan's grin goes wide.

"You're on, my dude."

CHAPTER FOUR

just a girl

IMOGEN

ONE WEEK BEFORE FALL SEMESTER

Arriving at Logan's place instantly makes me feel at home, though maybe a touch inadequate. It's a Victorian-style house with a beautiful yard, ornate windows, and a large balcony, but I think it's the two big gargoyle statues flanking the steps I *know* he got at Party City that really ties it all together.

Logan says he picked this place because it looks haunted, a motivation I'm sure some of his friends think was a joke, but I'm certain is 100% true. The man is obsessed with Halloween, an obsession we share.

"Thanks for letting me stay," I sigh as he kills the engine and we step out of the car.

"No problem. Need help with your stuff?"

"It's just one suitcase. I'm good, dude."

He pops the trunk and the two of us reach for my bag at the same time. I swat his hand away.

"Cut it out!"

"I'm just trying to be helpful!"

"Yeah? Well you're being annoying!" I laugh.

He rolls his eyes and snatches the suitcase out of my hand just as I lift it from the trunk.

"Logan!"

He's already taken off down the driveway, giggling like an asshole. I swear, this guy is emotionally seven years old.

"Close the trunk!" He shouts as he reaches the front door.

I bite back a smile, trying to look unimpressed as I take off after him.

My brother's been one of my closest friends since we were little, and even though we drifted apart a bit over the years, we never fully broke that bond. He gets on my nerves, like all siblings do, but I still look up to him. He's already a tenured professor who lectures all over the world, and he wrote a best-selling book about medically assisted death after he changed research areas when we lost our dad four years ago. Since then, he's been an advocate for the 'right to die' movement.

Mom is proud, and I know dad would be too.

My boots crunch along the gravel as I take in the smell of an early fall hanging thick in the air. It's crisp, with a sharp and sugary bite from the decaying leaves that litter the ground, all the way up the steps to the front door.

"C'mon. Take your shoes off, I'll show you to your half of the house." He ushers me inside, leaning my suitcase against the wall and taking my coat. "By the way, your stuff came in from New York the other day. How the hell did you afford to ship it?"

"You know, I *am* capable of saving money, Logan," I tease as we both kick off our shoes. "Even in a place as economically fucked as New York."

"Must not be genetic because I can't even go for a walk without spending thirty bucks," Logan grumbles.

"It's because you have the impulse control of a toddler in a toy store."

"Hey, these are *collector's items*!"

He gestures at a large cabinet in the foyer, filled with horror movie memorabilia.

"You do play with them, though, right?"

"That's besides the point," he grins. "Anyway, it helps me think sometimes."

Logan and I descend the long staircase, down into the basement.

"I gotta admit, dude, this is a little creepy."

I keep expecting some ghost in a nightgown to walk out and scare the shit out of me; that's just the vibe this place gives off.

"You say that like I designed the house."

"You kind of did, though, right?" I laugh.

He spent a good amount of time playing interior designer and it definitely shows. His personality bleeds into everything in this place.

At the bottom of the stairs is a small closet, next to a bathroom that connects to the guest room. If you turn left, it leads to a storage room that now holds what was left of my apartment in New York. There's not much, mostly clothes, books, and records. I sold all my furniture when Logan agreed to take me in, to make things easier on the both of us.

"Worry about that stuff later," his words slice through my thoughts. "I'll show you the bedroom."

"I've seen it."

"Yeah, well, I've improved it," he says with a wink. "Come on, it's so cool, Iggy!"

Logan knows to get in front of things before I fixate on a task, quickly leading me through the en suite bathroom. It's been scrubbed clean, and he's even put some toiletries out for me.

"Don't get distracted, you haven't even seen the best part."

He drags me into the bedroom and my jaw drops.

The room is luxurious without looking cluttered, with a leather chair, beautiful desk, and walls lined with Gothic-inspired art as well as framed posters of some of my favorite movies: Halloween, Nosferatu, The Exorcist, Carrie, all films we saw together growing up.

"Logan," I whisper. "This is..."

"I pulled the posters out of my collection." He slips his hands into his pockets. "I wanted this to feel like home, not just a place you were crashing."

All that said, the bed might be my favorite part of the room.

Four-poster, overflowing with silk pillows and a cozy navy duvet. I've slept on this thing before, when I was first here years ago, and it was like sleeping on a big cloud. I can hear the trees rustling outside, and I imagine the leaves falling, floating down daintily with the breeze. This place is pretty fucking magical.

"So, look, I know you were pretty crushed when you didn't get into NYU—"

"Or Princeton. Or Dartmouth."

"*But*," he takes a breath. "I'm glad it meant you could be here."

I wrap my arms around him, burying my face in his chest.

"Thanks, Logan."

His deep laugh ripples through me as he pats my back.

"No problem, Iggy."

Logan and I ended up even closer after dad died, once we got over some initial friction. It fucked both of us up, even if we were as prepared for it as we could be, but he took it especially hard. My dad was his hero, a world-renowned scholar who dedicated his life to breaking down barriers for people who couldn't afford higher education.

Declan Flynn had a vicious wit and an absurd sense of humor. He loved a good drink, a terrible joke, and a chess game where he could get one. I used to watch him play Logan for hours at the kitchen table while we all talked about... well, everything.

From moment one, dad said that he wouldn't let the cancer kill him. A while after things began to take a dire turn, he took matters into his own hands, contacting a doctor out in Oregon who could help him die with dignity.

We all flew out to be with him at the end, holding his hands as he took his last breath. My mom was a rock the whole time, very rarely talking to any of us about how she felt. I can't be sure, but I think she was relieved that he finally had some peace.

Still, it's hard to think about dad without feeling my heart break all over again.

"I'm gonna make some pasta for dinner," Logan says softly, pulling me once more from my thoughts. "You've gotta be starving."

I shrug.

"I ate on the plane."

"Ate what?"

"A bag of chips. Even got a complimentary can of coke."

"That's not eating, so let me make us some homemade pasta! I just got the machine!" He rubs his hands together and flashes me a goofy smile, doing a stupid little jig with his long, spindly legs.

Just like dad.

"I'll let you know when dinner's ready! No arguing!"

I grin, stretching my arms as he leaves, in preparation for the brutal task of unpacking. Most of my fetish gear ends up in the back of the closet, still tucked away at the bottom of my bag. Logan doesn't know what I've been up to, he thinks my interest in kink is strictly academic, and I want to keep it that way. I know he's friends with my supervisor, Frankie Hughes, and maybe that connection's opened him up to some of the concepts, but I'm just not ready to have that conversation quite yet.

One by one, I unpack the rest of my boxes, making sure to put everything in its new place. This is a fresh start. I'll clean this room every day, keep it organized, and make sure it stays that way. It's a promise I make every time I move into a new space, but inevitably my old habits take over and it's a disaster within a week. Maybe this time things will be different.

Logan left me an empty bookshelf next to the desk that I start to fill up. On the top is a framed picture of me and dad at Disneyland, both of us with pink glittery Mouse ears. He looks so young, with thick dark hair, stubble on his face, and the light in his eyes that the disease stole from him in the end.

I remember this trip so well. We rode the Haunted Mansion so many times that mom had to tell us it wasn't the only ride in the park. My dad always loved horror in any form, but it was movies he loved the most, and it's what a lot of his work revolved around. He was obsessed with pop culture and how people responded to it, but his true passion was studying *why* people enjoyed being scared.

I set the picture back down, grab my phone, and flop onto my bed, noticing one unread message.

PIPES: How's unpacking?

IMOGEN: Almost done. How's your amazing new apartment?

PIPES: Amazing! We have a washing machine?!

IMOGEN: So classy, are you out of my league now?

33

PIPES: Please, I'm gonna be eating butter noodles for the next four years. By the way, there's gonna be a mixer for the new PhD students! Pool, free beer, and hot professooooors!

IMOGEN: Gross, my brother's one of those "hot professors." Dude looks like Big Bird on a good day.

PIPES: Well, my supervisor looks like Tommy Lee Jones. They can't all be winners.

IMOGEN: Old Tommy Lee Jones or young Tommy Lee Jones?

PIPES: ANCIENT TOMMY LEE JONES.

I cackle and roll onto my back.

IMOGEN: That's not a bad thing, love an age gap.

PIPES: You need to be arrested!

IMOGEN: You need to start digging silver foxes, babe. When's the mixer?

PIPES: Next week. Friday before the first day of classes. You in?

IMOGEN: Sure. Could be fun.

It would be nice to meet my professors in a non-professional setting. Once you get up to this level, they start to treat you less like students and more like colleagues, because in a few years, you'll either be working together or competing for the same opportunities.

I smile and flip mindlessly through my phone for a couple minutes until I decide I want to check out the talent here. I open the KinkFinder app and set my location to Seattle to cast a slightly wider net. It's been a while since I got laid, and after all, sometimes a vibrator isn't enough.

My fear of losing the people closest to me has shut me off in a lot of ways, but especially romantically. I've convinced myself, and the people around me, that I've got too much shit going on for a relationship. I think the last time I had a boyfriend was just after dad died. It was intense, and things got serious fast because I found myself needing an anchor. Unfortunately, trauma isn't as strong of a bond as I thought and things ended with me hurt and alone.

Nowadays? It's all casual sex. A brief moment of connection, and you move on.

Or whatever people do.

Personally? I like a good high five after an orgasm.

The problem with this app is that there's very little vetting. So, I have to do a lot of it myself through conversation and in-person meetings before we start anything. I use a fake name, too. You can never be too careful.

I match with a couple of guys who shoot me a quick 'hey', but I keep searching until I'm compelled to stop on an unbelievably gorgeous man— well, a gorgeous mouth and chest because that's all I can see in his picture. He's got gray in his beard, full lips curled into a subtle grin, with a half opened dress shirt and tattoos peeking through. He's muscular, and he's even showing some scattered chest hair. I can feel my skin heat up, and suddenly the collar of my t-shirt feels really tight.

I scroll to his bio.

Henry. 43. Looking for a good teacher who can take control.

A lot of the guys I play with at parties are younger, but I *do* love an older man.

"Let's just hope you're not a creep, Henry."

I hear Logan thundering down the stairs just as I swipe right, looking up to see him looming in the doorway.

"Damn, you made that pasta fast!"

He runs a hand through his messy hair.

"Uh... turns out, I needed to read the instructions on the machine because I'm not as smart as I think I am. The dough *kinda* got stuck." He holds up a finger, now covered in a little Halloween-themed bandaid. "Almost died."

"Logan!" I choke down my laughter. "Are you okay?"

"Yeah, you know, just a cool scar to tell the chicks about." He grins, puffing his chest out a little. "Looks like we're having mac and cheese instead."

I gasp and lock my phone, tossing it down onto the bed.

"Dad's recipe?"

Logan grins.

His was always the best.

"Yep, with four kinds of extra gooey cheese. And after dinner... I was gonna ask you if you wanted to watch a movie?"

I beam up at him. We haven't had a movie night in years.

"I'm in."

"Cool," he breathes as he looks around to see that I've definitely made myself at home. "Room looks good already."

We might get on each other's nerves sometimes, but there's nobody else I'd rather have as a big brother than Logan Flynn.

"Hey, so... thanks. For letting me stay here."

"Well, I'm not gonna let you be homeless—" The oven beeps, cutting him off. "Shit! Okay, make it snappy, dinner's in five!"

His footsteps sound like a herd of wild horses as he sprints up the stairs. When we were kids, he used to purposely stomp around outside of my room just to piss me off. Now, I find it kind of endearing.

My phone chimes and I flip it back over, confident with Logan safely clomping around upstairs.

You matched with Henry!

I bite my lip and immediately open the app to send him a message.

> JADE: I like your tattoos.

Three dots appear and then disappear a couple times.

HENRY: Hi?

JADE: Hey? Did my message not send?

HENRY: Oh, okay, you're not a robot.

I giggle and roll onto my back.

JADE: Why would you think I was a robot?

HENRY: Some other bot account asked to be my sugar... mommy? I just had to send her my bank account information so she could direct deposit my allowance for the month.

JADE: Sounds like a good deal.

HENRY: Yeah, love to be a fraud victim.

JADE: Damn, I should have led with that, then.

HENRY: You might be $500 richer because that's all I got right now.

This dude is funny.

JADE: Oh, so you're saying I'd pass the bot check?

HENRY: Well, it helps that you're very pretty, and your competition was just a picture of someone's ass. I love an ass, but it does feel weird talking to one. It's nice to see a face.

JADE: Look who's talking.

HENRY: Hey, you get most of me.

JADE: Whatever you say, Mr. Chest.

HENRY: I was hoping it might be whatever YOU say, Miss Bot.

"Hey, Logan!" I call, scrambling off my bed. "I may need to borrow your car!"

CHAPTER FIVE

there she goes

IMOGEN

"So, tell me again how come you need to borrow the car?"

Last night, Logan and I stayed up way too late, eating junk food and drinking one too many beers. We got into that deep, drunken state of conversation about life and what it all means. My brother gets very philosophical when he's drunk, and it's only been recently that I've been able to keep up with how fast his mind works.

I swallow my cereal, not wanting to give too much away. There's no way in hell I'm telling Logan I'm going to hang out with a guy who's almost twice my age to see if he'd be a good submissive-slash-fuck buddy. Logan's protective of me, but I'm a big girl and I've been doing this for a long time.

"Piper, Jay, and I are going into Seattle for the weekend."

"I thought you'd want to explore Emerald Bay."

"I thought we kind of covered that when you said it takes 15 minutes to drive from one end of town to the other," I tease. "Jay wants to see some band, so we're making a weekend of it."

Lying to him doesn't feel good, but I want to get laid. Piper and Jay really are going to a concert, I just opted not to go with them.

"Do you even have a license?" Logan asks with a raised brow.

I feign shock.

"How can you even ask me that?"

"Uh, remember when you showed up at the airport with your expired passport?"

Not this shit again.

"It wasn't *that* expired."

"Two years, Iggy!"

I roll my eyes. I'm a forgetful person and I forgot to renew my passport and couldn't go to Mexico with Logan and my mom. They've never let me forget *that*. If I don't write things down, I'm fucked. The problem is, most of the time, I forget where I put the fucking list of shit I need to remember. I've tried my notes app and scheduling apps on my phone, but nothing really works.

I've tried medication, too, but it makes me crash hard. So, I'm managing my condition on my own now.

"I swear I have a license. I'm reckless, but I'm not a total idiot, Logan." I bat my eyelashes. "*Please* let me borrow your car?"

He sighs.

"Take the Toyota. It's old."

"Why can't I take the Jaguar?" I ask. "Don't think I didn't see that thing parked in the driveway."

Logan likes to fix up shitty cars in his spare time. He buys them cheap from people who want to junk them and puts every penny he can spare into them. By the time he's finished, they don't look anything like they did when they first graced his garage. Logan's always liked to take things apart and put them back together again. I think that's what makes him a good researcher. Everything's a puzzle to him.

"No way," he laughs. "That's my baby."

"Come on, dude! Let me look cool for once!"

Logan shakes his head and I already know I've lost this fight.

"You're taking the Toyota," he says firmly. "I just fixed it up, new paint job, gave it a tune-up, new tires, new plates. It's good to go."

"Great, I can drive around looking like a fucking soccer mom," I grumble.

"They drive vans, dipshit."

"Fair." I sigh dramatically. "Thanks, Logan."

"No problem. I'm just bummed out you're ditching me already."

I snort.

"Well, I am an adult and I'm allowed to have a life."

"Yeah, the SpongeBob pajamas really sell it," he mutters.

"Hey, fuck you!" I laugh. "And you have no right calling me out like this. You still had Star Wars bedsheets until last year."

"I know," he chuckles as he reaches over to ruffle my hair. "I'm just teasing you. It's really nice to have you here, Iggy."

"Yeah, you're pretty okay too."

He kicks me under the table, causing the milk in my cereal bowl to slosh out.

"Dude! Watch your gangly spider legs!" I yelp as I grab a napkin and mop it up.

Logan sips his coffee, staring at me like he's trying to figure me out. I wonder if he knows I'm lying about this weekend.

Or if he cares.

I clear my throat and take another spoonful, desperate to change the subject.

"What are you up to this weekend?"

"I've gotta finish the syllabus for this ethics course I'm teaching," he grumbles. "I still have to track down six more articles and figure out an assignment that's not a paper. I wish they could just make a diorama and call it a day, you know?"

Ethics are every academic's worst nightmare. You think you have a great methodology, and then you have to contend with the board. We all get how important it is, but it's still a minefield to navigate, and there's so much you have to think about.

"Sounds thrilling." I pause. "I thought you'd be hanging out with Abi."

Abi's the only one of Logan's friends that I've met, or even seen. Other than his goofy selfies and pictures of fall foliage, he's not one for social media. But last year, he brought Abi for Christmas dinner after her mom decided to go on one of those insane six month cruises. They definitely looked like they were more than just friends.

"Why?"

"Because you're close," I reply with a grin.

His eyes narrow.

"I don't like the way you said that."

"How long's it been since you dated?"

Logan drains his coffee and stands up, heading for the sink to rinse out his mug.

"I don't have time to date. I'm too busy."

I can tell by the way his shoulders are practically hunched up around his ears that he doesn't want to talk about it.

"Okay, that's cool."

I finish my breakfast and my coffee, and help Logan clean the kitchen. He's not charging me rent so that I can save up to find my own place. I am, however, helping to pay the utility bills, going halfsies on groceries, and doing my part to keep the house clean.

After breakfast, I head back down to my room to get a head start on some reading I have to do. In undergrad, I wouldn't start this shit until the first day of the first semester, but grad school is a totally different ballgame. You have to walk in prepared on the first day, and it's not just articles, it's full blown books.

Huge fucking books, and they're definitely not as interesting as the romance novels that line my shelves. It makes focusing next to impossible.

I sit at my new desk, pouring over Foucault and making notes when my phone buzzes, instantly pulling my focus away from what I should be doing. Honestly, I'm grateful for the distraction.

HENRY: Still on for mini golf tonight?

JADE: Of course! Looking forward to meeting you in person.

HENRY: You too.

He sends me a selfie and my jaw almost hits my desk.

HENRY: Just so you know who you're looking for. Hard to recognize a chest.

I'm giggling and spinning in my chair as I stare at the picture. He's got a rugged quality to him that makes butterflies swarm my stomach. Dark, messy hair, a long straight nose, and a lot of gray in his temples and his beard. But it's his eyes that really catch me. They're a warm hazel surrounded by crow's feet. For some reason I think he'd have a great laugh, something that puts you instantly at ease.

I text Piper the selfie, the details of our meetup, and his profile. It's partially bragging rights, and partially a safety measure.

> PIPES: Uhhh you're banging him, right?

> IMOGEN: I think it would be a disservice to humanity if I didn't. I just hope he's not a weirdo.

> PIPES: If he is, just hit him with a club. Problem solved!

> PIPES: I'll have my phone on all night. Text if you need, and be safe! If you need a place to crash, we rented an AirBnB for the weekend.

She sends me the address and the key code for the door. I smile, wondering what I'd do without a friend like Piper.

The sky looks like a watercolor painting with streaks of pink and orange spread out across an endless horizon. I've missed driving like this, with the windows down and fresh air filling my lungs. When I was at NYU, I used to drive Upstate and back just to think. I'm pretty sure I dictated ninety percent of my master's thesis with my foot on the gas while I screamed along to my playlists. It was a bitch to edit out all those song lyrics in the transcription, but in the end, it was worth it.

When I make it into Seattle, it's only another 10 minutes until I spot Lucky Strokes mini golf. There were a couple of other options, but this had the funniest name. I pull into the parking lot and kill the engine, pulling the sun visor down to make sure my hair and makeup still look decent. There's a bit of glitter smeared on my eyelids and perfectly carved wing liner with a pop of nude lipgloss. My hair is pulled back into two tiny buns on top of my head and my septum ring looks extra shiny in the light.

I look cute— casual, but cute. I chose a pair of tight blue jeans, a white crop top, and a soft purple hoodie that's a couple of shades darker than my hair. This isn't a date, so there's no point in going all out, but I still wanted to look presentable.

As I grab my stuff and climb out of the car, I hear a gravelly voice behind me.

"Jade?"

I turn my head, greeted with an image that's so much better than that selfie he sent me.

Henry's got to be at least 6'4", and he has the most bashful smile, his cheeks flushing when he sees me. In photos, he was hot, but in person, he makes my whole body feel like jelly. He's in a beaten up leather jacket and a pair of faded black jeans with a black v-neck t-shirt that exposes the tattoos on his chest.

This guy is exactly my type, and to top it all off, he's standing beside a black Thunderbird.

"Y— yeah," I stammer, quickly trying to regain my composure as I slide my phone back into my pocket. "I assume you're Henry?"

"Hope I'm not too disappointing," he chuckles.

I like a bit of self-deprecation, but there's nothing about this man that's disappointing to look at.

He takes a step toward me and stretches out his arm to shake my hand.

"It's nice to meet you."

"You too."

His hand is warm and I'm trying to carefully breathe through my nervousness. There's something about the way he's looking at me that makes me want to burst into giggles and twirl my hair like an idiot.

"You changed your hair," he remarks, yanking me out of my thoughts.

"What?"

"You were blonde in your pictures." He starts to stammer as I smile. "Not that— that's a bad thing or anything— I like— I like the hair. I like all kinds of hair— Sorry, is it obvious I haven't done this in a long time?"

"What, talked to a woman, or..."

"Oof. That's rough," he chuckles as the blush in his cheeks deepens.

"I'm kidding!" I exclaim before realizing that the two of us are still shaking hands. "This shit's awkward, I get it."

44

"You're tellin' me," he sighs as we break the handshake and he runs his fingers through his hair, messing it up a little more.

The more I look at this guy, the more I wonder what he'd look like tied to a hotel bed.

"Come on, let's play some mini golf and get to know each other," I offer. "We can ease into the other stuff."

As we head for the entrance, I immediately text Piper.

> IMOGEN: He's even hotter in person. I'll keep you updated if anything weird goes down.

We pay the entrance fee and head inside. The place looks like a theme park, and each of the 18 holes has a different vibe. As we line up for our equipment, Henry seems really nervous, his eyes dancing around and taking everything in.

"Do you wanna bail?" I ask. "I don't mind. I can golf by myself."

"No! No, it's..." He hangs his head. "Look, I wasn't joking when I said it's been a long time since I've done anything like this. Mostly, I just go to work and go home."

"Well, everyone needs a change of pace, right?" I ask as we get to the front of the line.

He nods and we rent a couple of clubs and a small basket of golf balls. The place is a little empty, but then again, it's a Tuesday night.

"So who goes first?" Henry asks as we approach the first hole.

"Rock, paper, scissors?"

I stick out my hand and he does the same, the two of us shaking our fists three times, and he throws out paper while I end up with scissors. Henry groans, tipping his head up to the sky as he laughs.

"I was so sure you were gonna pick rock!"

"Why did you think that?"

"You've just got a rock... vibe," he chuckles and then winces.

"What's a rock vibe?" I laugh, arching a brow.

"I don't really know. Kind of cool, uh... I don't know why I said that. I don't know what other qualities rocks have."

"*Kind* of cool?" I tease, elbowing him a little to help ease the tension.

I think I'm actually making it worse.

"You're killin' me, Jade."

I didn't expect this kind of bashfulness from a guy who looks like him. There's a lack of confidence in his posture that feels alien. But I bet when he's really comfortable around someone, he's relaxed and assertive. I'd like to see that.

I gently tap my club against his.

"You can go first."

"No, no. You won fair and square. Show me those mini golf skills."

The first hole has two giant soccer balls stationed as obstacles and you have to bounce your ball off of one of them in order to get it anywhere near the hole. I take a step back and swing hard, and the ball goes flying, bouncing off of one of the soccer balls and then into a little pond.

Henry turns to me with a sly smile, and a gleam in his eyes.

"Wow, it was your idea so I kind of assumed you'd be good at mini golf."

"Look, you almost gave your bank account information to a sex bot. I don't think you're in a place to judge me."

He chuckles and jogs after the ball.

"It's fine!" I laugh. "We have other ones!"

He ignores me, getting down on his knees and reaching out with his tiny golf club to pull the ball toward him, fishing it out of the pond. When he drops the ball into my palm, his fingers gently brush against mine. I swear I feel sparks, and my stomach flips as he takes a step backward. His club is way too small for him to actually lean on, so he rests it on his shoulder like he's holding a baseball bat. I line my shot up and try again.

"Try hitting it with a little less force this time," he says, taking a step behind me and leaning in, his lips just barely brushing my ear. "Might help there, sweetheart."

I shiver at the sudden boldness and glance over my shoulder as he steps back.

"You're a bit of a brat."

"Is that bad?" He asks.

"Not at all." I grin. "I know how to tame brats."

I hit the ball again, this time sinking it into the hole in one. Henry applauds behind me, and I hold my club above my head, spinning around to face him with a big smile.

"Just call me Tiger fuckin' Woods!"

CHAPTER SIX

tennessee whiskey

ROMAN

It's been a struggle to take my eyes off her.

Her long, lavender hair flows down her back, and her warm brown eyes shimmer with a touch of mischief. The thing I like most about her, though, is her smile. She's got a slightly crooked tooth that she doesn't seem at all ashamed to show off.

She showed up casual, dressed in a pair of light washed jeans, bright green sneakers, and a white crop top with her hoodie tied around her waist. She's also got a septum ring, and tattoos scattered across her arms; I keep finding my gaze wandering up and down her body, wanting to ask about them as I try to count them. I'm glad we didn't agree to a nice dinner at a place that's fancy enough to demand a dress code. I feel like I can be myself a little more.

Jade walks with confidence, swinging her club gently back and forth as we head to the next course. She puts her hands on her hips, staring at an obnoxious windmill lit up with neon lights, the whole thing surrounded by fake palm trees. There's a small, very thin path leading right to the hole that's flanked by large sand traps on either side, and the windmill's arms spin just quickly enough to force the timing. A little too late, or angled just slightly wrong, and you're digging your ball out of the sand.

"How do you want to approach this, Tiger?" I ask.

She drops her ball onto the ground, grinning at me.

"Carefully. Now step back and don't steal my strategy."

I give her some space, watching her take a breath as she figures out how to get the best shot.

"So, um, do you take all of your potential... partners to play mini golf?"

"No," she replies casually, kneeling down to better judge the position of the hole. "Coffee dates, lunch, sometimes a walk around the park. Anywhere where I can get a feel for someone."

"That's smart."

"Do you think you're ready for the 'what are you into' conversation?" She asks, still not looking up from the green.

I glance around, slightly paranoid. I've never really voiced these desires before, and no matter how foolish it sounds, this almost feels like I'm doing something I shouldn't.

"I... I like the idea of submission." My voice is shaky, and Jade's clearly noticed, glancing up at me with curiosity. "Spanking, humiliation, stuff like that."

"And domination? Any interest there?"

My mind flashes back to one video I saw of a woman on her knees with a tie wrapped around her eyes and her mouth gagged with a massive cock. She was choking, spittle dripping down her chin like honey while she rode a vibrator, coming over and over again until she was shaking.

"Yeah," I murmur. "Yeah, definitely."

Since research is my job it didn't feel odd to spend a lot of time googling shit that would make my internet company blush: Ball gags, blindfolds, rope bondage, spanking. I watched pain turn to ecstasy, a kind of joy I've never seen or experienced before. It made me envious. I wanted to do it, and I wanted it done to me.

"Okay, so you're a switch. That's cool." She takes her shot, watching the ball until it comes to a stop just in front of the windmill before turning back to me. "But I want to be up front: I don't sub for people I don't know well."

"I understand. I read somewhere that it's a good idea to be submissive first, before moving on to domination."

She smiles as I chip the ball, and it sails off the path and right into the sand.

"Very good, Henry."

I can't tell if she's talking about my submission comment, or if it was a jab at my shitty golf abilities, but the teasing nature of her tone makes me blush.

"That was terrible."

"True," she sighs dramatically. "Come on, I wanna see you hit that thing for real."

"Yeah?" I saunter into the sand trap, gearing up to take a swing. "You wanna watch complete and utter embarrassment?"

"It'll be good practice for when I'm calling you a slut one day."

I miss so hard I think I might need to join the mini golf witness protection program, and Jade raises her club as that rich laughter of hers rings through the night.

"Yes! Got you!"

"When did this become competitive?" I ask, shaking some of the sand off my boot.

"Isn't golf always competitive, or are you just afraid of losing?"

She wanders over to her ball and takes another shot, trying to inch it past the arms of the windmill. Unfortunately she hits it a *little* too hard, and we both watch it soar through the air, bouncing off the roof before nearly hitting her on the way down.

"It kinda looks like we're both losing."

She frowns, her hands on her hips as I stifle my own laughter.

"Well, now it's a competition to see who's losing worse and you…"

"You're saying I'm winning at losing?" I tease, getting the jab in before she can even finish her sentence.

Jade pauses, her eyes volleying between me and the golf ball.

"Fuck. Looks like you're right."

She strides over to pick up her ball and hurls it across the park, straight into the water; I stare at her with a look of total confusion as she tosses her hair back.

"New game strategy! Team work, we get this done together."

"Oh, now that I'm winning the humiliation game, you wanna change the rules?"

"Hey, I paid for the entry fee! My rules now."

Jade lifts her club and rests it on the back of her shoulders, giving me a playful shrug before licking her lips. That's when I spot her tongue ring.

"Fine, I can get on board with that," I reply, doing my best to seem calm.

"Perfect!"

She bounces back toward me and chips our remaining ball, sending sand flying up into the air as it sails across the path and into another trap.

"Chill out!"

"Well, I had to get out of the sand!" She shouts.

"And into more sand?"

"Just take your turn, tough guy."

I cross the path while she stays behind in the opposite sand trap, but it's hard to care about the ball when all I can think about is how gorgeous she looks, and I take a quick moment to steal a glance. Her little crop top rides up her stomach, giving me a good look at more tattoos. Flowers and leaves mostly, all disappearing into the waistband of her jeans.

I find myself unable to stop thinking about how much I'd like to trace them with my tongue.

"So." I clear my throat as I try and fail to focus on my shot. "What happens when you decide someone might be a good kink partner?"

"We'd start you out slow since it's your first time. We'd figure out limits, a safe word, and then get into our roles. Lots of teasing and getting you comfortable with submitting." I can hear her making her way over to me, but I keep my focus as best I can. "I'm here to guide you; you can say the safe word any time you want, and we stop."

I nod.

"How long are the sessions?"

"As long as you want," she replies, her voice coming from right behind me now. "I like meeting people in this scene and connecting with them. It doesn't always have to be kink or sex. But I... I don't do relationships. Just want to make that clear."

"So, it's friends with benefits."

"Pretty much, yeah."

We keep playing the hole for quite some time, resulting in a lot more failure and laughter trailing off into the evening. I was skeptical of a mini golf date to begin with, but I ended up having more fun than I've had in a long time.

Finally, on what has to be our hundredth combined attempt, I manage to hit the ball just right for it to slip past the arm of the windmill to the other side.

"Heeeey!" She laughs. "Does that make you our loser-winner, or winner-loser?"

As the night stretches on, and our focus moves further and further from the greens, I get to understand more about Jade and her limits. She draws the line at true sadism, doesn't enjoy making people bleed or truly hurt. She also doesn't do stuff like water sports, which I had to look up on my phone while her back was turned.

Definitely *not* my thing.

"What about you? What are your limits?" She asks.

"I don't really know. For now let's just say... don't punch me in the balls?"

"Got it. No ball punching." She snorts. "And turn ons? What do you like?"

I clear my throat and look around to make sure we're out of ear shot. Jade doesn't really seem to care, she's probably had these conversations dozens of times, but I'm still a bit flustered by the topic.

"I like the idea of getting slapped, some light humiliation. I also like um... compliments?"

I figured that out pretty fast from watching those videos.

"Praised *and* degraded. It's a fine line, but I can walk it," she replies, flashing me an approving grin.

"Does that kind of stuff work for you too?"

She slinks towards me, getting so close the toes of her sneakers touch my boots.

"There's a laundry list of shit that turns me on, Henry. Right now what I'm interested in is your pleasure."

She smells delicious. Amber, tobacco, and vanilla with a hint of something floral that I can't put my finger on.

"O— okay," I stammer. "So, you wanna do this?"

"Well, the night's not over yet, but I think it's going pretty well so far, don't you?"

"Yeah. You, uh..." She licks her lips as butterflies torment my stomach. "You seem really cool."

"You too."

"Now, I *know* you're bullshitting me," I chuckle.

I take in the soft freckles on her cheeks, the little sparkle in her eyes, and her long, thick lashes.

"Trust me, Henry. I've faked a lot of stuff, but—"

"Like being the Tiger Woods of mini golf?"

She snickers, her smile so big I find myself smiling right back.

"You're never gonna let me live that down, are you?"

"Not a chance, darlin'."

Blush cascades down her neck and onto her chest. Maybe I've still got it after all these years.

"I was going to say, I've faked a lot of stuff, but I've never faked interest in someone just to get some dick."

Before I can respond she turns around and takes a final putt. The two of us watch in silence as it creeps toward the hole, lingering for a moment on the edge before it slips in.

"Yes!"

Jade thrusts her arm in the air, full of excitement and glee.

"Nice job!" I exclaim, the two of us going in for an awkward high-five.

We debate going to another course, but ultimately decide against it, watching a few small groups of people play almost as bad as we did while we walk the grounds. Our conversation continues, quickly taking a left turn into our less private interests. Jade likes horror flicks, whereas I prefer my cooking shows and romantic comedies. She likes Stephen King, I like Virginia Woolf. It's a fun little exercise.

"Desert island. Top five movies," she says, grabbing my arm. "Go."

"That's too hard. Ten."

"Five!"

She's firm, in control even here.

"Fine, fine. I'll play along." I stroke my beard, racking my brain for an answer. "Okay, first one: When Harry Met Sally."

"Great pick."

"Thank you." I grimace, struggling for more. "Second... Erin Brockovich."

"Solid," she replies, nodding enthusiastically. "Julia Roberts is so good in that."

"She really is... but for my last three, let's say the Lord of the Rings trilogy."

Jade narrows her eyes.

"Extended version, or regular?"

"If you're not watching the extended version, is it even The Lord of the Rings?"

She grins.

"Amen."

We find a bench, sitting for a while as the conversation turns to music. She says she likes classic rock, although her definition of 'classic' is the stuff I listened to when I was 19 or 20. I tell her it stings a little, and she gets a kick out of that.

I'm 43, but I don't feel old, other than the fact that my knees suck, and if I sleep on one side for too long my hip goes numb. Most days, though, I still feel like I'm the same idiot I was when I was 20, and I'm not really sure what that says about me.

"Attention Lucky Strokes golfers, we'll be closing in 30 minutes."

The crackle of the PA system makes me jump, but Jade just sighs, scrolling through her phone as my anxiety begins to gnaw away at me. The last thing I want to do is go back to my empty apartment, alone, but before I can say a word she takes the reins.

"Are you hungry? I haven't eaten dinner yet, and I know a place nearby."

"Starved."

It's like she read my mind.

CHAPTER SEVEN

american girl

IMOGEN

We're tucked into a small booth in the back corner of the diner, with a teal table and shiny cherry-red seats. It's pretty chaotic for 11pm, packed with drunk college students and tourists, but I like the vibe. It kind of reminds me of a little diner that Piper and I used to go to in Queens. The whole place smells like fresh coffee, maple syrup, and french fries.

I'm digging into a stack of buttermilk pancakes, smothered in berries, whipped cream, and syrup. All the sugar and preservatives are probably going to liquify my organs by the time I'm 50, but I'm here for a good time, not a long time.

"How did you get into the whole dominatrix thing?" Henry asks, munching on a piece of bacon.

He's been surprisingly easy to talk to. I don't feel judged, and he really seems to consider what he's going to say before he says it. He's curious, but most importantly he's open in a way that puts me at ease. I like that kind of quality in a man.

"I went through something personal that made me feel like I was out of control and numb all at the same time. I was shutting down, and I didn't feel like I could express how I felt." I pause to take a sip of my scalding-hot coffee. "Anyway, I didn't want to feel powerless anymore. Kink gave me a way to take power back."

54

I wait for him to interject, but he just nods, encouraging me to continue.

"It was a shock at first, but subbing for someone and knowing I had the power to say no, and that it *meant no*, that was everything to me. Turned out I could set my own boundaries and be as involved or detached as I pleased. No feelings if I just wanted to play, and then nothing to be sad about if and when it came to an end. Just a handshake and a *'see you around, partner.'*"

I pull myself back, clearing my throat. Usually I just tell a curated version of the truth, and one that's got a lot less of *me* in it. I definitely didn't mean to go into that much detail, especially not to someone I only met a few hours ago.

Thankfully, Henry's light chuckle makes me feel a little less awkward about it.

"Partner? Like a cowboy?"

I lean back in my chair, grinning at him as I take another bite of my pancakes.

"Yeah, I keep a cowboy hat in my car just for the dramatic goodbye. Helps if it's at night and I'm under a streetlight so I look mysterious. Maybe whistle a little tune as I tip my hat and walk away."

Henry smirks, shaking his head as he slices off a piece of his waffle.

"You're quite the character."

"Just a bit," I reply with a little wink. "What about you? Were you always curious about kink, or..."

"Sort of. I was married for a while, but I've been alone for about two years now. It's given me a lot of time to think."

I can feel my guard raise a little; divorce can be a red flag with some guys. They say they want casual and then the next thing you know, they're trying to nail down a commitment, chasing you with an engagement ring.

"How long were you married?"

"Four and a half years."

"Any kids?"

"No," he whispers. "Never had time. She wanted them, but I didn't find that out until later. I work a lot, maybe too much."

I pick up my mug and raise it with a grin.

"To workaholics."

"Amen."

Suddenly Henry looks a bit uncomfortable. Maybe he sensed that the topic of divorce put me a little on edge.

"Are you and your ex on good terms?" I ask, immediately regretting the question.

His jaw clenches, and he clings to his mug like a life raft. I can almost feel the grief crashing against him, his body tensing as the words spill from his lips.

"She's– uh, she's passed. It was..." He blows out a breath. "Let's just say I didn't expect it."

"Oh I'm... Henry, I'm so sorry."

It's a struggle to even get the words out.

"No, it's— I probably should have been up front about it, it's just... you know, it's hard to—" He covers his mouth with one hand and stares out the window. I can see his eyes misting as he clears his throat, quickly regaining his composure while my stomach twists itself into knots. "Sorry, you probably don't wanna hear this shit. I'm sure I sound like a real goddamn sad sack."

I reach across the table, wrapping my fingers around his. He doesn't flinch, just squeezes back gently as he stares into his coffee.

"You don't sound like a sad sack at all, you sound like you're going through some pretty heavy shit. I never would have guessed."

"Yeah." He sniffles, his eyes rimmed red. "I guess grief gets comfortable to live in after a while."

I think about my own family, and how I can still see the pain in Logan's eyes when he talks about our dad. He's more open about his grief than I am. Mine lives in a deep, dark place that's hard to dig myself out of; I almost fell in last night, staring at that picture of dad and I at Disneyland.

"I lost someone, too, but we don't have to talk about this stuff. I'm probably making things worse."

He blinks away the tears in his eyes.

"You're not, I promise. I want to move on. I can't live in this place forever. It's..."

"Lonely," I finish.

Grief is like a wound that never quite heals. Some days, it's faded into the background, completely out of mind; others, you're buying apples at the store and a song comes on that brings you to your knees in the produce aisle.

"I tried dating, but it didn't work out so well." He offers a hollow laugh. "I think there's a part of me that's afraid I'm going to betray her by starting anything up with someone else. It's why I was big on the casual thing. I think this kink stuff could, I don't know... help me work through some of it, you know?"

"People get into this for all kinds of different reasons. I don't judge."

In fact, I probably understand more than he does.

"So, you grow up here?" He asks, changing the subject as he clears his throat.

"No," I reply, happy to move on from such a dour topic. "I'm here for school. What about you?"

"Been on the west coast for about 20 years, but I grew up in Montana on a big ranch. My dad was a bull rider."

I whistle and he smiles back at me. It feels like things are shifting back to the more playful dynamic we had on the golf course.

"Bull rider, huh? That's a tough gig."

"It's not for the faint of heart. Bruises, broken bones, dislocated shoulders, the works. My mom was always on his ass telling him to quit as he got older, but he loved it. He was on the road most summers while we stayed behind and looked after the ranch."

"Doing what?"

"Taking care of the horses and livestock, milking cows, basic repairs, stuff like that."

"Did you ever ride any bulls? Or horses?"

"Horses, definitely, but I wasn't really cut out for bull riding." There's a joyful twinkle in his eyes, like he's just recalled a distant memory. "Haven't ridden a horse in a few years now. Work kind of gets in the way."

Maybe it's the manners and the charm, or the fact that there's a tiny bit of twang buried under his West Coast accent, but the cowboy angle fits him.

"Do you miss that life?"

"Sometimes, yeah. One of my horses is stabled up at my friend's ranch in the Cascade Foothills. I try to get out there when I can." He pauses. "What about you? Spend any time in the country, or..."

"No," I laugh. "I'm definitely a city girl. But I've always been interested in horses. Maybe you could teach me how to ride someday."

"Oh, yeah of course. So, I'm assuming that means you want to meet up again?"

He sounds a little surprised and I'm not sure why. He's hot, we connect, he doesn't seem like a creep or a serial killer.

"I'd like to, if you're up for it." I clear my throat, bracing myself for the slightly awkward part. "Just so you know, though, I don't typically invite people over to my place. It's nothing against you, just a safety thing."

And now that I've moved, it's a nosy brother thing. I do not need Logan interrogating my hookups over coffee in the morning.

"Makes sense," he shrugs. "Lotta weirdos around."

"Definitely. It's just, some guys don't like it when I bring that up."

"Well, I figure if you're still fine with sharing a hotel room, I'm not too worried about it. Actually, I guess I'm still not really sure how this works. Do you do hotels?"

I can feel electricity lingering in the air between us, and my body is brimming with excitement.

"I usually meet up with guys at clubs, but I haven't really had the chance to get out to any since I got here." I lean forward, tapping my nails against my coffee mug. "How about this: if you promise to teach me how to ride a horse, I'll teach you *everything* you need to know about submission and domination. No strings attached, and none of that relationship shit. We can drop this any time we want. You in?"

Henry stares at me for a second, mulling things over in his head before offering his hand.

"You've got yourself a deal, Jade."

If I'm being honest with myself, I really like this guy. Piper tells me that my penchant for casual relationships is going to end up leaving me all alone. She may be right, but I'd rather protect my heart than have to glue it back together over and over again.

When the check comes, Henry snatches it away before I even have a chance to make a move, handing the waitress his credit card.

"You paid for golf, it's only fair I pay for pancakes."

"You drive a hard bargain, cowboy."

I get a flutter in my chest as he blushes at the nickname, feeling a little pang of regret as we slide out of the booth. I wish we'd eaten slower, or maybe ordered another round of coffee, anything to keep this going a bit longer.

"I'll walk you to your car," Henry says as we make our way outside.

The parking lot is empty, save for a few cars including our own, barely lit by the one or two overheard lights that are still glowing in the pitch-black. I pull my phone out, shocked at how late it's gotten.

"Jesus, it's past midnight," I laugh.

"You got a curfew?" Henry teases.

"Yep, I've got 30 minutes before I turn into a pumpkin." I gesture at myself, doing a little twirl. "This is all an illusion."

"You're doing great for a pumpkin," he chuckles. "It does explain your golf score, though."

"You want a rematch, smart ass?" I gently whack him in the arm. "I can get real competitive."

"Nah, I don't think so. The sand trap fiasco was enough humiliation for me."

We stop at my car and he stuffs his hands in his pockets, glancing around aimlessly. He's nervous again, but honestly, so am I. Usually, I just give guys a side-hug, maybe a quick kiss on the cheek, and quickly hash out an agreement to text each other for a second meetup. But this wasn't enough. I want more time with him.

"You know, I almost didn't come out tonight," he says softly. "But I'm really glad I did."

"I'm glad too. I had a really good time."

Neither of us really knows what to say, and all I can hear is the sound of the wind rustling the trees and the distant roar of cars on the freeway.

Should I ask him if he wants to get a hotel tonight?

Is that too forward?

I don't want to freak this guy out.

"Well, I guess I should..." He gestures toward his car.

"Yeah, me too."

My skin feels like it's on fire as his eyes lock with mine, burning into me. His smile fades a little, and suddenly I'm fully aware of just how close he's standing.

"I didn't want this night to end," he murmurs, his voice barely audible above the sound of my pounding heartbeat.

"Me neither."

I lean a little closer, and suddenly his hand is on my cheek, his thumb gently tracing my lip. I feel instant sparks, the tension so thick that it's getting hard to breathe.

"I had an *amazing* time with you tonight," he rumbles, a heavy silence lingering between us until he breaks it again with a laugh. "You know, I've spent my whole life talking and writing, and now I can't come up with anything charming to save my life. I feel like a pretty big dork right now."

I gaze up at him, taking in the deep hazel of his eyes.

"I kind of like the fact that you're a dork."

That smile is going to be the death of me.

"Fuck it," he growls. "I wanna kiss you."

"So quit running your mouth and do it."

He presses his lips to mine, his massive body pushing me up against the car and caging me in. He smells like musk and leather, but it's the undertone of soap and an unidentifiable warm sweetness that makes my knees wobble.

I'm ready to tell this man to bend me over the hood of this car and fucking *take me* right here. I don't give a shit who pulls up. I've always wanted to explore my exhibitionist streak a little more, but maybe on a second date.

"You wanna get a hotel room?" I ask, getting the question out before either of us has time to second guess it.

"For real?"

All I can do is nod as I tip my head up and part my lips, desperate for another kiss.

"For real."

"You're a bit wild, aren't you?" He chuckles.

I grin and cock my head.

"Just you wait, cowboy. I haven't even ridden you yet."

night moves

ROMAN

I'm standing in the lobby of a shitty motel on the interstate while the front desk clerk clicks away on his keyboard. I think about letting Frankie know how the date's going, but I don't need the thousand text messages that are going to blow up my phone, especially not tonight. Instead, I quickly text my neighbor and ask him if he can feed Mitzy in the morning and take her out with his dogs.

As I slide my phone into my pocket and take in my surroundings, the whole night catches up with me. Her laugh, her smile, that kiss...

What's gotten into me? I don't do this. I used to, back when I was a hell of a lot younger, but this is, what? Crazy? Irresponsible? Kind of makes me feel like I'm 20 again.

I feel like I've been blushing all damn night. I should be embarrassed but all I know is that I can still taste her cotton candy lip gloss, and I want more.

"Room 405." The front desk guy hands me two key cards, looking just as excited as you might think someone working a desk close to 12AM would be. "Have a good night."

I head outside, spotting Jade leaning up against her car on her phone and suddenly I'm all nerves. It's been four years since I've been with someone. I'm worried that I may have lost my edge.

But I've never been a quitter.

"Are you gonna take me to this motel room, or are we just gonna make eyes at each other all night?" She asks, lifting her head with a flirtatious grin.

If you asked me to list the qualities of my ideal woman, confidence would be at the top. It's a big turn-on for me, and Jade seems to have it in spades. It's like she lives and breathes this stuff. She doesn't just dominate in the bedroom, she's powerful, and a little intimidating.

"Room 405," I tell her, handing her a key card.

"Lead the way, handsome."

I take her around the building toward our room, my heart in my throat.

"I was just letting my friend know where I am, by the way. You seem like a great guy, but nobody wants to be the subject of a true crime documentary."

I chuckle, my heart still pounding as I hold up both hands.

"I assure you, all I'm interested in is..."

"Fucking?"

My face feels like it's on fire, and Jade leans to the side, looking past me.

"What?"

"Someone's staring at us."

I don't take my eyes off her. I don't give a shit.

"I wonder what he's thinking," she whispers scandalously as her eyes shine.

I slide my hand around her waist and I pull her in close.

"He's probably wondering how a beautiful girl like you wound up in his shitty hotel."

"Hey, it's a *motel*," she corrects me, keeping her voice low and sultry. "That's what the sign says outside."

Jade pins me against the wall to kiss me again. It's ferocious, the heat already beginning to consume us. I slowly unzip her hoodie as she slides her fingers underneath my t-shirt.

There's nothing hotter than a woman who looks like she wants to devour you.

I cannot *believe* how lucky I got with that app.

"We haven't even found our room yet," I laugh.

"It's your fault. You got me all distracted."

"I'm distracting you?"

"Yep. In those tight pants," she replies, playfully caging me in with her arms.

There's a buzz of electricity sparking between us, one that I feel creeping down my spine as I reach up and take her hand, leading her toward the room; neither of us speak for the short walk, staying silent even after I open the door.

I barely have a chance to take anything in before she's on me again, pulling me toward the bed by the sleeve of my jacket. She shoves me down, but takes a step back, giving me a second to drink everything in. The room is sparse, with only a bed, a shitty dresser, a nightstand, and a small desk near the window. It smells musty in here, like someone's tried to cover it with a cheap pine-scented air freshener.

Jade wastes no time in tossing her purse and hoodie aside before kicking off her sneakers.

"You just wanna fuck, or do you want me to dom you? Because I can do either. Or both."

"Both," I breathe as I slide my boots off.

"Stand up."

The command is gentle and sweet. I get to my feet, and she crooks her finger, making a little come hither motion.

"We're going to see how well you can follow orders, cowboy."

"Trust me, darlin'. I'll be good."

She cocks her head to the side, her eyes gleaming in a way that makes her look untouchable.

"Undress me."

I feel like I'm on fire, my heart thumping in the base of my throat as I reach for the hem of her shirt, and slowly reveal a canvas of tattoos on her torso. UFOs, horror movie icons, comic portraits of zombies, werewolves, and all sorts of other monsters, each of them tied together with intricate vines and flowers.

I dip my head and place soft kisses across her collarbone and down her breasts, stopping briefly to nibble on her stiff nipples through her flimsy lace bra, only to find...

"You've gotta be kidding me."

"Surpriiiise," she giggles.

Nipple rings. God bless this app.

I turn her around so that she's facing the mirror and glide my lips along her shoulders, taking my time and pulling her hair back so that I can suck gently on her neck.

"You're gorgeous."

My fingers work quickly to unclasp her bra and toss it aside. Slowly, I grind my cock against her ass, still frustrated by the layers of denim that separate us.

"You like this power play stuff, don't you?" She asks, her voice thick with desire.

"Mmhmm. It's nice to finally do it in real life."

Her smile is angelic, and the sliver of light pouring in from the half opened curtains makes her look ethereal. I want her to see herself, and I want to watch what her face looks like when I tease her pussy.

"You might not be as vanilla as I thought."

"Nothing wrong with vanilla," I reply, reaching around to pop open the button on her jeans. "But lately I've been finding I like a dash of something extra on top."

Her confidence seems to have rubbed off on me, because before I can even think, my hand is sliding into her panties. She's soaked, and I suck on her neck while I tease her clit in slow circles until her hips start to roll against my touch. Her cheeks are flushed and little pink splotches paint her chest like watercolor stains, but it's her moans that make me feel that primal desperation, like I'm clawing my way through the desert for a single drop of water.

"I told you to undress me and here you are, a little fucking slut with your hand down my pants," she purrs. "Is that what you are, Henry? A desperate little slut?"

She smiles, listening to the sound of pure sin leaving my mouth.

"Finish undressing me and I'll give you what you want."

"Yes, ma'am," I whisper.

I push her jeans past her hips and get down on my knees as she steps out of them. She's in a little pink thong that matches her bra, and I grab it with my teeth, pulling back until it snaps against her skin. She yelps at first, then lets out a soft giggle as she turns around and leans against the dresser. I move to stand, but she holds out her hand, keeping me exactly where I am.

On my knees.

"From here on out, you're *mine*. You do what I say when I say it."

Holy. Shit.

"Or what?" I ask, testing the boundaries of our new roles.

Jade leans over, her lavender hair tickling my face and her gorgeous tits just a few inches from my mouth as she grasps my chin.

"Or I'm the only one who gets to come tonight. And you'll only get to watch me while I take what I want."

"I'm not gonna lie to you, darlin', that sounds like heaven."

"So you're into edging, too, hmm?"

Jade releases me and slowly pushes the little triangle of fabric covering her pussy aside until I'm met with a patch of dark blonde hair.

"Answer me, cowboy."

"I think so."

I don't believe in God, but I might start after tonight.

"What else would you like?"

"Humiliate me. Punish me if I don't do what you want." I swallow hard, my heart in my throat. "I can take it."

"If anything gets too intense, you say red and we stop. That's your safe word for the night. If you can't say it, you squeeze my thigh twice, understand?"

"I understand."

There's a hungry look in her eyes that makes me ache. My cock is straining against my jeans and I want to ask her if I can take them off, but I know exactly what she'd say.

"Do you eat pussy?" She asks.

"Yes," I manage to rasp back.

"Do you want to eat mine?"

Her voice is like silk brushing against my skin, and the hairs on the back of my neck stand straight up.

"Y— yes. Very much."

She beams and strokes my cheek lovingly.

"You'll call me Mistress."

"Yes, Mistress."

"Good boy. Now, get to work."

Without thinking, I grab the string of her thong and yank it down her hips with my teeth while my hands glide up and down her thighs. Her skin is silky beneath my touch, with fine baby hairs that she's missed during shaving giving it a little extra friction.

I feel ready, but what if I'm terrible at this? The last thing I'd want to do is disappoint her. Jade seems to sense my anxiety, holding my chin gently in place as she flashes me a warm smile.

"It's okay," her words drip like honey. "I've got you."

There's something feral in her eyes that makes me crave her approval. Her praise.

"Tease me with your fingers first, like you did before." She leans up against the dresser. "I want you to touch every part of me, Henry."

My heart's hammering at the base of my throat as I slide my fingers between her pussy lips. She lets out a contented sigh and drapes one leg over my shoulder, her heel digging into my back.

"Yes," she moans. "Atta boy. Just like that."

I circle her clit lightly, feeling it stiffen and swell beneath my fingertips. Every so often, I put on a little extra pressure just to hear her rich, warm moans fill the room like a symphony.

"You can use your tongue now. Softly."

Jade looks enraptured, her head tipped back and her lips parted as she leans harder into the dresser. My mouth waters as I give her a long, slow lick, moaning at the sharpness that floods my tongue.

"That's it. *Good* fucking boy."

Her fingers knot themselves in my hair as I keep up the pace, nice slow licks that work her up until she's writhing against me, letting out raspy breaths.

"Faster." Her voice begins to break. "Oh, fuck!"

I oblige, but decide to throw in a little twist, wrapping my lips around her clit as I slide two fingers into her pussy. Jade holds my head in place as she writhes; if she suffocated me right now, I'd die a very happy man.

"Curl your fingers—*yes*! Oh, fuck, that's so good!" She whines.

Her hand slides a little further down the back of my head, fingernails gently scraping my neck. A tingle rushes down my spine. I want to reach into my jeans and stroke my cock so badly. I can feel precum soaking right through my briefs as my hips rock back and forth, desperate to alleviate the pressure that's building. I eat her pussy like I'm half-starved, my fingers pumping slowly in and out of her, leaving her trembling but clearly still in control.

"I'm gonna come," she moans.

I'm the one doing this for her. I'm her *good fucking boy*.

I pull my mouth away and look up at her.

"Do you want me to stop?"

She slaps me across the face, hard enough to send my head whipping to the side. Her eyes are dark and piercing when I look back at her, cheeks flushed as plump pink lips curl into a wicked smirk.

"Did I say stop?"

"No, Mistress."

"Good. You've got 30 seconds to make me come or you'll spend the entire night begging for mercy."

That familiar rush of heat ricochets through me like molten shrapnel and I'm overcome with desire, burying my face in her delicious cunt. I thought I would be a hell of a lot worse at this, but it turns out 'if you don't use it you lose it' doesn't apply here.

Her breathing becomes shallow and quick and suddenly she's clawing at my hair, fucking my face with a frenzied rhythm. For a moment, insecurity kicks in again, making me wonder if she's just trying to make me feel better, but Jade doesn't seem like the kind of woman who would fake it just to be polite.

"Fifteen seconds..."

Who am I to disobey this woman? I do exactly what she's told me, putting together all of her previous instructions until I can feel her legs quiver and strain. I slow the pace of my tongue and fingers as she groans, licking her until I've tasted every last drop.

When I'm finished Jade rewards me, stroking my hair and my face, bliss coating her every feature.

"You did so well."

She purrs, and my whole body sings.

"So, what would you like as a reward?"

I swallow hard, fighting the vulnerability that would normally hold me back from saying anything like this to anyone.

With her, though? I feel free.

"Mistress, would you want to... spank me?"

CHAPTER NINE
witchy woman
IMOGEN

I don't know where they make men like Henry, but I'd like to live there.

Where did he say he was born? Montana? Kansas? I'm too fucking horny to remember right now.

He leaves a trail of kisses up my thigh as he gets to his feet, each brush of his lips against my skin like tiny fireworks going off. His kiss is hungry as he reaches me, and I taste myself on his tongue.

I love it, but I give him a gentle push backward just the same.

There's a mischievous gleam in his eyes as he slowly unbuckles his belt, sliding it out of the loops and gazing longingly at the thick leather in his own hands. Some men get a little *too* bratty and forget who's in charge, but Henry walks that line well.

"Do you want me to hit you with that?"

I reach out to cup his cheek, his stubble rough and his skin warm. His throat bobs, eyes pleading as they flick back to me.

"Yes, Mistress."

"Take your clothes off, I want to see who you really are."

Henry steps back, peeling off his t-shirt and revealing exactly what I hoped was living under those clothes. He's muscular, his body a canvas of tattoos beneath a dusting of dark chest hair. The ink stretches across his chest, all the way down his toned arms, and I drink in every inch of him, my eyes lingering on the trail of hair that disappears into his jeans.

Henry unzips his pants, pushing them past his hips along with his briefs, and my jaw drops when I see the size of his cock. I want to get on my knees and worship it up close, licking and sucking him until he's shooting right down my throat, but right now we've got our roles to play.

"Keeping something like that all to yourself should be a crime."

He blushes and I take a step forward.

This electricity between us is addicting, and I *love* a bashful man.

"Do you think it'll fit?"

His voice is thick with desire, but all I want to hear is him moaning my name for the rest of the night.

"We'll make it fit." I reach down and glide a fingertip along his shaft, making him shiver. "*Cowboy.*"

Slowly, I ease him onto the bed, lowering myself to my knees in front of him and wrapping my fingers around his cock. My eyes flick upward to see his head tipping back. He's balanced on his elbows, almost statuesque as the moonlight carves out his features.

"I want you to shove your cock so far down my throat I can feel it in my fucking toes."

"Where'd you learn to talk like that?" He laughs. "I've never met a woman with a mouth like this before."

I drag my tongue along his shaft, base to tip.

"If you wanna do this on the regular, you're gonna hear a hell of a lot worse."

"Mmm. I can't wait."

I swirl my tongue around the tip, playfully teasing him as I squeeze the base of his cock.

"Christ," he groans, his hands finding their way into my hair as he pushes my head all the way down, setting the pace. "You look so pretty like this."

I let out a whine as I bob up and down. He's eager, and I can already tell by the way his body's tensing that he's close to coming, his hips snapping harder as a sinful melody fills the room.

Just as his breathing quickens, I pull away. A thin line of spittle dangles from my lips, still connected to his cock as he twitches, his face twisted up in exquisite agony.

"You thought I was gonna let you come?"

"You said I was a good boy," he whimpers.

I grin, and he flinches as I lightly smack his cock, an animal grunt escaping his lips.

"And *you* said you liked edging. Isn't that right?"

"Yes, Mistress." He sucks in a breath. "Fuck, I was so close."

I give his thigh a gentle tap.

"Get on all fours. On the bed."

There's an eagerness in his gaze as he shimmies backward, his cock still glistening with my saliva. I grab a condom out of my purse, tossing it onto the nightstand for easy access before I stand behind him with his belt, holding the buckle firmly in my palm.

"You get three hits," I tell him as he pushes himself up to all fours. "You're going to count them for me, do you understand?"

"Yes, Mistress," he breathes.

"Good. If it's too hard, you say red, remember? You won't be able to reach my thigh this time, so if you can't talk, I want you to hit the mattress twice."

He glances over his shoulder and flashes me a wicked grin that makes my knees wobble.

"I can take it."

I enjoy watching him flinch as I smack his ass hard with my free hand.

"Don't talk back to me, slut," I growl.

The rush of power that shoots through me feels exquisite. There's something we talk about in the kink scene called domspace. It's a kind of euphoria that you get from being in control, like a high.

"Keep talking to me like that," he groans.

I click my tongue, running my hand over his ass and giving it a gentle squeeze.

"Talk to you like what? Like the fucking whore you are?"

"Yes," he whimpers. "Just like that."

I give him another rough smack, a little test for what's about to come. It's all about watching someone's body language. On top of verbal communication, I do check-ins: light touches, praising the guy, and watching for any indication that they may want to stop. Right now, Henry's back is arched and he's rocking his hips toward me.

All good signs.

I fold the belt in half, dragging it along the place I plan to hit.

"You're going to feel it here. Breathe for me and remember to count."

"Yes, Mistress."

The crack of the leather against his ass makes me ache. I love how that sound almost becomes rhythmic once someone lets you *really* get going.

"One!" Henry cries out.

"Atta boy. You're well on your way to earning this pussy."

"Please, Mistress," he practically sobs. "I need more."

His body is vibrating and I take a brief moment, putting my hand on his lower back to soothe his frazzled nerves. This isn't easy for a first-time submissive, it's overwhelming letting someone have this much control over you, so I want to make it as smooth and as pleasurable as possible.

"Say red if you want me to stop," I whisper.

He glances over his shoulder again, his smile warm and soft. It looks like he's in the process of letting go of something that's been weighing on him. His eyes are a little gentler, the crease between his brows smoothed out, blush dusting the apples of his cheeks and the tip of his nose.

I looked the same during my first session. The dom got me to look in the mirror afterward; I barely recognized myself.

"I promise I can take it."

I soothe the welt on his ass with my palm, steadying his trembling body.

"Breathe in for me, remember?"

Henry drags in a deep, shaking breath and I swing my arm back, hitting him harder this time. He buries his head into the mattress, letting out another groan.

"Two!"

His muffled voice strains through the pile of fabric.

"You're okay," I murmur. "Just breathe."

He lifts his head, and all I hear is pure euphoria in the laugh that comes out.

"God, I almost came."

The crimson that was on his cheeks is spreading down his shoulders, and I rub the welt, making sure his breathing is still steady.

"One more?"

He nods, but doesn't look back at me, his toes digging into the mattress in anticipation.

"Gimme everything you've got, Mistress."

The leather sounds more like a gunshot this time, surprising even me as it bounces off of the walls along with his howl of pleasure. I immediately drop the belt and walk over to check in with him, running my hand through his hair while he breathes through the aftershock.

"Do you need anything?" I ask.

"Water," he rasps as he flops onto his back. "I can get—"

I bend down to kiss him, pressing one hand to his chest to keep him from moving.

"Relax, I've got it. I'll be right back."

"Take your time," he laughs. "It's just a dry throat."

"Yeah, the A/C sucks in here, huh?" I reply as I saunter into the bathroom, grabbing two glasses and holding them up to the light.

Piper used to clean hotel rooms for a while back in New York, and she'd come home with some fucking horror stories, so I always make sure to double-check absolutely everything in a room before using it.

"You need a break?" I ask, handing him the glass and watching him guzzle it down in a few seconds.

He shakes his head, and I set my own water on the bedside table before leaning over to whisper in his ear.

"I wanna fuck you, Henry."

I imagine his massive body eclipsing mine, cock pounding into me while the moonlight streaks through the curtains, enveloping us both.

"I don't come until you do," he groans.

I grab the condom off of the nightstand, quickly checking the expiration date. I'm sure the last thing either of us needs right now is an accident. I nestle between his legs and tear the wrapper open with my teeth as the unmistakable smell of latex and lubricant hits me. My heart races, pinching the tip gently as he watches me roll it onto his cock.

"Too tight?" I ask.

"No, it's—" He swallows. "It's good."

Slowly, I straddle him and start to glide my pussy along his shaft. The friction against my clit is fucking incredible, and soon my hands are resting on his shoulders, nails digging into his skin. I can tell he wants me to take all of him, but this man looks like he's on the brink of an explosion, and I want to see how far I can push that.

"Tell me what you fantasize about," I whisper.

His hands worship my body, twisting my nipples and flicking them gently, enthusiastically playing with my piercings. A shiver rushes down my spine and lust wraps itself around me like a blanket.

"How filthy do you want me to be?"

Henry's hand slowly slides around my back until his finger is pushing against my asshole. His lips glide past my jawline until he's nipping at my earlobe, and I let out a whine, savoring his deep, rumbling chuckle.

"Give me everything you've got, cowboy."

"I want to be blindfolded and tied to a tree." He grunts. "Naked."

I want to know exactly what makes him tick.

"Keep talking."

"I want to be kept on the edge until I'm begging for mercy, and even after that I still want to be told no."

I'm fully immersed in his fantasy. It's a cool autumn day, the leaves crunch beneath my feet as I wind the rope around his naked body. He's squirming as I praise him, his cock achingly-hard as he watches me take control.

Back in the reality of our motel room, I lean in, my nipples brushing against the hair on his chest before I finally sink down on his cock. I take my time, rocking back and forth on the head of his cock until I relax and manage to take all of him. Henry lets out a sinful moan as he stretches me.

"If you're a very good boy, maybe I'll make that little dream of yours come true." A broken whimper fills my ears as I roll my hips and smile. "And, eventually, when you've learned enough, I'll give you complete control."

He nods, mouth agape, and I grip his chin.

"You know what kind of dom I think you'd be? A pleasure dom."

His mouth twitches, like he's torn between curiosity and his desire to flip me over and pound me into the mattress.

"What's that?"

"Someone who gets off on praising his subs, who lives to make them come and watch them writhe around in complete fucking ecstasy. Because I bet that when you really let go, you fuck like an animal."

Henry growls, capturing my lips in another ferocious kiss. I'm bouncing on top of him now, the chorus of our combined moans filling the room. Heat travels down my thighs as he hits my G-spot, pushing his finger all the way inside of my ass in the same moment.

"I'm coming!" I press my forehead against his as my climax builds to the point of no return. "Fuck, Hen—"

I can't even manage to get his name out before my legs start to tremble and all I can utter are vowels. Henry keeps fingering my ass while his other hand rests on my hip, guiding me to fuck him the way he wants it. I let out a raspy moan, burying my face in the crook of his neck.

I'm letting him use me like a toy, finally giving up control.

With one massive slam of his hips, he's coming, holding me down on his cock as his head rolls back; I can feel his body twitching as I lift my gaze just in time to see complete and total ecstasy etched onto his face.

Both of us breathe hard as we come down from our high, finding a natural slow rhythm as I place sweet kisses on his cheeks and the tip of his nose.

"You did amazing."

"So did you." He exhales. "That was great."

I climb off of him and he removes the condom, tossing it into the trash before I snuggle up against him to rest my head on his chest. Aftercare is a big part of this scene. Sometimes it's checking in, sometimes it's talking things out, and sometimes it's lying in silence and just holding each other.

"You need anything?" I ask.

"No," he murmurs. "This is perfect."

CHAPTER TEN

the joker

ROMAN

"So?" Logan asks, barely keeping up with me.

We've been running partners for a long time. Well, sort of. Logan spends more time complaining about running than actually doing it. Me? I treat this like therapy. The second my feet hit the cold hardwood floor in the morning, I feel a drive to put on my running gear and head straight outside. I call it discipline, Logan calls it obsession.

It's probably a bit of both.

"So what?" I huff.

"What the hell do you think I want to know about? How was your date last night?"

"Is that the only reason you came running with me?"

He looks like a summer camp counselor, decked out in a pair of blue shorts, a red hoodie, mismatched socks pulled up to his calves, and all topped off with an 80s sweatband and a pair of battered sneakers.

"No, I just like to look at your gorgeous face, sweetheart!" He barks, in that fake Boston accent of his.

I smile as I shake my head, sweat trickling down my back.

"It was fine."

"*Just* fine?"

It was way more than fine.

We exchanged numbers and we texted all night and again early this morning. She's funny, and she loved the pictures of my dog, so that's a plus. We're meeting up again tomorrow. It was supposed to be tonight, but she's got plans and I got roped into this student teacher mixer. It's usually the one outing in a year I can't avoid. Frankie says the whole department needs to make an appearance, and at least pretend that they care about socializing.

"Yeah," I reply flatly, trying to focus on the run. "Like I said, it was fine."

It wouldn't be gentlemanly of me to divulge the details.

"You seem a little looser," he remarks. "You get laid?"

I raise a brow and glance over at him as sweat drips down his face. He looks like he might be sick, and we're not even running that fast.

"You good?" I laugh, grateful that his nausea allows me to seamlessly change the subject. "You look a little green around the gills."

"Yeah, ice cream for breakfast was probably a bad idea."

I snort as we round the corner. This fucking guy.

"Especially considering your relationship with dairy."

"And yet she calls to me, that temptress," Logan sighs. "But you still haven't answered my question."

"You know I don't kiss and tell," I mutter. "It's disrespectful."

What I don't want to tell him is that every time her name pops up on my phone, my heart leaps into my throat. She's so easy to talk to, and while I found myself nervous at first, multiple times now I've quickly melted into conversations about literally anything.

"Fine," Logan sighs. "I can respect that. But you *do* look different."

"Different how?"

"I don't know, just a little lighter."

I take my shot.

"Like with you and Abi?"

Logan lets out a deep sigh, shaking his head as I chuckle.

"Equivalent exchange. Don't dish it out if you can't take it, Flynn."

He lets out a frustrated groan as I push myself a little harder, relishing that deep burn in my thighs while I pull away from him. This afternoon, there's a little bit of fog clinging to the ground, giving the trail an eerie feeling. It gives the campus an ethereal feel.

"Come on, slow poke!" I shout.

"Did Frankie say something to you about that?" Logan pants as he struggles to catch up to me.

"What, that you're slow as molasses? Get those bird legs going, Flynn!"

He whines, lurching toward me like Frankenstein's monster on steroids.

"No, you asshole! About me and Abi!"

He's guarded, and a little more angry than I expected. That could be the running, though. He hates every second of working out, and only began when Abi started working here a couple of years ago.

"Nope. You two just seemed pretty chummy at her birthday the other night. It may have been a bit of a clue when you called her your date."

I'm almost certain he's got it bad for Abi, but whether or not it's just an unrequited crush remains to be seen.

"I was two beers deep!" Logan motions to me that he needs a break, putting his hands on his knees. "Nice deflection from talking about *your* date, by the way."

I lean up against a tree and stretch my quads.

"Thank you, I worked hard on that."

"Abi's just a friend," he mutters, pulling his hair back with both hands. "We're just friends, that's all."

There's something in his voice that makes me want to encourage him to be reckless. He and Abi always seemed closer than just colleagues. More than once, I've heard her giggles spill out from beneath the crack in Logan's office door as I walked past. I don't think it would come as a shock to anyone if they wound up together.

"I've got to be super careful with my sister in the house, too. I don't need her getting the wrong impression about all of this."

"About all of what? Your secret affair?" I tease.

He's smiling, but I can see I've gone too far, and raise my hands. It's our silent signal to show that we're done going at each other. I can see his body language relax a little as we return to running, and after a few minutes of silence, I speak up.

"I still can't believe your parents didn't stop at one kid after you."

"Iggy's not so bad," he laughs.

Logan's got some pictures of his dad on his desk, but that's pretty much it. Otherwise, it's horror movie posters, his degrees, and some plants, so I've never seen what she looks like; I'm assuming it's a hell of a lot like him.

"I believe you referred to her as 'a royal pain in my ass'. Did I get the quote right?"

"That's just the kind of shit you say about your sister. And she's gonna be *your* new TA, so you'd better be extra nice to her. I know you've made a couple of them cry over the years."

"That was because they weren't showing up to classes, and one was nearly a month behind on grading."

Frankie's rarely worked this quickly to get me a replacement in the past, so I was relieved when Imogen sent me a short message of introduction this morning. She seems perfectly normal over email, but then again, so does Logan.

And then he comes crashing into your life like the Kool-Aid Man.

"Yeah, well, she's coming to the mixer tonight, so you better be on your best behavior."

"You got it, doc."

We pause again as Logan doubles over, gasping for breath, with his hands pressed against his thighs. I know what comes next, so I point to some trees as I watch him suppress the urge to vomit.

"In there, and nowhere near my damn sneakers."

Logan stumbles over to the bushes and gags, but nothing comes out. He spits and wipes his mouth off with the back of his hand, taking a few deep breaths to steady himself.

My phone buzzes in my pocket and I pull it out.

> JADE: Something to tide you over until tomorrow.

I open the text messaging app to see her in a black leather bra complete with thick leather straps that cinch her waist. No panties, just her hand barely covering her pussy. My jaw hangs open, nearly dropping my phone as I stare.

"God, this sucks," Logan groans as he stumbles toward me.

I jam my phone into my pocket as quickly as I can.

"You offered to come. I didn't drag you out here by your hair."

"Yeah," he hisses, wincing with every step. "I'm trying to get more toned, you know? Pick up more chicks."

"Well, the Jack Skellington socks are really pulling the whole sickly Victorian child look together."

"Can't we walk the rest of it?" Logan whines. "I've got beer in the fridge at home. We can pregame before we get to the Hi-Dive."

"I'm 43, Logan. I think pregaming is out the window," I chuckle.

I forgot that I agreed to go to his place before the mixer. He texted during a moment of weakness and I agreed. Ever since last night, I've been thinking more and more about pushing myself beyond my comfort zone.

"Okay, so I'll get you a beer and a V8," he replies, ripping off his hoodie and slinging it over his shoulder. "I don't know why you do this to yourself."

"Again, you didn't have to come with me," I chuckle.

"Hey, you should bring your lady friend tonight," Logan says, ignoring my comment. "I'd like the chance to make fun of you for a change."

I pat him on the shoulder as we walk the rest of the way back to my car.

"Not a fuckin' chance."

The drive to Logan's place is short, although it certainly begins to stretch when he starts whistling along to the Prince song that's blaring from the speakers. I keep having to resist pulling my phone out to look at that picture of Jade one more time, going over the details in my head instead. By the time we get back to Logan's place I'm practically drooling at the thought of getting my hands on her again.

Logan ushers me into the house, and I can't help but notice it's deathly quiet as I kick my shoes off.

"Where's your sister?" I ask, glancing around.

There's no indication that another person besides him even lives here, other than a bright pink leather jacket that hangs on the coat rack. Definitely not Logan's color.

"She went out to some thrift store in Tacoma with her friends," he replies. "She'll be at the mixer, then you can say you've had the honor of meeting almost all the Flynns in person."

"Can't wait," I reply in a flat tone.

Logan punches me in the arm and I smirk, adjusting my small duffel bag on my shoulder.

"Is that bathroom downstairs still free?"

"It's Iggy's bathroom now, but you're welcome to use it," Logan replies as he heads toward the stairs, massaging the back of his thigh as he goes. "I've gotta put some Tiger Balm on these gams."

"I'm not sure anyone's used the word *gams* since the '30s."

"You're not sure? Isn't that when you were born?"

"I'm only seven years older than you, jackass!" I bark, feigning a lunge at him before peeling off and heading down to the basement.

It smells a hell of a lot better down here than it did when he first bought the place. This whole house was a dump and Logan *insisted* that he could fix it up himself. Three days later, he found a nest full of wolf spiders in the basement and decided to call in the professionals. Logan's the kind of guy who will trap spiders and set them free outside, but even he couldn't stomach that many of them all at once.

The door to the guest room is open, and I head towards it, unable to help myself. I linger in the doorway, taking in the ornate vintage furniture, the massive bed, and the horror movie posters lining the walls. It looks so personalized, infinitely more lived-in than the concrete husk of a room it was when I was last here.

It makes me wish I had the energy to do more around my own apartment. It's been two years and I barely have the emotional strength to look through Christa's things, let alone hang up a single one of her paintings.

I sigh and head into the bathroom, preparing myself for the second night in a row of stepping out of my comfort zone. I used to feel like I was trapped in this goddamn purgatory with no end in sight, but now...

Well, life goes on.

"Scratch!"

Frankie cackles as the cue ball bounces against the bumpers on the pool table.

"Goddamn, Flynn! I thought you said you were a shark!"

"Amateur hour," Abi calls across the table, shooting Logan a wink as his face goes bright red.

It's Logan and I versus Abi while Frankie provides colorful commentary from the sidelines. We initially thought it might even the playing field, but it's quickly becoming clear that more players does not equal more wins.

"I thought I had that one," Logan murmurs, passing me the cue.

Some grad students from the sociology department are already here, playing their own games of pool or mingling at the bar. It's the same every fall, we book the place and they shut it all down for the night. It's kind of like a company Christmas party, which we're no longer allowed to have after the 'bobbing for pigs' incident at the Hilton in Seattle.

That one was Frankie's fault. He got drunk off his ass, stole a tray full of pigs in a blanket from another Christmas party, and then started throwing them in the pool and telling people to dive for them. Like apples, he said. Abi's got the whole thing on video, which Frankie finds *very* not funny.

"Hey! Roman!" Abi barks as one of her balls just barely misses a pocket. "It's your turn!"

I pull myself out of my stroll down memory lane.

"Sorry, I was miles away."

"He's thinking about his *giiiirlfriend*," Logan teases, leaning forward.

Abi's eyes light up.

"Girlfriend?!" She squeaks. "You've been hiding a girlfriend from us?!"

"No! No, Flynn, don't start this shit."

"Look at him!" Logan shouts. "He's glowing!"

"That's the run we went on earlier," I bite back, moving in to line up my shot.

"I didn't know Logan could run, I thought he always just flapped his big bird arms and flew away," Abi replies.

Frankie chokes on his beer, high fiving her.

"Don't you have a house to haunt, Abi?" Logan fires back.

I use the laughter as an opportunity to take my shot, sinking one in the corner pocket.

"Ooooh!" Abi giggles into her drink. "Catching up!"

Abi's sunk all but three of her balls while Logan and I have sunk a *grand total* of three of our own. Frankie keeps saying he's about to take over the game, but he's all talk. The guy can't play pool for shit.

Logan begins slinking around the table like he's hunting for something, and I pass him the cue.

"Who's the girlfriend?" Abi asks, only half paying attention as she watches Logan with rapt amusement.

"Yeah, I'm curious who could possibly bag Roman Burke," Frankie chimes in.

"There's no girlfriend," I laugh. "It's just casual. We've just been... hanging out. We played mini golf once and we're texting. It's really not a big deal."

"Frankie?" Abi sips her drink, arching a brow. "Confirm for me, is he blushing?"

"Hard to tell. Logan, touch his face."

Logan looks up at me from across the table, grinning but quickly thinking better of it.

"Nah, I'm not getting hit tonight."

"Why didn't you bring her?" Frankie asks.

"Because I wouldn't want to subject her to the three of you and your asinine questions."

Frankie nods, sagely.

"As a researcher, I resemble that remark."

I smile as Logan takes the shot, hitting his target, but missing the center pocket by a mile. Instead, the ball ricochets off of the bumper, slamming Abi's solid orange one straight into a corner pocket.

"Yes!" Abi shouts, just as Frankie rushes over and tries to blow one of our balls into the pocket.

"Hey, outside interference!"

She shoves him away, the two of them laughing hysterically.

"I gotta help my friends!" Frankie insists.

"*I'm* your friend too, asshole!"

I glance over to see how Logan's taking the loss, but he's not even paying attention anymore. Instead, he's waving his hands in the air like a madman.

"Iggy!" He shouts. "C'mere!"

I turn around, expecting a carbon copy of Logan Flynn, but the image I'm met with causes a boulder to form in my gut. Long, lavender hair that flows down her back in gorgeous waves, those eyes that remind me of my favorite brand of smoky bourbon, and those lips that were wrapped around my cock and whispered the filthiest shit I've ever heard in my ear.

"Shit."

CHAPTER ELEVEN
i did something bad
IMOGEN

"Uh... is that the guy? Like, the sexy guy from your phone?" Piper whispers. "Am I hallucinating?"

I'm too dumbfounded to answer. Why the fuck is here, and why is he with my brother?

"I... I don't–"

She pulls out her phone and takes a quick look at the picture I sent her.

"That's definitely him, right?"

All I can do is give a little incoherent half-sob and flail my arms.

"I don't fucking know, Pipes!"

"Does he know your brother? Wait, *how* does he know your brother?" She hisses.

"I'm not sure! I don't know anything about the guy! I've just spanked him and had his dick in my mouth, we didn't go into his life's story!"

I'm hot with embarrassment, dizzy, the edges of my vision already going gray. This can't be happening. Maybe if I walk out of the bar and back in again, it'll be a different person.

Like when you reset a video game.

"He's staring at you," Piper whispers.

His friends at the pool table are doubled over laughing, shoving each

85

other back and forth, but he's only focused on me, his jaw clenched, ticking like a clock. It's definitely him, but luckily Logan hasn't noticed either of us staring yet.

I feel Jay's massive arm around me as he pushes his head between the two of us, probably confused why we haven't moved in beyond the entrance.

"What's going on? You scoping out all the old dudes, Iggy?" He asks with a smirk.

"Iggy!" My brother calls again.

This time, a few people in the bar turn to look at me. No chance to bail anymore.

"Come on, if we keep staring, your brother's going to start asking questions." She grasps my hand. "You can come up with an excuse to leave later if you really hate it."

Piper knows me, knows I won't go of my own volition, and so suddenly I'm being dragged forward to my doom. It could be a worse place to be doomed, though. The bar is kind of a dive, but it's cute. There are spots for people to mingle, along with pool tables, a dart board, and a big jukebox.

If this place were in Brooklyn, it would be packed every night.

"I'm gonna grab drinks!" Jay calls. "You ladies want beers, or something fancy?"

"Beer's fine! I don't think they do fancy here, baby!" Piper shouts back.

Jay bounces toward the bar as Piper and I approach the pool table.

Logan beams at me.

Henry tries not to stare.

My legs feel like they're filling up with lead.

I do *not* want to be here.

"You made it! Guys, this is my sister, Imogen, and her friend Piper. They're both starting their PhDs on Monday." He gestures to his friends. "Iggy, you've already met... Well, almost everyone, right?"

"I think so, but it helps to put names to faces," I chuckle, trying to squash my nerves.

"Sure, sure. This is Abi, Frankie, and this moody grump is Roman Burke. Hopefully he made a strong first impression."

My stomach knots and those tacos I ate before we got here start to creep up the back of my throat. Not Henry, Roman Burke. The professor I'm TAing for. When Frankie first emailed to offer me the contract, I tried doing a search to get an idea of what the professor I'd be working with was like, but all I got back was a bunch of articles. No pictures, and definitely no social media.

Roman's eyes briefly flash with panic, the same thing I'm feeling in every nerve ending in my body, but he quickly slips back into a neutral expression.

I sucked this man's cock. He had his *finger* in my *asshole* while I listened to him talk about his filthiest fantasies. Now I'm supposed to just work with him like nothing happened?

Thankfully, Frankie steps forward, giving me something new to focus on.

"Imogen, it's nice to finally meet you in person."

Frankie's really good looking, his intense blue eyes offset by golden hair and lightly tanned skin, a slightly crooked nose adding variety to the package. He's the head of the department, but more importantly for me he's my thesis supervisor. Now though, most importantly of all, he's another one of Roman's friends. I've got to get my head in the game. Nobody can know what the two of us did together.

"Hi, Frankie. It's nice to meet you too. I— I got your email about a meeting. I meant to reply, but things have been—"

I'm stammering, and my whole face feels like it's on fire, but Frankie only chuckles, holding his hand up in calm dismissal.

"Don't worry about it right now. This is super casual, just a way for students and staff to hang out, specifically without having to talk about work."

"Except it's academia and work is all we talk about," Abi chuckles as she sips her beer.

I let out a much-too-loud and awkward laugh, instantly wanting to die inside. Oh my God, Iggy, get it together.

Abi and I exchange pleasantries before I give my brother a hug, finally turning to face Roman. He stretches out his arm to shake my hand. There are beads of sweat forming on his forehead and he's staring at me as if to say *do not fuck this up.*

"Imogen, right? It's nice to meet you."

Hearing him say my real name is surreal, and even though I'm shaking, I can't stop thinking about how good those lips would feel.

"Nice to meet you too, Dr. Burke."

It doesn't help that he's in a tight white t-shirt and a pair of even tighter blue jeans. Now that I know what's under those clothes, I have to look at the space between his eyes to stay focused.

I swallow, finding myself desperate for a drink as I pull my hand away. I don't want to shake it for too long. Logan could start asking questions. How am I going to TA for this man for a whole semester? I have to quit. I'll move back to New York and, I don't know, sell pictures of my feet? Or my used underwear? Who needs a PhD in this economy?

"Hey, are we gonna finish this humiliation game or not?" Logan cuts in.

"Iggy!" Piper calls, offering a wonderful distraction as she floats toward an empty pool table. "Come on, let's play!"

Jay holds out a cue for me, but I need a fucking breather.

"Sure, but I need to hit the bathroom first!" I step past Roman. "Excuse me, Dr. Burke."

I try to force myself to breathe normally as I escape, turning down a long hallway that feels even longer in the moment. Along the walls are near-endless pictures of random sports teams, jerseys with names I don't recognize, and weird art that looks like it's from a thrift shop. This hallway is where memorabilia goes to die.

Finally, I reach the women's bathroom, shut the door behind me, and bury my head in my hands. I feel like I can't breathe, like something's crushing my chest. My heart is racing, and my vision is starting to blur.

I don't even care about the fact that Henry isn't his real name. My name's not fucking Jade. I picked the name because I own a pair of jade earrings and it was the first thing my eyes landed on when I was making my profile. I put my hands on my thighs and suck in a deep breath, trying not to give in to the panic attack.

"You're fine," I mutter. "You're fine. Just breathe."

The world isn't ending.

I head for the sink and twist the knob, sticking my mouth under the tap to try and soothe my throat. When I'm finished, I wet a paper towel, pressing it against my chest as I keep up my steady breathing.

"I'm touching the paper towel, I'm standing on the floor, my hand is holding the sink. I can see the tap, my reflection in the mirror, and my shoes. My heart is pounding, I can feel my t-shirt tag, and the cold towel."

I've been dealing with panic attacks since my master's program. The pressure was intense, working down to the wire and late into the night. One time, a professor of mine caught me mid-panic attack and taught me the paper towel trick. It's been my lifeline ever since.

Unfortunately, it can only do so much.

A week in Washington and I've managed to fuck my brother's friend, a man who just so happens to be my boss. I just wanted a hookup without consequences. This reaping and sowing shit sucks.

My phone buzzes in my pocket.

"Please don't be Roman."

I take a few more deep breaths before I toss the paper towel into the trash and check my messages.

> PIPES: You good?

"Oh, thank God."

> IMOGEN: Bad anxiety. Be out in a second.

> PIPES: Wanna leave?

> IMOGEN: No, I'm fine.

I drink a little more water, fix my hair, and step out into the hallway where my heart nearly stops. He's standing by the men's room with his hands in his pockets. I gulp, my heart hammering against my ribs as that horrible hand of anxiety squeezes hard. I almost expect him to give me shit, but when he looks uncomfortably down at his boots, I feel like I might be able to breathe again.

"So... this is awkward."

I laugh. What else *can* I do right now?

"Yeah, pretty much the worst case scenario for both of us, huh?"

"You got that right, darlin'– Er, sorry, Jade." He holds up his hands in frustration. "Fuck! Imogen, right? I– I'm sorry."

89

I want to tell him that I like the nickname, that it gives me butterflies, that I haven't stopped thinking about the way it rolls off his tongue. Just like I haven't stopped thinking about last night.

But all I can manage is...

"It's okay," I reply, shoving my hands into my pockets as I glance down the hallway, making sure nobody's coming around the corner.

"I didn't know you were a student here."

"Well that's fair. I didn't know you were a professor," I chuckle. "Or that you're pretty much my boss."

I spanked my boss with a belt and called him a desperate little slut.

I think I just found the new American dream.

"Yep. Feels like something I should've looked into," he sighs.

"We *both* fucked up." I try not to give away the disappointment in my voice. "It happens, right?"

"Yeah." He runs a hand through his hair, his cheeks bright pink and his jaw clenched. "Yeah, I guess it does."

I was really looking forward to getting to know this guy, exploring with him. Apparently, the universe has much more boring plans.

"So? What do we do?"

All either of us can do is stand there, chuckling awkwardly. I don't want to lose my spot at the only university that would accept me, but if my brother found out what happened between us, who knows how he'd react. Imagine fucking this thing up before even setting foot inside of a classroom.

"I think we can chalk this whole thing up to one incredible night, but this can't go any further."

He sounds regretful, and more than a little sad.

"Totally agree." Even though having to utter those words makes me hate this entire situation even more. "I think that's for the best considering we're probably going to be working together. A lot."

Roman stares at me, hands stuffed back into his pockets. I catch the little muscle flex in his arm and find it hard not to stare. Why did he have to wear such a tight shirt? *And* tight jeans? That, combined with the cowboy boots is... well, it's killing me frankly.

He glances quickly over his shoulder, taking a step toward me, but to my surprise he brushes my cheek with the back of his hand. It's gentle, but it still makes me shiver.

"I had an amazing time with you, Imogen. You're funny, you're bright, you're gorgeous... and I really wish things were different."

I maintain a neutral expression, but the softness in his eyes and the way he says my real name cuts straight through me.

"Me too."

"Let's keep what happened between us."

"Agreed."

"We'll be professional and we can be friends." He pauses, his throat bobbing. "If you want to, at least. I'd like to be your friend, Imogen."

I hate the weight he puts on that word.

Friend.

"I'd like to be yours too." I wince, and start to stammer. "I mean, friend– I'd like to–"

"I got what you were saying," Roman chuckles. "Thanks for being so good about all this."

I give him a little shrug.

"What other choice do we have?"

He grins at me, a small glint in his eyes.

"I'll see you out there."

Roman disappears back into the bar and I slump against the wall, my heart still pounding. I can do this. We can be co-workers. After a couple minutes, I take a deep breath and walk back out into the bar. Piper and Jay are chatting with Logan while Roman stands at the back, waiting for another drink.

It's going to be hard not to think about him on all fours on that hotel bed.

CHAPTER TWELVE

beast of burden

ROMAN

EMERALD BAY UNIVERSITY
FIRST DAY OF THE SEMESTER

The sprawling, castle-like architecture of Emerald Bay University reminds me of those Gothic novels that line Logan's bookshelves. The whole thing is surrounded by lush forests and cobblestone paths, but the cloudy skies add a certain somber weight to what would otherwise be a fantastical environment.

I check my watch. I still have half an hour before class starts.

That's enough time to fight with the projector.

My first class today is *The History of Criminal Punishment* in a place that both students and staff have dubbed "The Dungeon." It's an old, repurposed church building all the way on the other side of campus, tucked into a little patch of forest. It's a pain in the ass to get to, but the university won't tear it down despite the fact that everyone hates teaching in it. I fought tooth and nail to get the classroom changed, but the department wouldn't budge. Offering Frankie a hundred bucks didn't even work, he said his hands were tied.

I make a left and head down a long path toward the church, wondering if she's already waiting for me. My guts twist in anxious anticipation, but when I reach the clearing, the only sight I'm greeted with is one of magnificent cedar trees that surround the building.

And no Imogen.

All that's left of this building's former glory is a stained glass window, creating a kaleidoscope of colors that splash against the walls, floors, and desks as you walk in. This place might be cold and musty, but when the sun hits it just right, it's beautiful.

I head for the pulpit and take my laptop out of my bag, plugging it in and messing with the settings until the slides finally pop up on the screen.

When it comes to teaching in the dungeon, a lot of new students show up late. It used to piss me off, but over the years I've grown to accept it. A lot of the things that used to really irritate me started to fade away after Christa died. I was so focused on my own grief that I found myself becoming the 'chill' professor I'd always wanted to be. My RateMyProfessor numbers even went up; kind of a macabre silver lining. I'm sure Christa would have found that part really funny at least.

As I'm checking my email the church doors creak, swinging open, and Imogen rushes inside. My heart starts to race and I look up at the ceiling. God's got a cruel sense of humor. The purple in her hair looks a little darker than last I remember, and she's dressed in an oversized pink hoodie with a pair of black leggings, a bright blue backpack hanging from her shoulder. Coffee sloshes out of the disposable cup and runs down her knuckles, singeing her hand as she rushes toward me.

"Shit," she mutters, dropping her bag and setting her drink down on the desk to lick her hand clean. "Fucking whipped cream."

"It's a bitch, isn't it?"

She smiles at me, and I find it frustratingly impossible not to smile back.

"I'd say I'm not usually spilling my coffee on the first day of the semester, but that would be a lie," she chuckles, bending over to scoop up her bag.

It's really hard not to look at her ass, so I pretend to busy myself with random wires.

But like she said, it's the first day. Over the semester, my infatuation will fade.

It has to.

"You might be covered in whipped cream, but at least you're early."

The second the words leave my lips, I wish I could fall through the goddamn floor.

Blessedly, Imogen seems content pretending that she didn't hear anything. She heaves her backpack over her shoulder, picks up her coffee, and heads straight toward me.

"Logan told me the dungeon was a little hard to find, he didn't tell me it was a church. It's... nice."

I take a small step back as she approaches, realizing quickly that I don't have anywhere to go.

"Y—yeah. Yeah, it is."

She stops in front of me, keeping a respectable distance.

"I was actually hoping to catch you before class started."

"You were?" I ask, my body freezing in place.

"Yeah, uh... I don't want things to be weird between us, or for you to think that I can't be professional—"

She stops herself mid-sentence, letting out a big breath as we exchange pained smiles. I wish it didn't have to be this way; I'd give anything to go back to that night. I didn't expect sparks to fly the way that they did: the way she kissed, the way she felt in my arms, the way she held me with a tenderness I haven't felt in years.

"Anyway, I'm not gonna tell Logan about what happened, and I'm perfectly happy to leave all that stuff behind us. I had a great time, but I don't want you to lose your job and no other school would take me—"

As she's talking, I notice a small smear of whipped cream on the corner of her mouth. It's hard to focus on anything else, and if I was a much bolder man who didn't give a shit about my job, I'd—

"What are you looking at?" She asks.

"You've got whipped cream..."

"What? Where?"

I point at the spot it would be on my own mouth, and her hand flies up to her face in a panic, trying to wipe it away. She's not even close. I crane my neck to the side, shifting my head and pointing to the same spot on my face, just a little more aggressively.

"Right here."

She walks a little closer, trying to match exactly where I'm pointing. "Here?"

She swipes at her face again, just a few inches away from the target. "No– here, I'll—"

"Oh, it's—"

I take a step toward her, reaching out and wiping the speck of whipped cream away with my thumb. She seems to shrink as she stands in front of me.

"Got it," I murmur.

Her face was hot to the touch.

"Thanks."

Before I can say a word and assure her that everything's fine between us, the door opens and three students walk in. Imogen scoops up her bag, flashing me a big, confident smile, and any remnants of the awkwardness between us gets pushed aside. I have a job to do, and so does she.

"I got the rubric for the first assignment, by the way— do you mind if I sit up front?"

"That's perfect. It'll be easy to introduce you to the class."

More students file in, laughing and chatting as Imogen takes a seat right in front of me. She pulls out a laptop that's covered in stickers from different horror movies.

My God, she *is* a Flynn.

I busy myself, prepping my lecture notes and waiting for the chatter to die down. Imogen is alternating between working on her computer and getting distracted by each and every notification that pops up on her phone. I don't know how she deals with that shit. It drives me nuts when it happens to me.

"Welcome, everyone, to Sociology 2100, *The History of Criminal Punishment*. Some of you know who I am, but for those who don't, my name is Dr. Roman Burke and I've been teaching here for about fifteen years now. My work primarily revolves around grief, social stigma, and suicide, but I did my MA in criminology, which means I'm *technically* qualified to teach this course."

I pick up the remote, glad for the few laughs that my lame joke got, and advance the slides.

"In this course, we're going to be talking a lot about crime and punishment, and what it means from a sociological perspective as opposed to a legal one. We'll also be discussing crime as a social construct, and how different violations of social norms can either be justified or condemned when we look at punishment. This is a theory-heavy course, so the readings are mandatory, and I recommend using the supplementary material in the syllabus."

I start to slide into the same spiel I give every time I explain the course and the expectations, and I can already tell most of the students aren't even listening. They rarely do during introductory classes. They shop online, they work on readings for other courses, or they're texting. There's nothing you can really do to stop it when the subject's as dull as course expectations.

"Your TA this semester is going to be Imogen Flynn. Imogen, would you like to introduce yourself?"

"Totally!" She clears her throat and stands, sliding out of her desk and turning to face the class. "Hi. I'm Imogen, and I'm a first year PhD student. Um, my research is in subcultures. Specifically BDSM and identity management."

That explains a lot, and it might be why she chose Frankie as a supervisor.

"Uh, sorry, I'm a terrible public speaker," she says with a laugh, standing rigid and keeping her arms tucked at her sides. "But if you need help with anything this semester, I put my email up on Blackboard. You can get a hold of me pretty much any time, or schedule a meeting during office hours if you just want a quiet place to talk."

She turns to me with a look in her eyes that says, *please save me from this*, and I grant her wish with a quick nod of my head.

"That was great, thank you, Imogen."

Relieved, she flops back down in her seat, one of her legs bouncing up and down with some unresolved nervous tension.

"Okay, now we'll go over the syllabus and the learning expectations, and after class I'll post your first assignment on Blackboard."

I'm on autopilot for the most part, having memorized this after years of repetition. When I get to the end, many students have questions about the assignment: how long it is, what they have to do... you know, the usual. As the last of the students get their answers and file out the door, I shut my laptop and Imogen makes her way toward me.

She plays with the string on her hoodie, pulling it all the way to one side so that the fabric bunches up before pulling it all the way back. The little plastic string cap looks like it's been chewed to shit.

"Sorry, Dr. Burke—"

I used to do the same thing with my sweaters when I quit smoking.

"Roman," I say with a smile. "It's okay to call me Roman."

I'd actually prefer it. After all, this woman rode me like an animal less than a week ago. She can call me by my first name.

"Right." She blushes, twirling the string between her fingers now. "Uh, so I just looked at the rubric and the style guidelines are missing."

"Wait, missing? What do you mean missing?" I ask, suddenly feeling a bit frantic.

I'm precise with my work, and I was so sure I'd gone over everything with a fine tooth comb, but then again, a certain lavender-haired temptress has been invading my thoughts all damn week.

"I'll show you."

Imogen opens her laptop and pulls up the rubric, and she's right. I've completely forgotten to put that section in. I've been so busy thinking about her and this situation that I didn't even think to take a second look at it before I sent it out.

"Damnit. Sorry. My head's been—"

"Trust me," she laughs, cutting me off before I have a chance to self-flagellate even more than usual. "I forget shit all the time. I submitted my thesis without a bibliography and didn't realize it for two days."

I snort, grabbing my own computer and pulling up the correct file.

"Here, I can send you the full version, but do you mind going over it real quick with me to make sure I didn't miss anything else?"

"Sure."

She leans in a little too close, gnawing at her lip as she reads. The smell of vanilla and bergamot is so strong that I'm transported back to that little hotel room.

"What I'm looking for, format wise, is standard double-spaced 12 point font. Sometimes students will mess around with the commas or periods— you know, making them bigger, but not big enough that you'll notice right away."

"That's a good trick," she says with a smirk, tapping her index finger on the table. "My personal favorite is adjusting the margins."

"A classic! I've used that one too," I confess with a laugh. "Anyway, I'm really only looking for the paper to follow the style guidelines, APA format. It's not a test, but I want to spend my time figuring out where their analytical skills are, so I need you to focus on making sure their formatting is consistent and concise."

She nods, quickly straightening up before flashing me a tight-lipped smile.

"Makes sense. Thanks, Roman."

We're both just trying to get through this, but I can tell there's something on her mind. Before she turns to walk away, I reach out and grasp her wrist. I can't let this get weirder than it already is.

"Are you okay?" I ask. "You seem really nervous."

A pained laugh of disbelief tumbles from her lips and she stares at me like I've got two heads.

"Of course I'm fucking nervous." She shakes her head in disbelief. "I wasn't expecting to accidentally sleep with my boss."

"The last thing I want to do is make this situation difficult for you."

When I look down, I realize that I'm gliding my thumb along her wrist and quickly remove it.

"You're not," she whispers. "Although, Logan did ask me to give you this, and I was totally going to throw it in the bushes and tell him I lost it, so maybe things are a *little* awkward."

Imogen digs in her bag, pulling out a large black envelope with my name written in gold calligraphy and a wax seal on the back. I chuckle, already knowing what this is.

A faculty only dinner.

"Will you be there?" I ask.

He does it every damn semester, but this is the first time in a while I've had a real reason to go.

"Well, duh, I live there," she laughs.

"Alright, but do you want *me* there?"

"It's up to you," she replies, packing up her laptop and slinging her

bag back over her shoulder. "But Logan was insistent that you attend. So...
maybe I'll see you tomorrow?"

"Yeah. Maybe."

I watch her leave and pinch the bridge of my nose, trying not to smile.

Logan's not going to take no for an answer.

Looks like this one's not my call to make.

killer queen

ROMAN

A dinner party.

A *goddamn* dinner party.

I should turn back around, go home, and cuddle Mitzy on the couch. It's only a twenty minute walk. I can tell Logan I got sick, or I fell in the Bay. People fall in there all the time. Mostly drunk college students, but still.

Before I can come up with another hare-brained scheme to get out of this, I find myself grabbing the obnoxious bat-shaped door knocker and I bang it against the wood. I can feel the sweat trickling down my spine. It's not even hot out, but the thought of seeing her is sending me into a spiral.

"Please don't answer the door, please don't answer the door…"

A deep blue blouse and a pair of black dress pants greet me as the door whips open, but thankfully, it's Abi's face smiling back.

"Oh, thank God," I sigh.

The words are already out of my mouth before I can stop myself.

"Wow, Roman!" She laughs. "Should I pass that message along to the host?"

I roll my eyes and thrust a bottle of wine toward her, but Abi bypasses it completely, going in for a hug instead.

"He knows how I feel," I mutter as I wrap my arms around her.

Out of the corner of my eye I catch a flash of lavender, and my stomach tightens.

"You good, big guy?" Abi asks, finally taking the wine. "Looks like you've got something on your mind."

"Just the usual," I chuckle, hanging up my jacket near the door.

When I finally work up the courage to look, Imogen is there at the end of the hall. She's in a black long-sleeve dress that hits her mid-thigh, her hair flowing down her shoulders in loose curls. She flashes me a smile before disappearing, and I can see every single goddamn curve taunting me from afar as she goes, only to be quickly replaced by Logan trotting down the stairs. He's in an orange sweater with a pumpkin on the front. *And* he's got mismatched socks on.

"You look absolutely ridiculous," I chuckle, pulling him in for a hug.

"Well, you RSVP'd and I thought I'd wear your favorite sweater," he pats me on the shoulder. "Come on, into the living room. Everyone's there!"

Everyone including his sister.

This is going to be great.

The house is massive, an ostentatious Victorian-style monstrosity, but Logan has it packed with horror memorabilia, along with framed movie posters on the walls. I think he spends more money on this stuff than he does on groceries or clothes. It's a perfect encapsulation of him as a human being.

The living room is cozy and jammed full of people, but my eyes are immediately drawn to a large crimson sofa with Frankie conspicuously draped across it. He's loudly chatting to somebody halfway across the room, and then his gaze falls on me.

"Hey, you made it!" He chirps, raising his drink.

"Are you kidding? Miss my favorite sweater?" I elbow Logan in the ribs.

"Thought you'd be eyeball deep in a Chopped marathon or something," Frankie teases. "I was waiting for a text telling me how pissed off you were that they were using the ice cream machine."

"It's a poor use of the time you have," I reply. "And the damn thing's always broken anyway."

Frankie claps me on the shoulder while Logan grins, handing me a drink.

"Thought this might ease your nerves a little. Do the rounds real quick and slink your way back in here, I'll make sure you don't have to do any more fraternizing than necessary."

I move around the room, shaking hands with Dr. Richard Barnes, who writes about police corruption. It's some of the most brilliant work I've read in decades. Then there's Janine Rogers, who primarily works in the area of domestic violence. She's been instrumental in enacting policies that make it safer for women to leave abusive relationships. Janine has been around for as long as I can remember, and she's got to be close to retirement by now.

No matter how interesting the topics might be though, I'm distracted, trying my best not to stare at Imogen. She's sipping on a glass of white wine, chatting in the corner with Abi. She looks so casual, like she belongs here, and somehow way less nervous than me.

I begin to move toward her, but I'm interrupted just steps away.

"So, how's your new TA working out?" Logan walks up, gesturing to his sister with his drink. "Thought I'd bail you out, but you look like you're doing fine."

I want to guzzle my whiskey right here and now.

"Imogen and I are getting along great."

"Of course, you are. She's a Flynn, after all," he replies.

"My ears are burning," Imogen announces as she turns toward us.

"Relax, I wasn't going to embarrass you. I was just asking how things were going," Logan smirks. "But now that you're here, I'm not sure if he'll be honest."

"Roman's been very..." I catch her brow twitch as she holds back a sultry little smirk of her own. "Accommodating."

Is she fucking with me, or am I seeing everything she does as something flirtatious? Either way, it's a struggle to stop thinking about ripping that tight little dress off her.

As Logan and I filter our way through the room, I find myself content just to listen to the myriad conversations. Everyone's talking about work, journal submissions, and what they did over the summer besides teaching. Every so often, I catch Imogen's eye, the two of us immediately looking away each time. How the hell am I going to get through this dinner unscathed?

After doing the rounds, Logan stops and lets out a deep sigh, looking around the room with a warm smile.

"I love this," he says, gesturing between Imogen and I. "My best friends, my family, all in the same place..."

"Someone take the Pinot Grigio away from Flynn," Frankie calls out. "He's gonna start serenading us in a minute."

"You wish, buddy!" Logan points at himself. "I'm the *King* of karaoke in this town, I don't give it away for free."

"Dude, you sing like someone swung a cat around by its tail," Imogen teases, grinning from ear to ear.

I chuckle into my drink, trying not to laugh too hard.

"I refuse to be the punching bag tonight. Iggy, Abi! Get over here! Come and mingle with the rest of us!"

The word mingle makes her visibly cringe. I want to tell her that I know the feeling all too well, but things are about to get a hell of a lot more awkward as she sits down across from me, her dress riding up her thighs. I look around the room, searching for any conversation that will keep me from staring.

Frankie and Janine are talking about some upcoming conference in Aspen, and I pretend to take an interest. Unfortunately, it's easier said than done, as the conversations get muddled with all of us sitting in one area. It sounds like everyone's talking at once and I begin to feel like I'm drowning.

Focus. All I have to do is focus on something that's not Imogen, her laugh, her voice, *especially* not her gorgeous legs.

Even if I want to bury my face between them.

I try to pay attention to Logan, nodding and pretending to be fully invested in some conversation about an academic publishing company, but fail miserably when I spot Dr. Barnes sliding into the seat next to Imogen.

He takes a brief moment to look her up and down, his eyes lingering on her chest, then her thighs. Imogen shifts her body slightly, turning away from him as she crosses her legs. The jealousy feels like a hot knife twisting in my chest, initially worrying about my reaction only to be emboldened when I see Logan staring daggers at him as well.

"So, Imogen, what did you do your master's thesis on? Same topic?" Barnes asks.

"Oh, um, sort of. It was mainly around identity management in the kink scene. Specifically, people who work prestigious jobs where that sort of lifestyle is still seen as somewhat deviant or harmful."

Fuck this. I'm getting in there.

"What kind of jobs?" I ask, leaning in toward the pair.

Her eyes gleam as she swirls the wine in her glass.

"Doctors, lawyers, judges... professors."

My blood runs cold as Frankie grins, hopping into the conversation.

"How did you get that kind of access?" He asks, cutting in. "Like, did they talk to you in person?"

"No," Imogen replies. "I mostly had to go with social media posts and Reddit forums that talked about it. It wasn't an easy feat, but I got a couple of interviews with doms who worked with high profile clients, people seen as pillars of their communities."

She's looking at Frankie, but I can tell she's talking directly to me.

"They could lose their jobs if someone found out what they liked to do on the weekends. A lot of kink clubs have strict anonymity policies— the good ones, at least. And no phone rules. That can cut down on someone's day job being leaked, but there's still a risk, and so people have to navigate who they're going to be in that space."

Dr. Barnes, who's been getting more and more irritated with each additional person hopping into the conversation, opens his mouth to speak but is cut off when his phone rings.

"Apologies, folks. It's the missus." He begins to sheepishly scurry out of the room. "I've gotta take this."

Imogen sneers.

"Creep."

Frankie's beaming, staring at Imogen like he's proud of his great decision to take her on. He *should* be proud. She's already been answering emails about the assignment and the feedback I've gotten from students is overwhelmingly positive. Our little affair aside, she's really taken the initiative.

But I'm terrified that the lines could continue to blur. Especially if she keeps shooting me those coy little glances.

"I'll be right back. Need a refill."

Imogen gets to her feet, holding up her empty glass, and I try not to turn my head too much as I watch her long legs stalk toward the bar.

This is going to be a long night.

"So?" Logan asks me, resting his chin on his hand as Abi plunks herself into Barnes' chair.

"So what?" She asks before I can respond. "What did I miss?"

"He's not gonna give it up," Frankie laughs.

"Give up what?" I look around at the three of them, confused.

Do they know? Did Imogen say something?

No, she wouldn't.

Dr. Barnes wanders back inside, frowning when he sees Abi in his seat.

"They wanna know where your girlfriend is," she chuckles. "I told them you'd be coming alone."

I sigh, shaking my head as I stare into my empty glass. I wish I had about six more of these in my system, then maybe I wouldn't feel like such a trainwreck.

"There's no girlfriend," I insist. "We're just…"

"Just what?" Frankie asks. "Come on, this is your first relationship since–"

"It's not a relationship," I groan. "I don't know where the three of you knuckleheads are getting these ideas from, but as far as I'm concerned, I'm still single."

Logan frowns.

"You said you had a good time with her, right?"

"Yeah, I did, but that doesn't mean things automatically work out," I reply, frustration slowly creeping into my tone.

I wish this whole thing between Imogen and I hadn't turned into such a giant clusterfuck. But we can be professional. We can be cool about this. Besides, she's clearly not having these issues, it's me. I'm the problem. Maybe I've been alone for too long, and I forgot how to admit to myself that I might be falling for someone.

"So, things fizzled?" Abi asks. "That sucks. I'm sorry, Roman."

"They didn't fizzle–"

"Hey, guys!" Barnes calls, trying to snatch back the attention he'd lost. "We're playing a game! Top Ten Desert Island movies!"

"Oooh!" Frankie coos, getting to his feet. "I love this game. Logan has terrible taste."

"I do not!" Logan laughs, following him toward the group.

"You wanna watch 976-EVIL *and* the shitty sequel for the rest of your life, don't you?"

"Yes, I do!" Logan sings. "They're cult classics!"

"I'll never forgive you for making me sit through both of them," Frankie mutters as the two make their way back toward the rest of the guests.

Abi grins at me, still seated.

"You joining in?"

"Just gonna grab a drink first," I reply. "I'll meet you there."

I get to my feet and head toward an empty bar at the back of the living room. As I approach, Imogen pops up from behind it with a bottle of chilled white wine clutched in her fist.

Shit.

"Hey!" She chirps, pulling off the foil and tossing it aside.

I laugh, both nervous and excited to be alone with her again.

"So, you the bartender this evening?"

"As long as you're drinking something that's super easy to make. My limit is two ingredients, and you have to cut the lime yourself."

"Wow, you run a tight ship," I tease. "I think bourbon is pretty easy."

"We'll see, I bartended in college for a couple of months." She tries to flip the bottle and barely catches it with both hands. "Impressed?"

"With moves like that, how could I not be?"

She snorts, grabbing a corkscrew.

"I wanted one of those bartending jobs where I could commiserate with patrons, but all I could find was a nightclub that sold overpriced vodka."

I lean against the bar, watching her uncork the bottle with a violent twist. She winces as she jimmies the cork out.

"It's not champagne, you know. Nothing's gonna happen."

"I know, I just hate the squeaky sound it makes!"

She yanks at the cork one final time, the bottle finally letting out a satisfying pop, and she fills up her glass before grabbing two kinds of bourbon and resting them on the bartop.

"Pick your poison, cowboy." When my eyes meet hers, she blushes. "Sorry. It just slipped out."

"It's no trouble, ma'am," I murmur, pointing to the bourbon on the left like it makes a difference. I just need alcohol in my system. "I'll take that one."

"Excellent choice sir," she quips, pouring out a generous portion before sliding it across the bar. "Hope this whole thing isn't too awkward for you."

"Only a little. How are you holding up?"

She sighs, brushing a perfect curl off her shoulder. Up close, she looks even prettier, almost untouchable, like changing anything about her would be labeled a crime. There's some shimmer on her collarbones, making them stand out even more against her black dress.

"Oh, you know… just in a room with a bunch of people who are way smarter than me. It's super intimidating."

"Seems like you're doing just fine." I sip my drink. "Dr. Barnes has taken a shine to you."

"Richard? Logan says he fucks anything that breathes… except his own wife." She lowers her voice, leaning in and giving me a good whiff of her vanilla perfume. My mouth waters, remembering how she tasted that first night. "But you didn't hear that from me."

"Oh, don't worry. We've all heard the stories about him."

She quirks a brow.

"Makes what we did seem not so bad, huh?"

My cheeks burn. I want to respond but Imogen quickly straightens up.

"Frankie, six o'clock," she mutters.

"Wh–"

"You bartending tonight, Imogen?" Frankie asks as he approaches.

Shit. We were doing so well. Once we get going, we fall into a natural rhythm again, like back at the mini golf course.

"For a bit, yeah." She leans up against the bar, glancing at Frankie. "What are you drinking, Dr. Hughes?"

"Jack and Coke," he replies.

"Comin' right up!"

She takes his empty glass, grabbing a bottle by the neck.

"Should I do my Tom Cruise in Cocktail impression again?" She asks with a confident grin, her crooked little tooth adorably visible.

"Not unless you're paying for that bottle," I laugh.

Imogen rolls her eyes, fixing Frankie's drink as he turns to me.

"So? How's it going with you two?"

The question makes me nauseous, and I gulp down the rest of my bourbon, relishing the way it burns the back of my throat.

"Just fine," I reply. "Like I said to Logan, Imogen's great."

"And Roman's a great boss," she chimes in. "I'm learning a lot about what it means to be a good TA, you know? How to handle student concerns and other... mishaps."

Her eyes flick to me, almost challenging me to say something. Is she flirting with me? All of a sudden, I'm sweating again, heart thumping a little faster as I wish I still had something to drink. Frankie shoots me a look. Does he know? Only a few more hours and I can go home and jerk off in peace while I think about those pillowy thighs, but it could all come tumbling down any minute.

"There really are a lot of those more complex mishaps," Frankie chuckles. "One time, I was on a flight to Italy and accidentally deleted every single student's grade off of Blackboard. Instead of getting them to resubmit, I just gave them all an A and called myself a moron."

Imogen passes him his drink with a smile.

"Well, hopefully, I don't screw up *that* badly." Her voice is sweet and sugary. "Right, Dr. Burke?"

Christ, it's like she's *trying* to get caught.

"I'm—" I choke, my voice breaking. "I'm sure you'll be great."

"Hey, guys?" Logan calls from the doorway. "Dinner's up in ten, so get your asses into the dining room!" He yelps as Abi elbows him in the ribs. "Please?"

Saved by the bell.

CHAPTER FOURTEEN

off to the races

"Roman, that pork roast recipe you sent me? Turned out perfect."

My brother's carrying a massive tray covered with one of those ornate silver lids that he bought at some estate sale. Everything in his kitchen is some level of vintage; he said it should be illegal to pay $500 for a stand mixer, so he bought one from a woman who was selling everything in her house, appliances included. The only exception is his toaster; he was so excited he bought it brand new because it's shaped like a rocket ship.

"Tadaaaa!"

He sets the tray down on the table and unveils the most tender looking pork roast I've ever seen. It's honestly kind of shocking.

Roman whistles, clearly in agreement.

"Looks good, Flynn. Nice job with the presentation."

Logan takes a little bow before easing into the seat next to Abi.

"Dig in everyone!"

Just as we start loading up our plates, Roman and I brush fingers, the two of us reaching for the mashed potatoes at the same time. Of course, when we got to the table, the only seats left were right next to each other. My face burns in embarrassment, but he only chuckles.

"Great minds, huh?"

"Well, it's Logan's famous garlic mashed potatoes after all. You've gotta be quick if you even want *one* helping," I reply with a grin. "You go first."

"No, it's—"

"You're the guest, I insist."

This whole thing is starting to feel like a cruel joke, but I can handle this. We did great keeping things under wraps in the living room, aside from that little bit of teasing. I really can't help it, though, it's kind of addicting to mess with him; he does this thing where he rubs the back of his neck when he's all bashful.

Roman flashes me a smile, grabbing a big scoop of potatoes before passing me the bowl.

"You know, I actually gave your brother that recipe too."

"I know," I murmur, loading my plate up before passing the bowl down the line. "He told me that dirty secret this afternoon when he was prepping the food."

"Yeah? What else did he tell you?"

"Oh, just that you might be bringing a girlfriend," I tease.

Roman's eyes widen, but Logan clangs his fork against his wine glass, getting to his feet before he can say anything.

He looks so much like dad in this light, with his dorky little sweater and his mussed up sandy hair. My dad was big on family dinners and making sure that we all connected at least once a day over a good meal. Over the years Logan's taken some of his traditions on for himself.

It's a way of grieving.

Mine is crying in BDSM clubs because I've been avoiding my feelings everywhere else in my life. Not sure which is more healthy.

"Thank you all for coming tonight. I started these faculty dinners as a way for us to connect outside of work. Now, instead of complaining about the administration during department meetings, we can do it over a good meal and a lot of alcohol." He gestures to Roman with his glass. "I'm sure you've all noticed Dr. Burke's missed a couple of these over the last two years."

Roman looks a little nervous and reaches for his drink, taking a big sip.

"Well, *I'm* sure Logan's more than made up for my sparkling wit."

"Not quite," Logan replies with a grin. "But it's really good to see you back, man."

Roman forces a smile, and I can tell he wants to be anywhere in the world but this party. I don't blame him. If I had it my way, I'd be upstairs in that big clawfoot tub with a bottle of wine and a romance novel. *That's* the ideal way to spend a Friday.

"I'd also like to welcome my sister and brilliant scholar, Imogen Flynn. She'll be attending these for the next four to seven years." He winks at me. "It's too late to back out, by the way."

I make an exaggerated roll of my eyes as laughter fills the room.

"There's plenty more food in the kitchen, plenty more wine, and after this... how do we all feel about karaoke in the backyard?"

"Are you going to serenade us all with *Endless Love* again?" Frankie smirks.

"Yeah, we can duet," Logan replies. "I know how much you've been itching to get back on the microphone."

More laughter ripples through the room as Logan eases back down into his seat. Roman leans over, gently bumping my knee with his. Everyone around us is swallowed up in conversation, and I take the opportunity to stare back into his intense gaze.

"I had to tell them I was sort of seeing someone because, well..."

His voice is barely above a whisper.

"It's cool. Did you think I was mad?"

"No, I was just afraid it would be weird."

"Well, I mean it is." I flash him a quick little smile. "This whole situation is weird."

"You're tellin' me, darl—" He winces. "Sorry."

I swallow hard and look down at my plate, suddenly wondering how I'm going to choke all of this down. It looks delicious, but with Roman next to me, I'm feeling too nervous to eat. This was a bad idea. That *fucking* nickname still gets to me.

I wonder what it'll feel like when these gooey, giddy feelings I have for him finally fade away. God, I can't wait for that day.

"So, how are you enjoying Emerald Bay so far, Imogen?"

Abi's voice startles me, but it somehow manages to cut through the awkwardness. More importantly, it's something completely removed from Roman that I can focus on.

"I haven't really had the chance to see it. I've just been so busy, you know? New school, lots of work, still getting settled."

"You went to Seattle though, right?" Logan asks.

Roman visibly bristles beside me, covering it up with a sip of his wine. I clear my throat, trying to remember what lie I told Logan so that he'd let me borrow his car with as little fuss as possible.

"Yeah, just to hang out."

Smooth. Real smooth.

"What band did you see again?" He asks.

I swallow hard, the blood roaring in my head. As I shift in my seat, my foot accidentally bumps against Roman's, my heart skipping a beat. I swear, the universe is *trying* to get the two of us caught.

"Uh... The Commandos or something?" I laugh. "I don't really— it's Piper and Jay's thing, I was just kind of there."

"Oh, I thought you said you had a great time." Logan frowns.

As much as I love my brother, right now all I want him to do is shut up.

"Yeah, it was cool," I reply, trying to keep my voice steady. "I've never really been to Seattle before, so... you know, it was fun. I'd like to— uh, stay for longer, actually."

"All of us should go!" Logan suggests, nudging Abi. "There's this really cool board game bar! Oh, they have a mini golf course called Lucky Strokes—"

Roman starts to choke, covering his mouth and turning off to the side.

"It's the name, isn't it?" Logan laughs as Roman gasps for air.

Abi looks concerned, but Roman shakes his head, holding out a hand to keep her from standing up.

"I'm good, Abi." He clears his throat. "Wrong pipe, and poor timing on Flynn's part."

"Or perfect timing!" Logan chuckles. "You okay there, champ?"

"Yeah, I'm fine," Roman rasps. "Just... how about you try not to accidentally kill me again, okay?"

Logan raises his glass, everything returning to normal, but all I can think is that I've got to get the fuck out of this house. I wish Piper was here right now. If she was, she'd find some excuse to get me out of this dining room before I make an Imogen shaped hole in my brother's wall.

Now, I'm eating to distract myself, despite the bubbling in my gut. I can barely taste the food, but I need something to take my mind off of Roman, off my brother, and off of this entire circus.

"So, how are your classes going, Imogen?" Roman asks, trying to act normal.

"Uh, good. I'm only taking two—"

"'That's plenty," he assures me. "Especially with the workload. Two PhD courses is closer to four, especially with Abi teaching one of them."

Abi holds up both hands in mock-defense.

"Hey, Frankie's the one who said I needed to amend the syllabus! I think his exact words were: *it wouldn't be grad school without a little suffering.*"

"It's really not that bad," I laugh. "I don't feel like I'm drowning in work yet, but I'm sure that'll come soon enough."

Abi winks at me, giving a reassuring nod. She's close to my age, and to see someone as young as her already teaching graduate courses is inspiring. It makes me want to work harder.

"That's great to hear." Logan says, sounding relieved. "And I'm glad this whole thing between you and Roman is working out, too."

A rush of electricity shoots down my spine as my mind flashes back to that hotel room. The moans that filled it, the smell of sweat and sex that made me feel like I was drunk, and his filthy brand of sweetness as he fucked me.

"Yeah, he's teaching me a lot," I reply as Roman clears his throat, clearly desperate to shift the subject back to safer territory.

"You went to NYU before this, right?" He asks.

"Yeah. Didn't get into their PhD program, though," I chuckle. "Or Dartmouth. Or Princeton."

Abi nods.

"Those are good schools. Tough competition."

"Yeah, you're telling me."

Roman's foot is still touching mine. Do I move it? Do I leave it there? Why isn't *he* pulling his foot away?

"But I really like EBU, and Emerald Bay is cool. What I've seen of it, at least. I'm hoping to do some more exploring this week."

"There's great hiking," Roman says softly. "It's really beautiful around the bay. During the summer, the reflection from the trees makes the water look green— hence the nickname."

"Hiking, I'll look into it," I murmur. "Thanks."

He flashes me an awkward smile as Abi refills her wine glass. I can hear my brother's boisterous laughter as he leans away, chatting with another faculty member. He's barely touched his meal.

The Flynns are easily distracted.

Roman gives me a look, silently asking me if I want to move, but I ignore him as Abi lobs another question.

"It must be a big adjustment to go from living in New York to being here."

God bless her, this dinner would be physically painful without her here.

"It is. It's really quiet here. My first night, I kept waking up and thinking it was weird that I didn't hear horns honking or people screaming. And now I can't believe I used to sleep with all that noise going on."

After a while, it all started to sound like radio static. Unless someone was screaming right outside my bedroom window, I could fall asleep to pretty much anything.

"I did my PhD in Toronto," Abi chuckles. "Back in Canada. It's the same thing there, constant noise from the street. It's been bizarre to actually live in a place that's calm and quiet."

"It's amazing what you get used to," I sigh, noticing my foot bumping up against Roman's again. I've probably been doing it for the past five minutes and haven't even noticed.

I'm like a live wire, all of my adrenaline pumping as hard as it can, and I need to calm down. I let myself fade into the background as Frankie cuts in and the two of them carry on the conversation about Toronto, giving me a brief breather from the questions.

I glance over at Roman and he looks like he's in agony, but I can't help but notice he never pulled back his leg. I feel like we're playing some weird fucking game of chicken, and before long I begin to notice people clearing their plates. He clearly does as well, because he immediately takes the opportunity to lean in close.

"Are you trying to rile me up?"

Roman's voice is low and gravelly, making the hairs on the back of my neck stand up.

"What are you talking about?"

"The bar, the foot thing—"

"To be fair, you never moved your foot either."

His eyes dart around, and he looks like he wants to say something more but can't find the right words. Or maybe it's the right opportunity he's been waiting for.

"So, are we all finished?" Logan's voice cuts through the room as he looks around at the rest of us.

"Why? You got an itinerary for the evening?" Frankie shoots back.

"Duh!" Logan points toward the back of the house. "Backyard karaoke! It's the last time I'm going to get to use that patio furniture until next summer!"

There are a few groans around the table, the loudest ones from Frankie and Roman, but all I see is a perfect excuse to get out of the dining room.

"Logan?" I stand up, noticing that Roman's staring directly at my legs, eyes tracing my tattoos. I tug my dress down and smile. "The cupcakes—"

"Iggy, you have to sing!"

"I will, but we still have dessert, remember?"

"Okay, okay," he sighs. "Abi, Frankie, Roman? You wanna help me set things up?"

"Yeah." Roman gets to his feet as I start stacking plates. "Sounds great."

Thank god.

I'll finally get a fucking breather away from that man.

CHAPTER FIFTEEN

guilty as sin

IMOGEN

Dinner felt like an exercise in torture– so much so that trapping myself in the kitchen icing cupcakes seemed like the perfect escape.

The eye contact, the footsies, the way he smelled... maybe handing him that invitation *was* a mistake, but it's too late to rescind the invitation.

Right now, I have to focus on the present, and not how hot he looked holding a fork. There's something wrong with me. How does someone look hot holding a fork? It's not possible. I must be going insane.

I'm trying to concentrate on making icing for the cupcakes. For some people it would be easy, two simple steps: pull out the ingredients from the pantry and make the icing. With my brain, though, I have to break everything down into bite sized pieces, actionable little bullet points, before I can actually tackle the task at hand.

So making icing isn't *just* making icing. It's making sure I have the ingredients, the right measuring cups... everything needs to get done in the right order or I get all screwed up. But then, the fact that missing any one of the steps can fuck up the entire process makes the smallest task feel like climbing Everest.

How I got into research is a mystery to me.

For now, I focus on getting everything I need from the pantry. No distractions, even though my biggest one is sitting right outside in those *incredibly* tight jeans. I pull out a bowl and set it on the counter, but just as I've dropped a stick of butter in, I hear the kitchen door creak. When I glance over my shoulder, I spot Roman holding an empty glass.

He clears his throat.

"Need some ice."

I'm a puddle at the sound of his voice; I have to turn my attention back to the buttercream or something disastrous is going to happen.

"Sorry to intrude," he mutters, heading to the freezer.

"You're not intruding."

Out of the corner of my eye, I catch him pouring himself a drink. Those muscular forearms flex as he wraps his fingers around the glass. My heart is pounding, but I keep my head down. The less eye contact I make, the better.

"Listen, Imogen, I... didn't mean to make you uncomfortable at dinner."

I chuckle and shake my head as the butter starts to smooth out. I increase the speed on the mixer, hoping it'll get loud enough to drown out all the stupid ideas blossoming in my brain.

"You didn't. It's just an awkward situation."

Roman rubs his beard, struggling for the right words.

"I'm sure we can figure this out, right? We're both professionals."

My face is flushed now, sweat trickling down my back, and suddenly the only thing I can think about is the feeling of his lips on mine. My body is practically screaming at me, craving what we had back at the hotel room. I don't want to be thinking about him like this, it's going to screw everything up, but I haven't been able to get that night out of my head.

"We're cool," I reply, my voice trembling slightly.

I've got to get out of here. I need a few seconds to breathe.

When did it become a hundred degrees in this kitchen?

"Can you watch this for a second? I need to get the sugar."

I dust my hands off and head for the pantry, not even waiting for a response as I step inside and let the door swing shut behind me. I reach up and turn on the light, the bulb flickering with a pathetically dim glow. With one hand on a rickety shelf and the other on my chest, I take a minute to ground myself and breathe.

In for four.

Hold for four.

Out for four.

I picture my anxiety being squeezed into a tiny ball and push that ball down toward the floor with each breath. When my heart has calmed and the buzzing in my head has passed, I get up on my tiptoes and grab at the big bag of powdered sugar. I try to tug it down gently, but it doesn't move.

"Shit."

It must be stuck to the shelf. A small growl escapes my lips, and I pull harder.

"Come on, you motherfucker."

I glance around for a stool, but there's nothing. Out of sheer frustration, I grab it by the corner, tearing it down from the shelf as hard as I can. The bag explodes, because of course it does, covering me in powdered sugar.

"Son of a bitch!" I yelp, stumbling backward.

The door flies open and a big beam of light from the kitchen fills the tiny room. There's white powder all over the floor, on my dress, my thighs...

I turn to find Roman staring at me in the doorway.

He licks his lips and takes a step toward me, a microscopic grin on his face.

"It's not funny," I whisper, my face burning with humiliation.

"I wasn't laughing."

God, his *voice*. It's like warm honey.

"Looks like there's enough for the buttercream, but you got some in your hair."

"I bet I look like I just blew Frosty the Snowman."

He reaches up and pushes a strand of sugar-covered hair from my face.

"It's not a bad look," he whispers.

He takes a step forward and the door behind him starts to close.

"You're a bad liar, Dr. Burke."

He closes the gap between us, backing me up against the shelf as he cages me in with his arm. I smell whiskey, spice, and the faintest hint of leather.

"You've been staring at me all night." He rumbles, trailing his fingers up my bare arm. "Or was I imagining that?"

Roman's touch makes me feel like I'm standing on the surface of the sun, but I'm trying my hardest not to let him see how it's affecting me.

"Are you drunk?" I laugh.

"No," he breathes. "Not drunk, at least not enough that I'll forget."

"Forget what?"

He leans in close, staring at me like he wants to eat me alive.

"How much I want you."

He reaches up and turns the light off, taking a moment to ensure the door is fully shut. He's had enough booze to make him brazen, and I know damn well that someone could catch us any minute. But maybe that's what makes it fun; playing this game until something explodes.

"You're breaking your own rules, Dr. Burke."

A devilish smile tugs at the corners of his mouth as he dips his head, his tongue gently flicking against my neck.

"I forgot how good you taste."

I shiver, eyelids fluttering as he nips at me, pausing to gently suck on the skin. Just light enough not to leave a bruise. What the fuck is this guy's deal? Is he trying to break me? If so, I'm waving a white flag. I've *been* waving one since he walked in here.

"Must be the sugar."

It's hard not to let my voice shake.

"The sugar's got nothing to do with it."

Before I can respond, his mouth eclipses mine in a slow and sensual kiss. I whimper as he takes control, grabbing my hair and tugging my head back just enough to cause the perfect amount of pain. I've missed his mouth, even dreamed about it, and I've gotten off to thoughts of him eating me out more times than I can count.

I glide my hand over the front of his jeans, feeling an obvious bulge. Roman lets out a groan, pushing me harder into the shelf. The wood digs into my back, but it only adds to the desire that's coursing through me at breakneck speed.

If someone opens that door, this is all over.

He breaks the kiss, lowering himself to his knees. Calloused hands run up and down my bare thighs, leaving a trail of goosebumps as he pushes my dress up higher.

"What happened to professional?" I laugh.

"We'll start tomorrow."

I swallow another whimper, covering my mouth as Roman nips and nibbles his way up to my bare pussy.

"You didn't wear panties." His warm breath fans against my exposed cunt, sending shivers down my spine. "Can I taste you?"

His voice is raspy and a little unsure.

"We could get caught."

Roman dips one finger in the sugar on my skin before he gently glides it along the hood of my swollen clit.

"Then, I guess you'll have to be quiet and let me eat my dessert." He slides a hand around me, giving my ass a rough squeeze. "*Darlin'*."

I gasp as he dives between my thighs, and all the pressure that's been building the whole night finally snaps. Outside, I can hear someone howling along with a song I think I recognize, but am too distracted to put a name to.

"Fuck *me*," he groans.

"Oh, I'd love to, cowboy."

I roll my hips, desperate for more friction, and he stares up at me with blazing, hungry eyes. I'm shaking, scanning his face for any sign that he wants to stop, that this has all been one big mistake, but I don't see one. My mouth drops open as he wraps his lips around my clit and sucks down on it, the tip of his tongue lashing against my swollen bud like a velvet whip. I'm gripping the shelf so hard my fingers feel like they're going to break; it's taking everything in me not to scream.

He releases me with a pop, licking up more sugar from my thighs while he begins to fuck me with his fingers.

"I wanna make you come," he rasps.

"We blurred those boundaries pretty fast, didn't we?"

Roman says nothing, but he doesn't slow his thrusts either. It feels like he's walking a very fine line. I push the straps of my dress down, exposing my breasts and teasing my nipples.

"You still want me?" I whisper.

"More than anything."

"Then take me, cowboy."

His sinful little moan tumbles out on a rush of breath and he buries his face between my thighs again, the speed of his tongue as desperate and impatient as the two of us.

"Oh, god, keep doing that."

I grasp his hair and rock my hips against his face, keeping my voice crushed down into a whisper. I don't want him to lose his job, and I don't want to get caught, but this feels *so* good. When he adds a third finger, I almost come undone, greedy for everything he could give me.

"Good boy."

When I hear his belt buckle start to jingle I smile, remembering how good his cock felt in my hand, my mouth, my cunt. My pussy squeezes his fingers tight and I throw one leg over his shoulder.

"You wanna fuck me, don't you?"

All I get is a muffled grunt in reply. He's getting desperate, picking up the pace as he devours me. The only thing keeping me upright is the death grip I've kept on the shelf. Roman swirls his tongue around my clit playfully, lashing it quickly, and then backing off with gentle massages while he strokes my G-spot. There's not a single part of me that doesn't want him to turn me around, grab me by the hair, and fuck me like an animal.

"Oh, fuck. Right there, baby. Right *fucking there*." I swallow a moan. "Make me come."

My clit throbs and my back bows, and when he finally hits that perfect spot, I unravel. I have to stuff my knuckles into my mouth, biting down hard as pleasure crashes into me like a wave. When I open my eyes, he's already tugging my dress back down and getting to his feet. I grab his wrist and shove his fingers in my mouth to lick them clean.

"You have no idea how badly I want you right now," he whispers, chest heaving.

I release them with a soft pop, reaching down to play with my pussy.

"I *said* take me, cowboy."

He shakes his head, stuffing his cock back into his pants.

"I can't."

The regret in his voice makes me ache.

"What, all of a sudden you're mister chivalry?"

He sighs, brushing his fingers against my cheek. Even in the dark, I can feel his eyes dig into mine, an anchor that I can't seem to let go of. I don't know if eating me out suddenly made him sober, but it certainly made him reflective.

It feels like he's going to end things here, and that pisses me off. Because *I'm* the one who's always walked away, and having someone uno-reverse this shit on me feels like a slap in the face.

I thought I could do this, I really thought we could make this work, but now there's a part of me that thinks this whole thing was the universe playing a cruel joke. Now he gets to treat me like some toy that he can abandon any time he wants, reduced to the secret he finger fucks in closets.

"I should go," he breathes. "I crossed one too many lines with you, darlin'."

Even if it was expected, rejection is like a knife plunged deep into my gut. I know he's right, and I know it's for the best. But it doesn't mean it doesn't hurt. I swallow it, along with my pride, and take a deep breath.

"Sure. That was fun."

But this part's not.

"I don't regret that date," he sighs. "I just wish things were different."

I'm not sure if him trying to soften the blow is better or worse.

"Me too."

"I think it's best if I talk to Frankie about swapping you with another TA."

I want to laugh in his face. He wants to talk about this *now*? After he just ate my pussy like it was a goddamn cupcake? I swallow the anger building inside of me and nod.

"Whatever you think is best."

"I'll be in touch, okay?"

And then he's out the door, shutting it behind him and leaving me alone. All alone with this fucking mess we made.

the song remains the same

ROMAN

"Where did you run off to on Friday night?" Logan asks, spinning one of my pens around his fingers. He's made himself right at home in my office. "You missed Frankie and I doing Bohemian Rhapsody."

Logan called to check on me after I left the party early. I could barely pick up the phone, not after what I did with his sister. To his sister. Even seeing his name come up on the call display sent me into a spiral. I tried to find distractions over the rest of the weekend: immersed myself in new recipes, went to the farmer's market, and cooked enough to feed a small army, but nothing really helped.

"Felt sick," I reply flatly as I avoid his gaze, staring at the email I've drafted to Frankie about swapping TAs.

It's been blank for the past hour.

"I hope it wasn't the food," Logan sighs.

"No," I murmur, closing out of my draft and shutting my laptop. "Had a little too much to drink. Didn't want to be hung over the next day."

"That was a good plan. Wish I'd thought of that."

"Yeah?" I say with a wry smile. "Feeling a little rough?"

"Yep. Apparently, a few glasses of wine and one measly beer turns me into a husk of a human being these days."

"That's what drinking in your 30s will get you, and with a body like yours you'll need at least six business days to recover."

"It was fun, though. Worth it."

"It was. Good food, good people, and from what little I heard of your duet, maybe even *great* music."

Logan grins, leaning back with his hands cradled behind his head.

"I'm telling you, man, you're looking at a future Grammy winner here. The first one Emerald Bay's ever seen."

I cock my head to the side, grinning at him. The thing I love the most about Logan is that he's powered by a combination of delusion and the utmost confidence.

"What about Daphne Carmichael?" I ask. "Didn't she win like three last year?"

"You mean your guilty pleasure?" Logan laughs. "I've seen your Spotify playlists."

"Nosy fucker," I chuckle.

Daphne was born and raised in Emerald Bay. She started singing at the Hi-Dive on karaoke nights, and eventually sold out stadiums. Even though I've been a fan for a long time, the only one of us who's ever met her is Frankie. Apparently, they grew up together, but he never really talks about it.

"Anyway, do you really need a Grammy? Aren't all those awards and accolades from academia enough?"

"Maybe combine the two for lectures," Logan suggests. "A full concert on Durkheim."

"I'm sure students would be *super* responsive to that," I chuckle.

There's a light knock on my door and I immediately shift into professional mode, furrowing my brow. I don't have office hours scheduled this morning, but students tend to find their way here regardless.

"Come in."

The door swings open and Imogen pokes her head inside. She looks startled for a moment when she sees her brother but she quickly shifts into a pleasant smile. Damn, she's good. I could stand to learn a thing or two from her.

"Hey, Iggy!" Logan calls, spinning around in the chair. "How's it going?"

"G– good– uh, yeah. It's…" She clears her throat. "Just working on uh… something for Roman."

Alright, maybe she's not *quite* as good as I thought.

"Running her ragged already, huh, Burke?" Logan grins.

Oh my God, Imogen mouths squeezing her eyes shut as I shake my head. She's about 500 shades of red right now.

"You might wanna rethink that turn of phrase there, Dr. Flynn."

Logan shifts in his chair awkwardly, a little uncomfortable with the energy he's added to the room.

"You're right, that did sound kind of gross. Sorry, Iggy."

"It's cool, I can, uh… I can come back–"

"No, no, no. I've gotta get back to work anyway." Logan stands up and heads for the exit, patting her on the shoulder as he slips by. "You look really stressed, though. You need to learn how to chill out."

"Why do you have to say such weird shit?" Imogen hisses.

"I said I was sorry!" Logan calls back, already halfway down the hall.

"Sure," she sighs, smoothing out her clothes. "Whatever."

She's dressed more casually today, in a pale-purple t-shirt that matches her hair and black leggings that cling to her thighs, leaving little to the imagination. An awkward, almost choking silence fills the air as she glances down at the floor, twisting a silver ring around her finger. She looks like she doesn't know why she came in here; maybe she was compelled by the same thing that made me walk into that pantry on Friday.

"You wanted to see me?" I ask, trying to cut through the awkwardness.

Her jaw twitches and she takes a moment to breathe. She's got to be pissed at me for leaving her like that.

"Do you think I led you on?" Imogen asks.

"What?"

Led me on? Where did she get that idea?

"The other night in the pantry. Do you think I led you on?"

"I–"

She takes a step forward.

I was wrong. She's not nervous, she's pissed.

"Then why did you do it?" She asks. "We said we were going to be cool about this, that we were going to put it behind us. I want to know if you think that I led you on, that it's my fault."

This isn't how I wanted things to go, and before I can make sense of it, I've already rounded my desk, taking up her hands in mine.

"Friday night was my fault," I whisper, soft enough that she has to lean in a little to hear, and I catch a whiff of rich vanilla and something citrusy. That scent combined with the taste of powdered sugar has haunted me for two days.

"Imogen, I cr—"

"Crossed a line." She repeats my bottled words from the other night, glancing down at my hands in hers. "Yeah, you already said that."

There's a storm in her eyes, her face twisted up in an expression that fills me with terror. I can't tell what she's thinking, but I have to end this. It's the right thing to do.

"I can't jeopardize your spot here, and I *can't* lose my job."

"You said *that* already, too." Her gaze is steely and cold. "So, is that why you went down on me in my brother's fucking pantry and then walked away? One last taste?"

In her eyes I've been flip flopping, unable to make a decision about whether or not this game continues between us, and she's not wrong.

"I had a lot of time to think on the weekend, Roman, and I want to know what your problem is."

"My problem...?"

"I'm not going to be treated like I'm just some dirty fucking secret."

There are tears in her eyes, and suddenly I can feel a blade twist deep in my gut. I didn't even think about what this would do to her, I just *wanted her* that night.

"I'm sorry."

"You're fucking right you're sorry," she spits. "You say you're afraid of the consequences, that we blurred boundaries, but we were cool, Roman. It was fine, even with the little bit of flirting we were doing. It didn't have to escalate, but then you decided to have your little *fuck it* moment. So you want to end this? Go ahead and end it like you should have done before. For both of our sakes."

She might as well have just slapped me in the face. I want to be angry, but with the truth laid bare, all I feel is guilt. I didn't mean to do this. I calm my breathing, refusing to let go of her trembling hands.

"A transfer request is going to take a while," I whisper. "I'm going to have to talk to another professor and see what I'm able to do."

She gives me an indignant look.

"I'm sorry." I say it as sincerely as I can. "I am, Imogen. If things were different—"

"Just fix it. I can't keep doing this."

Her tone is venomous but her gaze is practically pleading. I feel an immediate compulsion to hold her and tell her everything's going to be okay, that I can fix this for the two of us, and—

No.

Hell no.

I'm not making that mistake again. I don't know anything about this woman other than her name, her kinks, and the way she tastes. That's not love, that's hormones.

"It's like I said, it'll take a while, maybe a couple of weeks. I have to figure out what to tell the department and we may have to have a meeting to discuss everything, but I'll put the wheels in motion and let you know when we're ready to take the next steps."

"What are you going to tell them?" She asks. "The department, I mean."

I laugh and shake my head.

"I'm sure I can think up some personal problem I have that would make the swap necessary. Frankie already thinks I'm a grumpy asshole, so it shouldn't be too hard. None of it will fall on you."

I flash her what I hope is an encouraging smile, but she only nods coldly in response.

"Alright, so it's done then."

"It's done. I'll send Frankie the email right away."

And now I've got a secret to bury.

What a great start to the semester.

"Okay then. I'll see you in class," she says softly before shutting the door behind her.

I let out a groan and grab my laptop, opening it up to face the email I don't want to write. Things could have been so much simpler, but it's too late now; it's time to figure out a way to dig myself out of this hole.

Frankie,
I need to have a meeting with you about Imogen.

"No. Delete."

I pinch the bridge of my nose, cursing myself as I try to come up with an explanation. Anything other than the truth. Maybe I can say I don't need the help. I can grade papers and give lectures all on my own. I only have the one class after all, plus the two master's students I'm supervising. But really, I can't tell him I don't need an assistant because I do. I even made a big deal out of it when my other TA quit, and it wasn't for nothing. I've been slowly reintegrating back into the department since Christa, and there's no way I could handle it alone. Not yet.

"I wish I'd never joined that app," I mutter, sinking lower into my chair and staring at the cursor, blinking like it's taunting me.

I need to stand up, move around and get my blood flowing. Maybe that'll get my brain working. I slam my laptop shut, getting to my feet and heading for my coffee machine. This'll be my third cup of the day. Or is it the fourth?

"Think of something, man. Think."

The problem is it's more complicated than just explaining away a TA transfer request. She's Logan's sister, and as long as she's here, I'm going to have to see her every day. She'll be at parties, karaoke at the Hi-Dive, in the halls. She'll be *here* and there's nothing I can do to change that. Nor would I really want to.

She's woven into my life now, whether I like it or not.

CHAPTER SEVENTEEN

illicit affairs

IMOGEN

I'm starting to go a little crazy. It's been two weeks since I stormed into Roman's office and I've heard nothing from him about a transfer. All my emails about *the situation* have gone unanswered, but he's more than happy to copy me on emails where students are requesting meetings with him.

A bead of sweat trickles down my back as I force the image of Roman Burke on his knees out of my mind, continuing down the path that leads to The Dungeon. I want to catch him before class starts and get a definitive answer. How hard can it be to confirm a transfer? How long can it take?

My ADHD makes me impatient. Delayed gratification isn't really something that my brain recognizes. It's part of that whole impulsivity deal, and it's gotten me into a lot of trouble.

When I finally reach the building, I push past the heavy wooden doors to find Roman bent over a small table, his brows knit together as he swears under his breath. The room is empty, the projector screen behind him still blank.

"Morning, Dr. Burke!" I call.

He turns around, dressed in that same white t-shirt and a pair of jeans. There's a leather jacket draped over one of the chairs, and his sunglasses hang off his collar, pulling the fabric down and exposing a little more of his chest.

Why does he always have to dress like that? It's going to make professionalism on my end extremely difficult.

"Morning," he grumbles, giving me a brief wave before turning back to his computer. "The cable's in, just won't fucking work."

"You're having technical difficulties?" I ask, setting my bag down on a desk up front and pulling out my laptop.

"Yeah." He runs a hand through his hair and sighs, straightening up. "So the cable is connected to the computer, but I can't seem to get the *computer* to connect to the *projector*. It usually just does it automatically, but..." He lets out a soft chuckle, his cheeks going pink and my knees going weak. "Well, I guess I'm not so great with technology sometimes."

"You want help?"

His body tenses, the smile fading as quickly as it arrived.

"No, I think I can figure it out."

I shrug and slide into my seat, opening up my laptop. I have a paper to work on that I was planning on outlining during Roman's lecture. *If* I can concentrate.

After only a couple minutes of working in silence, Roman starts cursing again. As adorable as it is to watch him be frustrated like this, I have to help him before this entire class turns into one big tech support session.

"Let me help you," I laugh.

"No, really, it's—"

"Come on. I'm good at this stuff." I put my hands on my hips. "Besides, do you really want to get shown up by a bunch of eighteen-year-olds? You know they're going to have it fixed in like 5 seconds when they get here."

Roman sighs again.

"I just want this damn thing to work, I don't really care how it happens."

"Then let me help, I promise I can figure it out. My mom calls me all the time when her Netflix isn't working and I've got a 100% success rate."

He chuckles, taking a step back and gesturing at his laptop.

"Who am I to argue with success?"

"Thank you."

I head toward his computer and take a look at his settings, messing around with them until I find what I think I'm looking for.

"What's the projector called?" I ask, glancing over my shoulder.

"A... projector?" Roman asks.

I giggle and roll my eyes.

"No, the *name* of the projector. Your laptop disconnected from it somehow, which happens, but you've got a couple of bluetooth devices around here as well. I just want to make sure I'm connecting to the right thing."

"Oh." Roman rubs the back of his neck and walks over to a small box tucked behind the pulpit. "I think it's this white thing? Try SR792?"

I try, but can't connect.

"Nope. Got anything else back there?"

I watch him as he struggles to find the right device, getting a good look at his ass in those jeans and his shirt riding up his back, exposing lightly tanned skin.

"I think this is it. Star Projector, and the model is... XI90YT."

I scroll down past a list of letters and numbers until I find it, hitting connect with a little prayer. After a moment Roman jumps up, clapping his hands together as the device whirs to life.

"You did it!" He laughs.

"Easy peasy lemon squeezy," I reply, straightening up and dusting my hands off.

Roman looks relieved, and for a split second it's like nothing happened between us. But only for a second.

"Okay, uh, thanks, Imogen."

"No problem!" I chirp, hoping to keep things light, mostly because I'm about to launch into an incredibly awkward question. "Listen, Roman—"

"I want to apologize," he cuts me off. "For the way I acted at the party, and then leaving you— that wasn't... that wasn't okay, and you didn't deserve that. I was being selfish, and I didn't consider how it might make you feel. I know—"

The door creaks open and some students come piling in, their overlapping conversations cutting through our little moment.

"Can we talk after class?" I ask, lowering my voice to just above a whisper.

Roman blinks, his throat bobbing.

"Sure, but... can I ask why?"

He looks paranoid and I think I can see sweat forming on his forehead. The reluctance hurts a little, but I swallow it.

"Because I have a question?" I laugh. "Is that okay?"

"Yeah— yeah, I'm— I'm sorry. I'm just all over the place lately."

"I know the feeling."

More students pile in, some of them making their way toward Roman with awkward smiles on their faces. When they start asking him questions about assignments, I slink back to my desk and open up the outline for my paper.

Just sink into the work, Iggy. It'll be there no matter how messy this shit gets.

It's kind of my solace right now, and it should be my main focus, not some *dude.*

He's just a guy.

Just a guy.

A very hot guy—

Stop it. Focus.

Not only do I have a paper due, but a huge discussion on Bourdieu coming up for Abi's class. I want to be well-versed, and it feels like I should have started this book two weeks ago, but I've also got papers due for other classes.

More reading, TAing, all of it.

Sometimes it feels like I'm teaching myself. But what if I'm a bad teacher?

That doesn't bode well for my future.

I nibble at my thumb nail, trying to focus on my outline while Roman starts his lecture. It's difficult to concentrate, my eyes flicking back up to take him in as he advances his slides, quickly dropping back to my laptop in shame each and every time.

"Today, we're going to be talking about the history of the modern prison, but don't get too comfortable, because we'll be following that subject to its natural conclusion: punishment and its sociological implications."

He launches into the lecture with ease, so charismatic when he's in front of the class, presenting information in a way that's engaging and relatable. I'll be honest, I've been reading this shit for a long time, and understanding academic jargon never really gets easier. I can tell his jokes about the dense material are going a long way to make the students more comfortable.

I look back down at my outline and sigh. I'm only at the first argument with no idea what I'm supposed to be talking about. Most of the time, I just start writing, sort of wing the assignment and end up where I end up. If I had to identify my writing style, I'd say it's like a combination of stream of consciousness mixed with a deep desperation to get to the finish line. Unfortunately, I've been told this can lead to arguments that aren't exactly... cogent, so I've been trying a different method.

My brain isn't used to this new format of bullet points and headings, notes and prep that will have to be translated into a fully structured essay. It's hard for me to work in a way that's organized. My ADHD really does make it easier to thrive in chaos, and besides, leaving an assignment to the last minute might spell disaster, but there's a thrill in it that I kind of love. Chasing the clock has always been a huge dopamine hit. But I vowed that I would be more organized during my PhD. More calm.

So, that's what I'm doing.

At least trying to.

Roman continues the lecture, using Foucault as his primary example of the history of the modern prison. The guy basically invented the way we think about all of this stuff now, and if you're going to study prisons, leaving him out of your reading list would be a huge mistake.

"The Panopticon was a concept derived from the mind of Jeremy Bentham... can anyone tell me who he was?"

Nobody answers, but Roman only grins, probably excited to get a chance to dive into more detail.

"He was one of the main contributors to the school of Classical Criminology and Penology. In theory, the Panopticon allowed all prisoners in a single facility to be observed by one guard in a tower. The trick is, this would be done without the prisoners knowing *when* they're being watched, only that they *could be* at any time. Later, you'll read Foucault's metaphor for the panopticon that stretches beyond the walls of

Bentham's theoretical prison, but we'll cross that bridge when we get to it."

He continues on for another hour, the students raising their hands every once in a while as they get used to his style. By the end, everyone including Roman seems at least a little bit more confident in the material, but the students are still clearly relieved to be dismissed for the day.

I wait off to the side as a few of them linger around to ask him about the readings. He's patient, taking the time to listen to their questions and concerns and I find myself kind of wishing he was a total douche so I could hate him. It would make this whole thing so much less complicated. When the last student wanders out the door, Roman slowly packs his bag, smiling up at me as he does.

"I'm actually supposed to be meeting your brother for a run." He motions toward the door. "Walk and talk?"

"Sure."

We head for the exit, and for a moment I'm worried I'll let the awkward silence take over, but we're only a few steps from the door before I manage to speak up.

"I was wondering why you haven't been answering my emails about the transfer."

Roman strokes his beard, a contemplative look on his face as he holds the heavy door open for me.

"I did say it would take a while," he replies.

"Two weeks, yeah, and it's been two weeks. So you're saying you haven't heard anything back yet? Is that why you're avoiding talking to me?"

"I'm not avoiding—"

"Yes, you are, dude!" I laugh. "Look, I have no problem being chill about this with you, but as it stands you're barely answering my emails unless it's forwarding me students to deal with. That's not—"

He sighs, nodding. Roman always seems to know exactly when he's fucked up, which somehow makes things even more annoying.

"I'm sorry," he replies.

And he's always sorry.

"I didn't answer you because I don't *have* an answer for you right now."

I snort.

"Then you should have been up front with that."

I'm supposed to be meeting some of my cohort in the library right now, but I knew I wouldn't be able to concentrate unless Roman and I had this discussion. It'd eat into all of my other thoughts, gotta get it out and done with.

"I'd just appreciate more communication, I think that's fair considering this is my job and basically my life."

He stops as we reach the clearing, sun breaking through the massive cedar trees that wrap around us. I can't help but feel a little sorry for him. It's that forlorn look in his eyes. Sometimes, when I find myself getting frustrated with other people, I try to remember something my mom taught me: *It's everybody else's first time being a human being, too.*

The thought washes over me and allows me to breathe.

"I get that, and it's why I'm trying to make sure that this doesn't reflect poorly on you in any way." He tugs at the collar of his shirt like it's choking him, a flush of red creeping up his neck and disappearing under his beard. "I swear I'm working on it. You have nothing to worry about."

I raise a brow, carefully considering his words.

Trying to make sure this doesn't reflect poorly on you.

I want to dive a little deeper, but that's probably not such a good idea. He seems flustered enough. Maybe getting rid of me isn't his main priority. Maybe there's more going on with him.

It irritates me that the thought gives me a bit of hope. I like seeing him in class once a week, and I wish we could both have just said *fuck it*, but...

There's too much at stake for the both of us.

He reaches out and puts his hand on my shoulder, and a warm tingle rushes down my spine, making the butterflies in my stomach begin to storm.

"I promise I'll email you once I hear something, but I also want to do better than I have been. If you need anything, I'll answer."

I don't quite believe him, but I nod all the same.

"Thank you, Dr. Burke." I motion to the campus with my thumb. "Now, believe it or not, I've gotta get to the library."

"And I've gotta teach your brother the importance of long distance running."

"Want him to really remember it? Go for the backs of his knees!" I call, slipping my sunglasses on. "Long-ass legs like that? You'll fuck up his whole day!"

Roman laughs and gives me the thumbs up.

"Thanks for the tip!"

I reluctantly turn toward the library, that feeling in my stomach refusing to go away. It's cruel that things can't be different between us, and it's going to be a real struggle to work my way through this.

But all the same, I find it impossible not to smile.

CHAPTER EIGHTEEN
monster mash
IMOGEN

HALLOWEEN

This is the worst party I've ever been to.

Whoever's in control of the music has the worst fucking taste of all time. Five Pitbull songs in a row is just a little too much, and the house is packed so full that everyone's bleeding out into the backyard along with the music. I have to admit though, the unscheduled entertainment's been surprisingly good. Who'd have thought drunk frat boys continuously screaming *'Mr. Worldwide!'* while they hurl themselves off the balcony onto some mattresses would be so much fun to watch.

"Piper, no offense to Jay, but next time we pick the party."

"Agreed," she mutters, checking the time on her phone and letting out a frustrated groan. "God, we've been here for 45 minutes."

"Does that mean we can go home?"

"I'll have to ask the keg master," she chuckles, gesturing off to the side.

Jay's all the way across the yard helping people do keg stands; he's keeping a very organized lineup, kind of like an amusement park ride. Looks like this might be his true calling.

"Well, maybe you can get a word in after this and we can—" Someone slams into me from behind, spilling my drink all down the front of my dress. "Fuck!"

"Sorry!" A girl calls, flashing me a pained smile as she slips past me.

"She's lucky this is latex," I mutter, wiping the wine off.

I'm dressed like Barbie, in a bright pink dress that's about two sizes too small for me, and a pair of matching stilettos that have been slicing into my feet all night. I even changed my phone case to match the color of my dress. When I do a costume, I go all-out.

I miss my dad's Halloween parties. You couldn't get in the house without a costume and if you didn't have one, he'd find something stupid for you to wear. Obnoxiously, other than the three of us, most people here aren't even dressed up.

I pull out my phone as we sit on the sidelines, the chaos of the night unfurling around us. I open a reading for Abi's class, trying to get as much out of it as I can while Piper takes a bunch of selfies from different angles. I've got a paper due next week that I've barely started because I've been struggling with the material.

And hey, since we're killing time, why not try to comprehend Pierre Bourdieu with some THC and a couple glasses of wine in my system?

"We need a selfie." Piper elbows me in the ribs. "Evey from the Mummy meets Dominatrix Barbie."

Grateful for the distraction, I set my phone down in my lap, laying a kiss on her cheek just as she snaps a picture.

"Oh, that's a cute one!" She gushes, already touching the photo up to be posted.

"Hey, ladies!" Jay calls, dragging a bewildered looking man toward us. "This is my friend Ryan!"

I look up into a pair of stunning blue eyes that take me a little by surprise.

"Your friend," I reply, staring Jay down. "Known him long?"

"Yeah, totally, and you guys have a lot in common!"

It's sweet that Jay's trying to help me get over my whole... situation, but I'm not really sure about this, even if Ryan is really cute. That said, I'm not *with* Roman, so it's fine right? Maybe this'll be a fun way to get him out of my head.

"Hey, Jay?" Piper asks, a very intentional tone in her voice as she gets to her feet. "Can you teach me how to do a keg stand?"

I want to roll my eyes, but resist the urge. She's so obvious.

"Sure," Jay replies, grinning from ear to ear as he stares over at me. "You need anything?"

"Nope." I raise my glass. "All stocked up."

He throws me a wink, flashing finger guns for good measure as he and Piper disappear into the crowd. They always think they're going to introduce me to Mr. Right at these kinds of parties. It's never going to happen, but I'm not the sort of girl who says no to a potential good time.

"Sorry," Ryan clears his throat. "I didn't mean to interrupt. I was just telling... was it Jay?"

"You mean your good friend?" I chuckle.

"Hey, I firmly believe you can learn a lot about someone on a keg stand. It's life changing," Ryan replies, sipping his drink. "The truth is, I've kind of been wanting to talk to you all night and I meant to wander over here earlier, but you just looked..."

"Bored?" I ask.

"Angry."

"Unfortunately, that's just my face."

"Ah, I see. Well, it's a very good face," Ryan laughs.

I toss some curls behind my shoulder.

"Actually I was trying to get some reading done for class. Resting bitch face is just a tragic side effect."

"You're studying? At a Halloween party?"

He looks gobsmacked.

"I mean, what else am I supposed to be doing? Beer pong? Jump off the roof?"

"Oh, I don't know, how about you make friends with someone new and interesting?" He puffs out his chest. "What's your name anyway?"

"Imogen."

"Pretty name."

"Thanks. Got it from my dad."

"Oh, cool, was his name Imogen, too?"

He's got a real All-American-Boy thing going on that's surprisingly appealing. It helps that he's decently quick too, even after one of Jay's keg stands.

"Hey, I'm not gonna take that from—" I look him up and down. "What are you supposed to be dressed as?"

He glances down at his football jersey with a sly grin.

"My scholarship." He gestures to the empty seat next to me. "Can I sit?"

There's a little twinkle in his eyes that reminds me of Roman. I kind of hate how much space that guy occupies in my head.

"You've earned it, I guess."

"Do you go to EBU?" Ryan asks, leaning back in the chair.

"Yeah. I'm a PhD student."

"That's cool. Are you in, like, medicine, or..."

"Sociology." I rub the back of my neck, already regretting the direction the conversation's taken. "I, uh... I research the kink scene."

"Oh wow, that's intense."

Sometimes when I tell men my dissertation topic, they get a little... well, creepy. Even other academics. I did a whole presentation on it for a class at NYU and one of my classmates followed me all the way back to the subway asking me questions about it, while not-so-subtly trying to get my number.

"So, are you, uh... a practicing kinky... person?" he asks with a shy smile.

I grab a bottle of wine from my purse, one I nabbed from the kitchen before it got overwhelmed by the stink of over-enthusiastic dancing, and take a swig straight from it.

"I've been known to be. For the right partner."

A cheer erupts from the kegs, and I glance over to see Piper raise both arms before letting out a primal roar that garners even further applause. I've never seen Jay look more proud.

Ryan shifts in his seat a little, trying to grab my attention back.

"So, uh, what would a guy have to do to be the right partner?" He purrs.

As his eyes dance up and down my body, I don't find myself responding the way I did with Roman. The butterflies have flown away, there's no heat in my cheeks, and even though I think this guy's cute, I'd much rather be spending the evening spanking my boss with his own belt.

"I'm sorry." I'm flooded with guilt as I watch the disappointment in his eyes. "I'm kind of... waiting for someone."

I really should have just stayed home tonight. Lying in bed watching Netflix and avoiding my assignments would have been a lot better than having to look at Ryan's big puppy dog eyes.

"Damn, I could have sworn Josh told me you were single."

"You mean Jay." I elbow him gently. "And I sort of am— it's... complicated."

"I get it," he murmurs, pulling his phone out of his pocket, his fingers flying across the keyboard. "I don't want to stand in the way of true love, but if he keeps you waiting for too long, let me know?"

He hands me his phone and I see the word 'Barbie' written at the top.

"You're a bold guy, Ryan."

"I think it's my best quality."

I chuckle, taking the phone and punching in my number.

"Thanks for not being a jerk."

"Had to shoot my shot, right?"

"Yeah, you did a pretty good–"

Suddenly, I hear angry shouting from inside the house, dragging my attention away. It's so loud it cuts right through the music, and I look up just in time to see the glass of the back door practically explode as someone is thrown through it. Screams erupt as a guy in a football jersey comes barrelling through the shattered glass.

He's fucking huge. Hulk-level huge. The guy looks like he pops steroids like Skittles.

"You motherfucker!" He bellows, picking up the second guy by the collar of his shirt and punching him in the face. "You fuck my fucking girl-friend?! I'm gonna fucking kill you!"

Everyone rushes for the action, Ryan and Jay included. Fists are flying and it's hard to tell what's going on until I manage to catch another glimpse of Jay trying to break up the fight. He leaps onto Hulk, trying to pull him away but it only makes the guy angrier. He throws Jay off of him, grabbing him by the shoulders and kneeing him in the face before Jay's body goes limp.

"Oh hell no."

I sprint for the packed crowd as Piper's bloodcurdling scream echoes through the backyard.

"Get away from him!" She roars.

I make my way toward them, pushing through a crush of football players who smell like the inside of a brewery. When I get there, I'm immediately greeted by the sight of Jay covered in blood, with a gash above his nose the size of the Grand Canyon.

"Pinch the bridge and tip your head forward— oh, fuck, Jay! I think it's broken!" Piper turns around, her face twisted into a snarl as she stares at the group of people fighting on the lawn. "Who the fuck did this?! I'm gonna fuck you up!"

"Babe–"

The piercing screech of a police siren slices through the noise.

"Emerald Bay Police Department!"

It's only seconds before people are scattered like leaves in the wind, and we're quickly caught up in a stampede scrambling for the back gate, the two of us struggling to keep Jay on his feet.

"We have to get him to a hospital!" Piper shouts.

Behind us, more screams, cursing, and the sounds of police radios swirl together in a chaotic din. We keep going, pushing through the crowd until we get to a back alley. People split off into every direction, some of them laughing, others shouting out the location of another party a few blocks away.

"I don't need a hospital!" Jay laughs. "We can keep partying. I'll just text—"

"No the fuck we can't!" Piper snaps. "Your nose is broken."

I can see exposed bone in the glow of the street lights, and his eyes are already starting to swell up. He's trying to act tough, but he's blinking a lot, wiping away tears as he stumbles.

"Piper—"

The venom in her eyes makes Jay freeze, clearly much more concerning to him than the blood dripping down his face.

"Jay, baby, I love you so much, but if you don't let me take you to the hospital, I'm gonna send you there myself," she snaps. "Now pinch your fucking nose!"

I already know that I do *not* want to be in that waiting room. It'll just be hours of Piper reaming Jay out, and him telling her that he 'had no choice.' If Jay sees a fight, he immediately involves himself; it's like he's got a compulsion to get his ass kicked.

"Piper!" He groans. "Come on, can't we talk about this?"

Unfortunately for Jay, she's already on the phone with the taxi service, and I take that as my cue to get the hell out of dodge.

"I'm going home!" I shout. "Text me, Pipes!"

"I will!" She waves. "Love you, babe!"

"Love you too! And Jay, let her take care of you!"

I can hear him groan as I plug my brother's address into a map app and start the trek home. A few years ago, I might have followed some people to another party, even after my friends had to bail, but now all I really want to do is crawl into bed ASAP.

The air is chilly and I immediately regret not bringing my jacket with me. After about ten minutes, my feet are killing me as well. I can feel the faux leather slicing up my skin and I slide my shoes off, wincing at the sight of my toes now looking like little sausages.

The GPS says Logan's place is only another 15 minutes. I can walk barefoot for 15 minutes. I just need some music or a podcast, something to distract me. I dig through my purse, trying to find my AirPods, but after a few moments I can tell something's wrong. I stop, my stomach churning and toss my purse onto the ground, crouching down and using my phone as a flashlight as I push things aside, feeling around for something sharp and metal.

"Come on," I murmur. "I know you're in there."

I take out the bottle of wine I brought to the party, my charger, wallet, pepper spray, asthma inhaler, and... that's it.

No keys.

"No fucking way."

I dump my purse upside down and shake it like a madwoman. Nothing comes out, but I only shake harder, letting out a desperate whimper when I get the same devastating result.

That's when the memory hits me like a freight train: I put my keys down on my nightstand, just for a second, when I was grabbing my phone. I never picked them up. How the fuck did I forget to pick them back up? Logan even *asked me* if I had them before I left because...

He was going to lock up after me.

Because he was going to be out of town for a couple days.

I dial his number. He's in San Francisco for a conference for the weekend but it's not *that* late at night. It's only... well, I guess it's technically morning.

The call goes straight to voicemail.

"Shit."

I remember having this fight with dad so many times. I would do things too fast without thinking, and always wind up losing something: Keys, my debit card, my wallet, my homework. I left my very first phone at a fucking bus stop and sobbed until I was sick. My dad was pissed. He told me that if I wanted to keep nice things, I had to make sure that I didn't misplace them.

I let out a frustrated sob, years of self-hatred bubbling up in my chest. It's not like I did it on purpose. Sometimes I still feel like a kid who just can't get it together. I sit down on the pavement and grab the half-empty wine bottle, flicking the cap off and tossing it behind me as I take a deep swig. Everything's finally started to come crashing down.

I moved to a place I barely know, I can't find an apartment to save my life, I slept with my brother's best friend, and I still can't get him out of my head.

And the cherry on top? I'm locked outside with nowhere to go.

I sniffle, digging for my phone to text Piper when I hear a sound that makes me jolt straight up.

"Imogen?"

Roman's standing behind me, bathed in the gentle golden glow of the street lamps.

My goddamn hero, somehow looking perfect at 1 AM on a Friday.

"You've *got* to be fucking kidding me."

CHAPTER NINETEEN
just what i needed
ROMAN

There she is, in a tiny dress with blue eyeshadow smeared up to her temples and mascara running down her cheeks. Her feet are bloodied and sliced up, but it looks like that's the least of her concerns. The entire contents of her purse are spilled out on the pavement, save for the wine bottle that's sitting next to her.

Why is it that when you're trying not to think about someone, all of a sudden, they show up right in front of you? She's the most beautiful disaster I've ever laid eyes on.

"Cute dog."

She sniffles as Mitzy licks her arm.

"Imogen, what are you doing out here? It's past midnight."

She gestures vaguely, a bitter laugh escaping her lips.

"Oh, you know! Just enjoying Emerald Bay as a drunken disaster."

She's got tears streaming down her face.

"Did something happen?"

"Yeah, some guy got tossed through a glass door, and then the cops showed up at this stupid Halloween party that nobody else was dressed up for." She lets out a long sigh. "And then I lost my keys, and my *stupid swollen feet* won't fit back into my *tiny fucking shoes*!"

She takes a swig from the wine bottle and I frown. Should I sit with her? Should I ask her if she wants to stay at my—

No. No, I can't do that.

She would turn me down, anyway.

"I'm having a great fucking night!" She shouts to no one in particular before turning back. "But enough about me, how are things with you?"

"Did you call your brother?"

Her groan echoes through the empty street.

"Logan's in San Francisco for some conference, and he puts his phone on Do Not Disturb after 9:00. He left me the spare key, which is, of course, sitting cozily on my nightstand."

Son of a bitch. I can't leave her out here.

"Do you have a place to stay?"

"Uh, no. I was thinking about downing the rest of this wine and going to the hospital. Maybe I can beg Piper and Jay to let me sleep on their couch."

"Hospital?"

"It's a long story." She buries her face in her hands. "I always do this! I always lose shit, and I'm always fucking things up!"

A deep sob ripples through her and she drops the wine bottle, startling herself as it clatters onto the concrete.

"Son of a bitch!"

Shit.

I care about her too much to leave her by the side of the road, but I'm not great at this whole comforting thing. I feel awful, and she looks so damn helpless but it's probably too forward to sit down and wrap my arm around her. Getting close tends to lead to poor decisions on my part.

Mitzy pulls me toward her again, licking her and nudging her in the arm.

"Can she smell a trainwreck a mile away, or is she just a big sweetheart?"

"Both," I joke, trying to lighten the mood. "She picked me out of a crowd, and I'm a complete mess."

More laughter, but this time there's no irony; it's bright despite the tears in her eyes.

"Roman, you don't have to stick around. I can go meet up with my friends."

She gives Mitzy a little scratch behind the ears.

"In your bare feet?"

They look swollen and beat up, and they're only going to get worse if she tries to walk half the town with no shoes on.

"Well, unless you wanna swap shoes..." She points to the bright pink stilettos that sit next to her. "Honestly, I can't even joke. You'd probably look good in these heels."

"Well, I'm a size 13, so..."

Even with bloodshot, tear-stained eyes, she's still kind of looking at me like she wants to jump my bones. Every time we're around each other the tension feels like it might choke me. It's been a month now of barely communicating via email. She's waiting for an answer, and I don't have one for her. I've gotten sick of pushing the feelings away, sick of thinking about her every ten seconds.

"Come home with me."

She snorts, flashing me a look of disbelief. I barely believe it myself, it just sort of slipped out.

"What?"

"Your feet are swollen, you've got makeup running down your face, and it's the middle of the night. I can't leave you out here. It wouldn't be right."

She opens up her camera app and checks herself out, looking briefly disgusted before glancing back up at me.

"I look fine! And anyway, I can walk, just... you know, I'll do it carefully."

Mitzy sniffs at her purse as I kneel down next to Imogen, shoving the dog lightly away from the spilt wine on the pavement. Imogen stares at me in silence, those big brown eyes burning into mine, and I reach out and wipe away some of the dried mascara on her cheek. I'm a little surprised how willingly she leans into my touch.

"You can sleep on the couch and go to your friend's place in the morning. We can even wash your dress."

"It's latex," she says, wiping her nose with the back of her hand. "Hard to clean."

"Okay, well, then you can wear my sweats. I can call a locksmith in the morning. I'll cover the bill, too."

This isn't a good idea. Staying away from her, that was a good idea. Putting her up in a hotel? That would be a good idea. The whole plan was to stay as far apart as possible until all of this stuff is resolved. But then again, I still haven't sent that transfer email, have I?

She takes my hand and stumbles a little, wincing as Mitzy paws at her calves.

"Mitz, cut it out." I grab Imogen's waist to hold her steady. "Can you walk, darlin'?"

"Yeah, I–" She takes a step and hisses in pain. "Ah, fuck!"

"Put your shit back in your purse and grab your shoes, I'm carrying you."

"Roman, no!" She yelps. "That's ridiculous!"

I tilt my head.

"I'm not going to let you hurt yourself, at least not anymore than you already have. I *won't* tell you again."

There's a moment when I think she's going to fight me, tell me off and limp out into the night, but she doesn't. She just hobbles back toward her things with a little grumble. This is *not* a good idea, and I'm fighting against every instinct that I have, but I can't let her sit out here by herself. Not like this.

I let Mitzy off her leash, giving her a quick command to keep close before hoisting Imogen up into my arms with relative ease.

"I wasn't ready!" She squeaks, quickly trying to cover up how pleased she sounded just now. "Fine, fine, let's get this over with."

"Here, wrap an arm around my neck."

She looks around, avidly avoiding my gaze as I start toward my place.

"You must work out a lot. How often are you carrying damsels in distress home?"

I scoff, my face burning.

I've never done this before. The most I've done was help Christa back to the car when she sprained her ankle playing badminton. She bailed within the first ten minutes, tripped over her own shoelace, and hit herself in the head with her racket. The two of us were laughing so hard we could barely breathe. It's a beautifully painful memory.

"Okay," she mutters. "The strong, silent type routine. Got it."

The streets are quiet, and all I can hear is the wind rusting the trees and the sound of Mitzy's little claws clicking on the pavement as she trots beside us. That and Imogen's steady breathing.

"I'm so used to New York and horns blaring constantly, or people screaming outside my window," Imogen sighs. "It's so quiet here."

"I went to UCLA for my MA and PhD. When I first got the job here, it took us a while to adjust."

"Us?"

I can feel my stomach lurch at the thought of that word.

"Me. I meant me."

Gracefully, Imogen doesn't press the matter, shifting back to the previous subject.

"So you like it here?"

Despite the fact that she has a couple of friends in town, there's a part of her that looks just as lonely as I feel.

"It was hard to adjust at first, but you'll find your people. This town's full of good ones."

She smiles, adjusting her grip on the back of my neck and staring up at the infinite sky. There's not a lot of light pollution in Emerald Bay, and the stars are especially beautiful out at Guardian Point. If things were different, I'd probably have already taken her there.

But that nagging sensation keeps digging its claws into me, over and over.

You can't do this.

This is wrong.

You could lose everything.

I set her down at my apartment door, and she bends over to give Mitzy a scratch as I fish out my keys.

"Thanks for being our fearless leader, uh— what's her name again?"

"Mitzy."

Imogen smiles.

"Mitzy. I love that."

With the front door open, I scoop her back into my arms and carry her up two small flights of stairs to my apartment.

"Wow, did you *just* move in?"

She whistles, making me a little self-conscious as she surveys the place.

"Ha-ha." I roll my eyes and make my way toward the kitchen as she follows, hobbling behind me. "Don't forget, I've seen *your* house. I know how that brother of yours lives."

"What?" She giggles with a confused expression. "I was genuinely asking, I thought this might have been a new place."

I bite my lip, embarrassment tickling the back of my neck as I try to focus on the task at hand. She needs ice. And water, if she has any hope of waking up without a ridiculous hangover.

"Sorry, sometimes it's hard to tell when people are joking— uh, I moved in here after Christa passed away. I never really had the heart to..."

"I get it," she murmurs.

Imogen bites her lip, not sure where to look as Mitzy happily dances around her new friend.

"Hey, so I don't want to impose, but do you mind if I use your shower?" She asks, folding her arms around her body. "I'm kind of freezing and I feel gross."

"There are towels in the closet, and uh... I'll see if I can scrounge up some sweats for you to wear. Bathroom's down the hall to your left, unless you need me to–"

I move to pick her up again but she grasps my hands, leaving me staring helplessly into her eyes.

"It's like, what, two feet away?"

"Yeah," I laugh. "Sorry."

I take a step back, watching her hobble down the hallway with Mitzy carefully walking beside her, checking in on her every few seconds. When I finally hear the bathroom door shut, I head for my room to rifle through my drawers for something she can wear.

All of Christa's clothes were finally donated last year. Logan and Frankie helped me clean everything out, pack it all up, and send it off to Goodwill. I felt so stupid tearing up just putting things in boxes, but they were there for me through it all.

I manage to find one of my old UCLA sweaters and a pair of shorts with a drawstring that Mitzy hasn't chewed to shit, heading for the bathroom with my heart in my throat. The door is ajar, and Mitzy is sitting outside.

"You like her, huh?" I ask.

She yawns and flops onto her side.

"Yeah, me too," I whisper. "It's a real problem."

I knock gently, leaning in to listen for her over the sound of the shower.

"Hey, Imogen? I've got those clothes for you."

"Can you put them on the counter?"

I quickly slip into the bathroom, trying my best to avert my eyes but still catch her silhouetted figure through the semi-translucent shower curtain.

"I'll get a first aid kit for your feet, and, uh..." Her back arches and I can see the perfect outline of her tits as she rinses the water from her hair. "I'll get you some painkillers."

She pulls part of the shower curtain back, mascara streaked and smeared beneath her eyes.

"You don't have to do that."

I frown and lean against the counter.

"Will you just let me help?"

She flashes me a resigned smile, and her gaze lands on the clothes sitting on the counter.

"I'll be out in five minutes."

I nod, standing stock-still until she quirks a brow.

"Oh, right, sure, and I'll be in the living room."

I rush out of the room, shutting the door and taking in a deep breath. This might be it, I might be doomed. The fact is, I can't stop this chemistry from firing between us. She makes me feel alive. Even just being around her has my heart pounding and my palms clammy. Sure, I can transfer her, I *should* transfer her, but I'm still going to have to see her.

There will be more dinners, more parties, more mixers.

It's not something we can easily run from.

And if we've already crossed a line, what's a few more steps?

CHAPTER TWENTY

your woman

IMOGEN

It's been a while since I've been this hung-up on someone. No matter what I do or where I go, I keep finding Roman Burke.

Or he keeps finding me.

I finish up in the shower and shut the water off, stepping out to dry myself off with one of his big fluffy towels. I stare at myself in the mirror and wonder what the fuck I'm doing here as the remnants of my makeup linger beneath my eyes. I should have just texted Piper, but instead I let my boss carry me back to his apartment like a damsel in distress.

I want him.

I root through my purse, finding a frayed hair tie and pulling my hair back before I change into the soft shorts and giant sweater that Roman gave me. The clothes are so big that I have to push the sleeves up to use my hands, but they'll do for now.

By the time I head back into the living room, Roman has a first aid kit set out and ready, along with a couple of ice packs. I hobble to the couch, trying not to wince as I ease myself down, and he crouches in front of me without a word.

"Give me your foot."

I extend my leg and he gently cradles my heel, running a damp cotton ball over the deep cut on my big toe.

"Does it hurt?" He asks.

"Yeah, but it's fine. I've had worse."

I didn't realize how badly the skin was split until now. It stings a little, but the pain fades within a few seconds.

"You've gotta stop wearing shoes that are too small for you."

"They look good, though."

He smiles.

"You know, I've heard a lot of women say the same thing."

"About my shoes?" I ask. "That's awfully nice of them."

He snorts as he bandages me up, one warm hand sliding up my calf as he checks my foot for any other nicks and cuts. I can't help but let out a gentle, contented sigh, my eyes closing as his fingers work the muscle.

"Hurt?"

"No," I murmur. "Feels good after being in those heels all night."

Warmth trickles down my spine as my muscles start to relax. I know this is weird, and he probably knows we shouldn't be doing this, but I'm not one to turn down a free massage. With those hands? He could charge good money.

I open my eyes to find him staring at me, lips parted, and his eyes brimming with desire. He doesn't drop my leg, in fact, his fingers glide a little higher.

"Funny how we keep ending up like this," he says softly.

There's no point in beating around the bush. We either do this, or we end it. There's no room in between, and we both know it.

"You never emailed me back. About transferring to another professor."

"Is that what you want to talk about right now?"

God, his voice, velvety and rich like caramel or honey. Or both. Either way I could drown in it.

"I think we should, considering I haven't stopped thinking about us in that pantry for the past month."

"You haven't?"

I shake my head slowly; he almost sounds proud of himself.

His gaze rests on my thighs and he takes a breath.

Fuck the rules. Fuck the administration. I *want* this man, and I want him now.

"We shouldn't be doing this," he sighs.

"You keep saying that, but that's not the vibe I'm getting from you right now."

His eyes flash with regret, but the look is quickly overshadowed by something dark and sinful; something I want to press tight against my chest and hold onto.

"You make it sound like I don't—" He shakes his head, turning away from me to look out the window. "Forget it."

I reach out and grasp his chin, forcing him to look me in the eye.

"Say what you need to say, but you're going to *look at me* when you say it," I reply, my voice soft but commanding.

His hand slides higher up my leg, like he's trying to savor what little time we have before he finally cuts me out of his life.

"You make it sound like I don't want you," he finally manages to choke out.

I say nothing, the silence clawing at him until he caves.

"The reason I haven't sent you another email is because I never talked to anyone about transferring you."

"Why not?"

"I wanted to be careful about it, take it slow so that no one would get suspicious. I was worried that your brother could find out, that the department could find out, but..."

"But what?"

I grin, flames burning inside me as I watch his pupils expand and feel his calloused palms gliding higher until one hand slips between my legs.

"But everyone keeps secrets."

Oh, shit. Are we doing this? He could turn on a dime. He has before.

"Can *you* keep a secret, cowboy?"

"That depends on you, darlin'. What do you want to do?"

Breath passes between us, and that fire grows hotter by the second. I try not to rock against his hand, but it feels so good to give in.

"Take me to bed."

His lips hover over mine, curling into a wicked grin as his fingers brush against my clit.

"I want to be in charge tonight."

It's a welcome surprise, although I *was* looking forward to tormenting him a little.

"Do you know how? To dom, I mean."

"I'm a researcher, aren't I?" He asks, his smile growing wider by the second.

"Clever boy," I whisper, trying my best to stay composed as he increases the pressure of his fingers. "What are you waiting for, then?"

"Be a good girl and ask nicely."

I bat my eyelashes, half-mocking him as I press a kiss to his lips.

"*Please* take me to bed, sir?"

Roman pulls his fingers from my aching pussy and licks them clean, all while refusing to take his eyes off of me. Pent up desire makes me shiver as he stands, grasping me by the waist and hauling me over his shoulder in one fluid motion.

"Roman!"

He gives my ass a rough smack and I yelp.

"You like that, huh?" He asks, his voice laced with a dash of arrogance.

He carries me to his bedroom, tossing me onto the bed before kicking the door closed and peeling off his t-shirt. My mouth hangs open in complete awe of the confidence that's flooded into him. His shoulders are pulled back, his head held high, and he's staring at me with a hunger that I haven't seen since that night in the pantry.

Slowly, I spread my legs, playing with the drawstring on my shorts.

"I've been thinking," he rumbles as he takes a step towards me.

"About?"

"What kind of dom I would be."

Roman's voice is what I'd imagine an expensive glass of brandy sounds like.

"And what conclusion did you come to?"

He slowly unbuckles his belt and slips it out of the loops, his eyes fixed on mine as he flips it in half and drags the leather across his palm. I've never wanted to shove my hand down my pants so fast.

"I think I'm someone who gets off on *getting* people off." He smirks.

"A pleasure dom."

"That sounds right. But with that in mind, I need some information from you, darlin'."

His muscles ripple as I watch him squeeze the stiff leather in his hands, his eyes darting around as he contemplates how he's going to use it on me.

"And what information is that?"

"I want to know exactly how you'd like to be fucked tonight."

He towers over me, stepping closer.

"Nice and sweet like a good girl, or spanked and fucked stupid like a dirty little slut."

How much research did he do? He's a natural.

Roman slowly drapes the belt across the back of my neck. He holds it there gingerly, even tenderly, as he stares down and pulls me closer to him.

"Do you like to be spanked?"

"Of course."

"Good, because you're going to be bent over my knee tonight."

His eyes are electric, searing away whatever willpower I might have had left. I want this man to fucking *destroy* me.

"So what's our safe word?"

"Tonight, I was thinking strawberry," he grins.

"Strawberry?" I ask, raising a brow.

"It's what you tasted like that first night. Can't get it out of my head."

Roman sits on the edge of the bed, his back to me, patting his thigh with the belt still in his hand. I can see his expression in the full length mirror across the room, and I can tell he's hungry. All he has to do is inject a little bit of that authoritative presence and I'm putty in his hands.

"Come here and tell me what else you want," he purrs.

For a second, I don't want to move. I just want to stare at him, imposing and confident, even statuesque as he sits bathed in moonlight. I *knew* this side of him existed, and I wonder how long he's been fantasizing about doing something like this. Slowly, I crawl across the bed toward him, snaking my arms around his waist and staring at him in the mirror.

"Start with your hand first so you can feel how hard you have to hit me."

"I can do that," he murmurs.

I reach down and squeeze his cock through his pants, savoring the deep rumbling growl in his chest that makes me ache.

"I want praise," I purr. "Lots of it. Things like: *you're doing so well, good girl, that's my girl*. Understand?"

He nods.

"Are you ready?"

"Yes, sir."

"Good girl. First, I want you to strip. Let me see all of you."

I roll off the bed and stand in front of him, letting my hair down and shaking it out. Roman watches with rapt attention, blush creeping down his neck as he grips the edge of the bed.

I decide to give him a show, tossing my sweater onto the floor and taking a step toward him, lingering just out of reach. I'm fucking loving the power I have over him as his fingers twitch and his eyes dance all around me. I slowly peel off my shorts, turning around and bending over to give him a nice view of my pussy as I slide them down.

When I lift myself back up I find Roman staring at me like it's the first time he's ever seen me naked. My nipples pebble and goosebumps rise on my skin as he licks his lips.

"You're so goddamn beautiful," he whispers.

I take another step toward him, running my hand through his hair.

"Look who's talking, cowboy."

Roman grabs me by the waist, the cool metal of the buckle pushed against my skin. He presses his lips to my stomach, kissing his way up and nipping at my breasts. It's been too long since I've felt his hands on my body, and I fully give in to him, to the temptation, to all of it.

"Lay across my lap."

I follow his command immediately, crawling back onto the bed and laying across him. He briefly caresses my ass before moving between my legs and beginning to tease my pussy.

"How many do you want to start with?"

I wiggle my hips, breathing in deep as I ready myself for what's to come.

"Three with your hand, and then three with the belt."

He gives my ass a rough squeeze as he lets out a growl from deep inside.

"Start counting."

CHAPTER TWENTY-ONE

wicked game

IMOGEN

"Fuck— One!"

He slips his hand between my thighs again, fingers sliding into my pussy while the sting of his palm against my ass is still fresh in my mind.

"Good girl," he groans. "You're already nice and wet for me, aren't you?"

I feel myself quiver around him for a moment, turning my head to see him grinning triumphantly in the mirror.

"Harder sir," I grunt, rolling my hips as the heat from his first strike starts to dissipate, radiating down my legs. "Please."

Roman's taking his time, carefully gauging how much I can handle while doing his best to keep up his new dom persona.

But I need more.

"Be a doll and keep counting for me," he growls.

He pulls his fingers out, licking them clean before going back for the second strike. I hear a sound like a gunshot before I feel it.

"Two, sir!"

I moan, wiggling in his lap as he soothes the welt on my ass with his hand.

"Can you take one more?"

"Yes, sir."

He grabs my hair with his free hand, knotting it in his fist as his other one comes down even harder than before. A ragged grunt breaks free of me as my body jolts from the impact.

"Three!"

I get the word out as clear as I can before my voice starts to shake.

"Atta girl."

I can feel him getting harder beneath me, my spike of adrenaline already fading slightly, but then I hear the telltale jingle of his buckle. He shows off his grip in the mirror, making sure I can see it as he clutches the belt in his fist.

"Is this okay?" He asks.

I give him a small, approving nod, and only a moment later I feel another razor-like sting on my backside. I forgot how good this kind of pain feels. It's a beautiful sensation that always makes my head spin.

"Keep counting."

I remember the first time somebody spanked me: I cried, not because of the pain exactly, although the sensation was a little overwhelming, but because it made me feel so fucking free.

"That was one, sir."

He hits me a second time, almost the moment the words leave my lips, maintaining the same amount of force. My hands curl into tight fists and tears well in my eyes and I feel like I might combust.

"Two!"

Another hit and my eyes roll back, my clit aching to be touched as I whine through the pain. The last strike stings the most, ripping through me like a bullet.

"Three!"

The leather produces an entirely different sensation than his palm, but no less exquisite.

"You did so good," he whispers. "What a good girl."

Roman sets the belt aside, gently soothing the welts he's made. He slides his fingers into my pussy once more, thrusting them slowly to satiate the ravenous hunger that's growing inside me. Soon, the slick sounds of him fucking me become the only thing I can focus on, and I give in, writhing like an animal.

"That's my girl. You needed this as much as I did, huh?" He crooks his fingers. "Look at how wet that made you."

"Fuck me," my words practically come out as a sob. "Please, Roman."

He gives my ass one more sharp smack, his raspy growl making me quiver as he slips his fingers out of me.

"Stand up."

I scramble to my feet, pushing my hair out of my face as what feels like a brand new man gazes up at me.

"You are a work of art, Imogen."

God, I think he means it. I can tell by the look in his eye.

"Thank you, sir."

He pats his leg like it's an invitation.

"Now, straddle my thigh."

Slowly, I ease myself down, the rough denim creating the perfect amount of friction against my clit. Roman grasps my chin, studying me like a painting. The sheer intensity of the eye contact compels me to straighten my spine. I want to be good for him—

But no, not just good.

Perfect.

He takes his time with me, both hands guiding my hips as I grind my swollen clit against his thigh. I put my hands on his shoulders, practically breathing his name as he places soft kisses up and down my neck.

"God, I love the sound of that," he grunts. "You're my girl, aren't you?"

"Yes, sir."

"My *good girl.*"

My head falls back and I cry out into the ceiling. I could listen to him call me that every night. It's almost better than sex.

Not quite, but almost.

Roman dips his head, biting down gently on my nipple.

"Next time we do this, I'm going to make you beg for my pussy," I moan.

He lets out a mocking laugh that nearly sends me over the edge. I want to come. I *need* to come.

"Oh, darlin'. I'd let you ruin me."

"I don't need you to *let me* do anything, cowboy."

He rocks me faster, and my toes slip against the hardwood as I try to keep up, biting down on his shoulder and struggling to maintain control. His jeans are so fucking wet I'm practically gliding across them, and I can't stop myself from letting out a loud keen as the orgasm catches me by surprise.

We share a kiss that's messy and carnal. It's everything we want to say but can't.

"Fuck me," I whisper.

"Not quite yet."

He taps my hip, helping me stand up before stripping off his jeans and laying on his back.

"Hands on the headboard. And sit on my face."

I'm ready to go again just looking at him, crawling across the bed like a starving animal. Roman purrs as I toy with the waistband of his briefs, all too eager to get that cock inside of me. I straddle his hips, pausing for a moment to drag my nails down his chest.

"How much research did you do?" I ask with a smirk.

"I may have dedicated a couple of days to it." He bites his lip. "Now do as you were told, I'll give you what you need."

He slides down the bed a little, making it easier for me to hover over his mouth. I grip the headboard tight, lowering myself down until I can feel his stubble.

"Oh, fuck!"

And then his tongue sliding all the way inside me.

I move slowly, savoring the way he glides over every inch of my pussy. My head spins, and I can feel sweat begin to drip as I'm forced to focus on keeping myself from coming.

Roman's lips wrap around my clit, rough hands squeezing my ass and moving my body like he owns it, yet each touch is surprisingly tender. The remaining uncertainty that's still clinging to him is endearing, but it's holding him back. I want to teach this man to *really* let go.

"Roman!" I gasp. "Roman, I'm—"

But my pleasure is cut short when he lifts me up and flips me onto my back. I let out a sharp gasp as he snatches my wrists, pinning them above my head. That cocky smirk on his face makes me want to scream bloody murder as my body tries to recover from being denied.

"You'd better hope I don't get my hands on that belt of yours."

He smirks.

"Don't threaten me with a good time, darlin'."

"I was so close!"

"I know." He dips his head, giving me a mocking kiss. "But I want to look in your eyes when I make you scream."

He climbs off of the bed, hooking his thumbs into the waistband of his briefs and slowly slipping them off as that wicked look in his eyes refuses to fade.

"You're such a fucking tease," I laugh.

"It's no fun if you're not squirming for me," he rumbles as he wraps his hand around his cock. "You got condoms?"

"They're in my bag, don't worry I'll handle things while you're gone."

I reach between my thighs but Roman grips my chin tightly, my heart thumping wildly as my fingers hover frozen, inches from relief.

"Don't," he growls. "You keep acting up and you're not gonna be able to walk straight tomorrow, sweet thing."

I'm giddy at the thought; I've been dying to test his limits.

"Stop teasing and do it."

"God, you're a fucking brat."

"Takes one to know one," I purr.

Roman's hand moves down to rest at the base of my throat, fingers squeezing my neck just enough to make me shiver.

"Move that hand."

"How about you choke me while you fuck me, and I'll do anything you want." I lick my lips. "It's important to be able to negotiate, *sir*."

He releases my throat, grinning like I've just given him the best idea in the world.

"Your bag's out in the living room, right? I'll be right back, so don't move a muscle."

Roman steps out, shutting the door behind him as he goes, and I take the opportunity to look around his bedroom for the first time. It's certainly lacking in decor, save for one plant hanging near the window.

There's a small pile of textbooks on the nightstand, with his reading glasses resting on top of them. A book on dom/sub relationships I've never read before sits at the top of the stack, and Roman has made extensive notes in the margins. He's even highlighted some passages on the importance of consent, and being a good play partner.

"What a good boy you are, Dr. Burke," I chuckle, flipping the pages.

Suddenly, the door creaks and my heart rate skyrockets once more.

"Did you behave while I was gone?" Roman asks as he stands in the doorway.

"Yes, sir," I reply, setting the book aside. "Just doing some reading."

He smirks, tearing at the condom wrapper before it slips from his fingers.

"Shit. That was smooth."

I roll onto my side, propping myself up on one arm as he bends down to scoop it up.

"You're doing great, cowboy."

"Thanks," he chuckles. "It's, uh... it's been fun."

"Feels good to be in control sometimes, huh?"

"Yeah." He rolls the condom down his cock. "Are you ready for round two?"

"Absolutely. We're nowhere near my limits yet."

Roman looks like he wants to devour me, and there's no way in hell I'm going to pump the breaks on that.

"Legs against your stomach." His voice is gentle but commanding as he climbs on top of me. "And grab me that pillow beside you."

He slides it beneath my lower back, one hand on my thigh while he lines himself up.

"Are you ready?" He asks.

"I'm all yours."

He pushes inside of me with one slow thrust, and I shiver, letting out a whimper.

"Louder," he rasps. "I wanna hear it all."

I hiss, moaning his name while he stretches me.

"That's a good girl."

With both hands on my thighs he dives in deeper and deeper, until I can feel the pressure on my G-spot. From there, every stroke makes my eyelids flutter.

"Put your hand on my throat again," I groan.

Roman doesn't hesitate, squeezing my neck until my head starts to feel fuzzy.

"God, you're beautiful. I could do this every day."

He pulls most of the way out before thrusting all the way back in with one rough snap of his hips. Suddenly I can't help the sounds I'm making.

Pathetic.

Desperate.

All for him.

"I wish you could see how you look right now."

My muscles are weak, and my whole body tingles as it screams for release, only needing one more thing to push me right over the edge.

I want to see just how filthy this man can get.

"Spit in my mouth," I moan.

Roman's eyes light up as I part my lips.

"You're a goddamn animal," he snarls, pounding into me with a force that has me gripping the bed sheets for dear life.

A wad of spit lands on my tongue and Roman squeezes my throat harder, making me flush even more.

"Be a good girl and swallow."

I follow his instructions and he rewards me with a ferocious kiss, pinning my arms above my head and sinking all the way into me.

"Eyes on me, darlin'."

Roman doesn't take his eyes off of me as I fall apart, pounding with a relentless force that keeps my climax rippling through me until he finally stills, letting out a deep groan.

"Christ."

He collapses the moment he pulls out, both of us panting as we stare at the ceiling. Without a word, he wraps his arms around me, like they were meant to be there all along.

"We'll talk tomorrow," he mumbles, burying his face in my hair. "I'm exhausted."

"Yeah, me too."

We stay like that for a while, breathing softly until he pulls the blankets over the two of us and drifts off to sleep. Alone in the afterglow, I can't help but feel like we've crossed into something bigger, something more than I thought we could ever have when this all began.

There's no going back now.

CHAPTER TWENTY-TWO
crimson and clover
ROMAN

I thought I'd be filled with regret after last night, but I feel the same way I did when we woke up in that hotel: content and peaceful, like I'm right on the edge of something that could change the entire course of my life.

My phone lights up from the nightstand and I see a notification from KinkFinder pop up.

You have a match!

"Yeah, she's sitting outside," I grumble, unlocking my phone and deleting the app without a second thought.

I made my choice last night.

I roll out of bed and tug on a pair of sweats and a t-shirt before heading out into the living room where the first thing that hits me is the smell of coffee and bacon. Imogen is curled up on my couch, trying to eat a piece of crispy bacon as Mitzy paws at her.

"I said no!" She laughs. "You had kibble already! Come on, you're going to wake your dad up!"

I lean up against the wall and watch, crossing my arms over my chest as I find myself grinning like a fool. Mitzy is fully invested, not even bothering to spare me a glance as her tail thumps against the back of the couch. She licks her chops and tries to take a bite as Imogen giggles, playing keepaway with her delicious prize. My heart feels like it's going to burst as she turns to Mitzy and holds out a piece of bacon.

"You get *one* piece," she says with a total lack of firmness. "And don't sell me out to your dad."

"Oh, he already knows," I announce. "And don't worry, she's very accustomed to getting turkey bacon. It's a special weekend treat."

Imogen glances up as Mitzy snatches the strip from her fingers, gobbling it down with lightning speed.

"Oh, thank God. I made extra for you, it's just warming up in the oven."

"Thanks." I trudge out of the living room to the machine and pour myself a fresh cup of coffee.

When I look down, I notice a Polaroid of Christa that I'd hung on the fridge is sitting on the counter. She's frozen in time, her long dark hair, intense green eyes, and boisterous laugh captured on film. That was only six months before she died.

"Oh! Um... she— uh, the picture fell down when I was making all this, and I just forgot to put it back." Imogen winces. "Sorry."

"It's fine," I murmur, sliding it back under the magnet. "That's Christa."

"Yeah, I– I figured. She was beautiful."

"She was."

I grab some bacon off of the pan, tossing a couple of pieces onto a plate before sitting down next to her in the living room. Mitzy's tail is sticking straight up, wagging enthusiastically as she pants and paws at Imogen's leg.

"I swear I fed her. I hope that's okay."

"Oh, definitely. But if there's people-food, she won't even consider her kibble."

"She's very polite though. She didn't even lunge for the bacon."

"Yeah, I had to get her out of that habit quick," I chuckle.

All of a sudden, Imogen seems to realize something and starts scrolling through her phone.

"Oh, hey, I got an appointment with a locksmith, but he can't come by until around 4:00. Also, it seems like he's going to charge me double since it's the weekend."

"I'll pay it—"

"Roman—"

I raise my eyebrow.

"Let me pay it, and you can stay here for as long as you need." I take a bite of my bacon, hoping she'll be content to drop the subject. "By the way, Is this all you made?"

"I didn't want to start fucking with all of your nice pots and pans. I was just hungry, and bacon felt like the perfect..." She shrugs. "Well, it was quick."

I chuckle softly and motion for her to follow me.

"I'll whip us something more substantial up and we can talk."

The two of us head into the kitchen and Imogen climbs on to one of the bar stools, her coffee in her hand and her phone resting next to her. I grab a bowl and some ingredients for some homemade waffles.

We *have* to talk. For real this time. No more hushed conversations in hallways and pantries. No more running.

"Didn't know you cooked."

"Yeah," I reply. "Picked it up after Christa died. It's been therapeutic."

"It's always good to find something that takes your mind off the grief."

She gets it, I can hear the compassion stitched into her voice. She's been where I am. Everyone who's lost someone understands this kind of pain, maybe not in the same way but it's the story we all share. It's the loneliness, the anger, the wondering what could have been had things turned out differently.

"Cooking gave me something to focus on," I continue as Imogen sips her coffee. "A totally new learning experience. I went all in: bought a bunch of knives, brand new pots and pans, special oils, and I started watching all these great chefs on YouTube. I think I made... I don't know, a hundred different desserts in the month after the funeral."

When someone dies, you don't just grieve their loss, you ache for the moments you missed out on: the calls you didn't answer because you were too busy, the times you said no to dinner, and the messages you forgot to reply to. It's cruel the way life swallows us up and we stop connecting with each other.

Imogen chuckles, bringing me back to the present.

"Man, I wish we'd done that. People just kept dropping off casseroles."

I grin, pointing at her with the whisk.

"Hey, don't underestimate a good casserole."

"Yeah, but sixteen is excessive."

Her eyes drift over to the fridge and I follow her gaze. She's looking at the picture of Christa again.

"I only recently put that up. It's hard to look at her sometimes. The guilt just... it doesn't go away."

Imogen reaches for me, placing her hand on my forearm.

"After my dad died, my mom took all of the pictures of the two of them out of her room. Said it was too hard to go to sleep looking at him..." Her voice wobbles and cracks, her eyes misting. "Sorry."

"It's okay," I rasp, my own voice wavering as well.

Imogen taps her fingernails on the counter and clears her throat. I find myself focusing on the intense pink polish that adorns her hands. And the glitter. It's a welcome distraction, keeping me from falling apart right along with her.

"Logan and I always thought that we didn't fight hard enough. That there must have been some treatment we missed, like a miracle drug or something. We'd stay up into the early morning reading science journals, trying to find anything the doctors might have missed. I don't know what we thought we were doing. Dad had made his choice, to leave on his terms."

She takes a breath, steadying herself.

"I was angry when he died, but I wasn't angry at him. I was angry at this *thing* that took him away. His disease was like another person in the room with us, standing in the corner with a timer that was just ticking down. As much as I logically agreed with his decision, watching the man who raised me take his last breath... it was so fucking unfair."

Imogen keeps her eyes fixed on the cup in her hand, staring deep into the coffee as tears roll down her face. It's only at that moment when I realize she's using the Snoopy mug that I found buried in a box of Christa's stuff. I don't even remember if it was hers, but at the very least it reminded me of her. It's been hidden away in the cupboard ever since.

"Christa, uh... she was in pain. I found bottles, booze and pills, and her appointment book had meetings with psychiatrists that I never knew about. I was angry at the invisible monster that caused all of it; the darkness that swirled inside of her head that she didn't talk about. Not with me." I clear my throat as all of the pain I'd buried slowly dislodges, slipping out between each word. "I was the one who found her."

Immediately I wish I could take it all back. It's too much to spring on someone, too vulnerable and open. God, the only people who know all this are Logan and Frankie. I start to panic, some kind of fight or flight kicking in.

I take a small step back but Imogen's eyes are locked on me, holding me in place. Her gaze is soft and empathetic, calming my pounding heart. She slides her hand across the counter and slowly turns it over, palm facing upward.

"I don't mean to dredge all that stuff up for you again, that wasn't–"

I place my hand in hers.

"I... found this piece of writing by a guy named Aaron Freeman. It's called *Eulogy from a Physicist*. He says that energy isn't created or destroyed in the universe, so the people we lose are still here in a way. Their vibrations, their particles and atoms and all the things I can't understand. I like to think that it's our love being dispersed into the universe when our physical bodies die. That way we're always here."

A long silence nestles between us until finally I hear her laugh, looking up at me with a tear-stained face.

"You got me, you fucker."

I chuckle, grabbing us more paper towels and pointing out my own red eyes.

"Got myself, too."

She dabs at her face and I give her hand a gentle squeeze. Usually, after I talk about Christa, my grief feels like an albatross around my neck, but not now.

Not with her.

"I used to try and be upfront about it in the beginning, but people got weird so I ended up not talking about her much. I tried to market myself as damage-free after that."

"You loved her," she smiles. "And you still love her."

"I do. It just hurts."

"Silver lining? We're like a buy one get one free when it comes to emotional damage," she jokes. "But, since I'm the master of awkward subject changes, you wanna talk about last night?"

I nod, adding a splash of vanilla to the waffle mix, along with some cinnamon. It's not the most ideal change of pace for a conversation, but it needs to happen.

"Anything specific?"

"About how indecisive you are," she laughs.

I'd have to be blind not to see this coming a mile away.

Setting the mixing bowl aside, I walk around the kitchen counter and grasp both of her hands. My heart is pounding, and I can't believe I'm doing this, what I'm risking.

"Look, I thought that we could be professional, but I was kidding myself."

Imogen arches an eyebrow, and I can tell she's trying not to get her hopes up.

"So, last night when you said you wanted to do this... did you mean *just* last night, or did you mean—"

"I want to do this. Us. Dating, friends with benefits, or whatever this is. Just like we wanted to at the start."

This feels like I'm walking into an abyss with no way of knowing if I'm going to get out of it unscathed.

"After what happened with us in the pantry, I felt like an asshole, and when you asked me if I thought you led me on, I felt like an even bigger one."

"I get it, Roman. You have your job, and—"

"I couldn't stop thinking about you, it was driving me crazy. I'd try to work or go for a run and..." I tap my temple. "There you were, darlin'. Front and center."

She smiles at me, her fingers playing with the hem of my shirt.

"*I* was driving *you* crazy?"

"More than you know." I reach up and brush her cheek. She's still got flecks of glitter on her skin from last night. "I haven't connected with a person this fast in a long time and I was stupid to try and ignore it."

The butterflies in my stomach swirl to life every time she's near me; I don't know if this feeling is just a base desire, or if it's already starting to blossom into something deeper.

She bites her lip.

Right now, I'm not going to question it.

"So we're jumping in with both feet?" She asks.

"Looks that way," I sigh.

"Friends with benefits?"

"Friends with benefits," I repeat the words back to her, like some sort of pact. "And we keep it secret."

"Secrets make it way more exciting."

I feel myself heat up, blushing furiously as her fingers slide underneath my shirt.

"Yeah," I agree, my voice low and raspy. "They do."

Casual might be the most that either of us can handle right now, because if I fall for this woman, there's no chance I make it out unscathed.

I grasp her face in my hands, my lips meeting hers. Her mouth is soft, moving slowly against mine, but when her fingernails drag down my biceps I can feel every hair on my body stand straight on end. When we finally break the kiss, we're both gasping for breath. I can still taste the remnants of cheap wine on her tongue, and I groan, craving more of her.

I could spend all day doing this.

"Well," she sighs. "I'm glad that's settled."

"Me too." I grin. "You hungry?"

"Fucking starved."

CHAPTER TWENTY-THREE

sparks

IMOGEN

MONDAY

> ROMAN: Wear a dress today. I don't want to have to rip those pesky leggings off of you.

I'm staring at the message, my jaw slack as my brain tries to catch up with what I'm reading. He sent this an hour ago. Has he been up that early thinking about fucking me? I snicker to myself as my eyes land on my closet. I have a bunch of toys in my suitcase, including some discrete ones that could be perfect for a little surprise. Roman said he wanted to learn more about kink, and this could be just the thing.

> IMOGEN: What time are you getting to campus?

> ROMAN: Already here. Why?

> IMOGEN: Can we meet in your office? I have something to show you.

I don't even wait for the response, already rolling out of bed and rushing for the shower the moment I hit send. I shave everything, condition my hair, and then spend way too long blow drying and curling it. By the time I'm finished, I'm sweating bullets.

"Logan needs to put a fan in here," I grumble.

Back in my bedroom I'm standing in front of my closet in nothing but my underwear, trying to find the perfect dress. I need to strike a balance between *'I'm railing my boss,'* and *'I'm a respectable PhD student, please take me seriously.'*

It's a hard line to walk.

I settle on a pale yellow sundress with tiny white flowers scattered across it, pairing it with combat boots and a denim jacket, and moving on to haul out my kinky little suitcase from its hiding spot. Just as I start getting to the good stuff, my phone buzzes.

> LOGAN: Hey, Ig! I'm still gonna be back in town today, but it'll be later than I thought. You might want to order yourself a pizza or something.

> IMOGEN: Sick, I'll take any excuse for pizza. Maybe I'll save a few slices for you, if I'm feeling generous.

I toss the phone aside to continue rooting through my suitcase until my fingers wrap around a soft silk bag. I open it up and grin, pulling out a discreet vibrator and remote.

Roman's going to fucking love this.

I stare at the toy, wondering if I should slip it into my panties now, or wait until I get to campus, but before I can make that decision, my phone lights up again.

> ROMAN: Are you going to tell me what you're planning?

> IMOGEN: Nope. That's half the fun.

> ROMAN: You're a damn tease.

> IMOGEN: Watch your mouth, cowboy, or I'll give you something real to complain about.

I head upstairs to make myself some breakfast, rooting through the cupboards until I find some bagels. I drop one into the toaster and as I'm waiting for it to pop, I get an idea. Pulling out my phone, I set a timer on the camera-app, leaning it up against the wall before sliding the vibrator into my panties and bending over the kitchen island. I flip my skirt, bunching my underwear up so that Roman gets a little taste before I arrive. It's uncomfortable, but it's totally worth the thought of him checking his phone in a packed elevator, or in class.

I arch my back and turn my head so that he gets a partial view of my face as well. When the shutter finally clicks, I rush over and check my work with an excited squeal, zooming in to make sure the vibrator isn't obvious in the shot. I want that to be a special surprise.

When I've deemed the photo worthy, I fire it off, along with a text.

> IMOGEN: You said wear a dress, right?

Triumphant, I grab my breakfast and head out the door, ignoring the buzzing of my phone as I hop onto my bike and head toward the university. The sun peeks through the clouds, and I smile, taking a deep breath of fresh air. I love New York, and it'll always be my home, but there's something so charming about this place to me. That is, until I hit the first pothole of the ride and immediately regret shoving this thing into my panties.

Unfortunately, I can't stomach the idea of climbing off and fishing it out in the middle of a residential street; I think I'd wind up on some kind of list. So, I trek onward, the peaceful bike ride short lived as I shift into the proper gear. My legs burn and sweat trickles down my back as cars whiz past and the end of my journey comes into sight.

The Flynns have never been a particularly sporty family. My dad used to say that the only way he'd turn into a serious athlete is if they finally let competitive drinking into the Olympics.

At least downhill on the way back will be easier.

I arrive at the campus, stopping at the sociology building and locking up my bike before finally checking my phone. I should be prepping for Abi's class, but the only thing I'm focused on is Roman and all those texts he sent.

ROMAN: Are you kidding me?

ROMAN: I'll be in my office.

ROMAN: Hurry up.

ROMAN: Please?

ROMAN: Don't make me send you one of those emoji things.

IMOGEN: Are you sure you can find them, cowboy? This softer approach won't let you off the hook, by the way. I remember how demanding you were earlier.

ROMAN: You're killing me.

I smile and head inside, taking the elevator all the way up to the tenth floor. The department's still fairly empty and I check a clock on the wall as I approach Roman's office. It's 7:58. The door's closed, and I glance around, making sure the coast is clear before making my move.

It's not like I could get in trouble, right now it just looks like I'm meeting my boss before class. Still, my brain is rifling through a laundry list of excuses I can give as to why I'm here. Sometimes it's fun to pretend.

I knock softly on the door, bouncing on the balls of my feet.

But he doesn't answer.

Is he messing with me?

I try again, louder this time, wincing as it echoes through the hall.

"Come in," he calls from the other side.

I turn the doorknob and step inside. Roman is at his desk, gaze fixed on his phone in his hand. I can feel my heart beat faster at the sight of him, looking fine in a tight navy blue t-shirt, his tattooed arms on full display. His hair is pushed back, artfully unkempt, and he's even shaved his beard down a little.

That'll feel good between my legs.

"Good morning, Dr. Burke."

The look he gives me could melt a goddamn iceberg.

"Close the door," he commands, standing and circling the desk. "Lock it."

When I turn around to twist the deadbolt, one hand wraps around my waist, sliding up to cup my breast while he wraps his other hand around my throat. My breath hitches and my heart pounds harder as his lips brush against my ear, his half-erect cock pushing against my ass.

"What the hell were you thinking sending me that picture?"

He squeezes a bit harder, and I start to feel that rush that comes along with the lightheadedness.

"Answer me."

"How about I show you?" I gasp, somehow managing to sound defiant while his fingers are wrapped around my throat.

Roman releases me, taking a step back to give me some breathing room, his chest heaving as I shrug my backpack off and place it on a chair. My excitement and apprehension are building at the same rate; I don't know how thin these walls are, and Frankie's office is next door. What if he decides to pay Roman a visit?

But Roman doesn't seem to be focused on that right now, so I guess I won't either. Instead I push him up against the desk and press my body against his, sliding one of my hands down to squeeze his cock.

"You're a very bad girl," he rumbles.

I lower myself to my knees and reach up to unbutton his jeans.

"I thought we were just having fun." I gaze at his newly freed cock, licking my lips at the sight. "Are you not having fun, cowboy?"

He's got an iron grip on his desk, his eyes stormy with desire. Fuck, I love a man who's falling apart for me, even when I've barely even touched him. I part my lips, swirling my tongue over his tip while he knots his fingers tighter and tighter in my hair.

"Don't tease," he begs, giving a desperate tug. "I've been thinking about this all morning. Hell, I woke up thinking about you."

Another flick of my tongue causes his cock to twitch, and I grin with satisfaction.

"Did you touch yourself?"

He moans.

"In the shower."

I wrap my lips tightly around the crown, sucking in tiny pulses before I release him with a pop, beginning to slide my hand up and down his shaft. Roman lets out a soft growl that makes me shiver; I want him to bend me over his desk and take what he wants.

"Did you come? In the shower I mean."

He shakes his head.

"Poor baby," I taunt. "You must be aching."

He tugs a little harder on my hair, and suddenly I'm even more aware of the vibrator between my legs. I could just reach over and give him the remote, push things forward a little quicker, but that would mean giving up my position in this game. There's something about the way he looks at me, like he'd collapse if I stood up and walked away right now.

"Please, darlin'."

"What do you call me?"

I've just decided Roman's getting a crash course in how I dominate today.

"I'm sorry, Mistress," he chokes.

"That's right, slut."

I part my lips and take him all the way down my throat, my eyes flicking up in time to see his head tip toward the ceiling. There's something so beautiful about a man losing himself in the throes of ecstasy.

I set the pace: slow and steady, with my hand firmly wrapped around his cock and my other resting on his thigh. I close my eyes as he hits the back of my throat, feeling tears stream down my cheeks until I'm choking on him. His breath sounds like a rushing river as he rolls his hips, and he struggles to control his moans.

"More. Please."

He's throbbing and heavy on my tongue, and when he pulls me back, I sputter, sucking in a sharp breath before I go back for more. The pace becomes frantic, and his hips snap, both hands gripping my hair. We lock eyes and I keep one hand on his thigh to anchor myself using the other to tease my nipple through my clothes.

"Imogen, I–"

A sharp knock on his office door causes both of us to immediately freeze in place, like deer in headlights.

"Dr. Burke?"

It's a voice I don't recognize. Younger. Probably a student.

Roman releases my hair in a split second, and I get to my feet adjusting my clothes and making sure nothing looks out of place. I've been so worried about Logan catching us that I didn't even think about a fucking student. Did they hear us? I don't think we were that loud, but when you're in the heat of the moment, it's hard to judge those kinds of things.

"I'm just in a meeting!" He calls, his voice shaky and unsure. "Give me five minutes!"

My heart thunders and my legs wobble beneath me.

"No problem, I'll just be out here!"

The two of us wait, counting the footsteps before we let out a collective sigh of relief.

"Christ..."

I take a step back toward him, his cock glistening with my saliva, and I gently run my finger up and down his shaft.

"I should go," I whisper. "I've gotta finish a paper for Abi."

Roman clenches his teeth, his eyes blazing. I turn away and bend over, making sure to give him a little show as I dig the remote out of my backpack and hand it to him.

"A present for you."

So far it's been cute to see him a little flustered, but I want to see what he can really do.

"What is it?"

His tone is measured, trying to stay in control.

"It's for this." I reach into my panties and pull out the vibrator. "Try it."

Roman pushes the button on the remote and the vibrator buzzes in my hand. He licks his lips like a hungry dog as I slip it back in, placing it right next to my clit. My eyes slide shut and I let out the softest moan I can manage, feeling him grab me by the waist and ghost his lips along my neck.

"Press the button, and you turn up the intensity. I think even someone as new as you could make it work."

"You shouldn't have told me that."

The vibrations get more intense and my eyelids flutter, laughter tumbling from my lips. I forgot how powerful this thing is. I'm trying to think about crime statistics to combat the throbbing between my legs.

"Is that all you've got, Dr. Burke?"

Roman says nothing, only sliding a hand down my body and reaching underneath my dress to give my ass a rough squeeze. Electricity ripples down my spine. This man knows exactly how to turn me on, but I refuse to give in no matter how much I want to. I want to see how brazen he can get.

"Well, if you have some time before I see you this afternoon, I'll be at Déjà Brew."

"This is dangerous." He grumbles.

"Of course it is. That's what makes it fun."

His eyes are burning, the animal hunger he has for me evident in the way his mouth twitches as he zips up his pants. I grab my stuff and head for the door, but not before giving him one last flirtatious glance over my shoulder.

"Catch me later, cowboy."

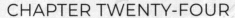

CHAPTER TWENTY-FOUR

down bad

ROMAN

Déjà Brew is *the* most popular place to go near campus aside from The Hi-Dive. Two business grads decided to open it up last year and they make a killing selling overpriced lavender oat milk lattes to their peers. It's cozy, with minimalist decor, the interior has dark red brick walls, and the place always smells like freshly brewed coffee and pastries. It kind of reminds me of a coffee shop you'd find in Brooklyn.

The place is packed this morning, with students crowding around tables, madly typing away on their laptops and scrolling through their phones. There's even a little shop cat named Butterball who's currently passed out on top of one of the bookshelves.

But the thing I'm the most interested in is sitting all alone out front, her computer on a little cafe table and a pair of giant headphones on her head. She's managed to tuck herself into a somewhat secluded spot at the edge of the seating area, but I'd recognize that hair anywhere.

I do my best to ignore her for now, making my way toward the front counter and ordering a black coffee along with something called a cronut. The name makes me frown, but it's the only pastry in the display that looks even half-palatable.

And then there's the unfortunate fact that it's ten goddamn dollars.

I take my overpriced treat and settle in at a table by the front window, with a great view of Imogen. Her long tattooed legs look so striking stretched out in front of her, and even her hair is shimmering, more luminous than usual in the morning sun.

I distract myself by biting into the pastry, hoping to keep from looking desperate as she glances in at me with a little smile. It's delicious, crispy and flaky without being too heavy. There's even a sugary sour cream glaze on top that allows the entire thing to melt on my tongue.

"Son of a bitch..."

I shove a whole half of it into my mouth, washing it down with a big gulp of perfectly bitter black coffee. It's even better than the stuff I make in my Keurig, and ends up costing about the same. I guess if I'm going to spend $15 on coffee and a donut, it makes sense to get my money's worth.

Imogen's head is still partially turned toward me, and I can tell she's trying to get a glimpse. Even now, just casually relaxing in the cafe, I feel like I'm doing something I shouldn't be. I guess that's part of the game. It's exciting— so exciting, in fact, that it's hard to keep my mind from wandering back to the feeling of her mouth around my cock.

I'm about to reach into my pocket to press the button on the little remote, but I catch myself just in time to stop when I see Frankie strolling up to me.

"Roman? What the hell are you doing here?" He asks, looking sincerely baffled.

I chuckle, taking in the surroundings.

"Am I not allowed?"

He grins and arches a brow, his curly golden hair looking like a halo around his head before he twists his face up in mock frustration.

"I distinctly remember you saying, and I quote, *why would I spend 20 bucks at a coffee shop when I have a perfectly good Keurig in my office?*"

"You do a horrible impression of me."

"Logan thinks it's great."

It's actually pretty great.

"He would, wouldn't he?" I say, leaning back in my chair. "Well, I've decided I'm turning over a new leaf this year. Going out more. Just like you two razzed me about."

"It's that new girlfriend, isn't it?"

"She's *not* a girlfriend," I remind him. "And it's really none of your business."

"You're practically glowing, my friend."

"It's the stress of being around you," I reply flatly. "Makes me sweat."

My eyes dart back to Imogen for just a moment, finding her head buried in her book, both hands in a position that I call *The Graduate Student*. It's a lot like that famous sculpture *The Thinker*, but if you look at the finer details, there always tends to be more tears and hair pulling. At the very least, she looks like she could use some stress relief.

I reach into my pocket and wrap my fingers around the remote, just as Frankie slides into the seat across from me.

"Well, it just so happens you're the man I've been looking for this morning."

"Fancy that. Am I in trouble again?" I click the button, watching her out of the corner of my eye as she sits up a little straighter.

"Nope," Frankie replies. "*But* I have an opportunity I want you to consider."

Imogen adjusts her position, shifting her laptop and crossing one leg over the other.

"Roman, are you listening?"

I'm pretending to look out the window at the fallen autumn foliage that's made the ground look like a sea of intense reds and golds. It's pretty, but she's prettier.

"Yeah." My eyes flick back to him. "What's the opportunity?"

"There's a big conference in Aspen. A whole weekend, all expenses paid by the department."

"Wow, you're really going all out."

"My buddy Glen's got connections at Oxford University Press, and he's looking for academics with research that's off the beaten path."

"Grief and stigma aren't exactly unique," I chuckle as I quickly glance over at Imogen. She's hunched over her laptop, looking like she's about to fall apart.

"But the way that you approach it, theory-wise, *is*. Dramaturgy and identity management? That's—"

"Just Goffman."

I hit the button again, raising the intensity just as Frankie leans sideways, cutting into my field of view.

"What are you looking at?"

"I saw a rabbit. Outside."

It's not a particularly wild lie, and luckily Frankie seems to accept it, just shaking his head as he lets out an exasperated sigh.

"Look, man. The department had a meeting and there's a list of professors that they want to put pressure on to publish this year. You're one of them. When was the last time you put out a paper?"

I press and hold the button to turn the vibrator off for a bit, opting to give her a short break.

"About two years ago."

Imogen's body relaxes and she takes the opportunity to cool herself down. Even from inside the coffee shop, I can see her bright red cheeks and her hot heavy breath in the crisp autumn air.

"You know that's how you stay employed."

I run a hand through my hair while keeping my other wrapped firmly around the remote. The pressure to publish, teach, mentor, attend conferences, and sit in on thesis defenses is insane. Frankly, I don't know how any of us keep up with it.

Logan and Abi can pump out papers like crazy, but they're still pretty young and inspired. You can still see the passion in their eyes when they talk about academia. Some days I don't know if I have anything left. After almost 20 years, I've been sucked dry.

"There just aren't enough hours in the day." I shake my head. "And it's not like this job encourages a reasonable work life balance. How many of us have our goddamn emails on our phones?"

Frankie leans forward, his face awash with compassion. He hates having to give these talks, and I don't blame him. Publish or perish is pretty much the motto if you want to keep your job.

"Look, man. This conference might be a good way for you to network, okay? EBU prides itself on its *active* academics, not dinosaurs who sit around still trying to pitch shit they wrote 30 years ago."

Frankie taps the table gently.

"Logan's going, Abi's going, and I'm planning to ask some students to submit papers as well."

"What about you?" I ask, clicking the remote back to medium.

"Got my cousin's wedding to go to that weekend, all the way out in Florida."

I shift in my seat, gazing back out the window while trying to keep my eyes from lingering for too long. She's still got one leg crossed over the other, staring intently at her laptop. Every few seconds, she adjusts her position, fidgeting to make it look like she's slightly uncomfortable, but I know the truth. I want to text her and ask her what payback feels like, but I think it might tip Frankie off.

"So?" Frankie asks. "Aspen?"

"When is it?"

"Late November, so no excuses."

"You mean aside from grading, drowning in papers, and students having nervous breakdowns during finals?"

Frankie shrugs.

"They're actually not called nervous breakdowns anymore. They're called mental health crises." He clicks his tongue. "Gotta get up to speed, old man."

"I'll work on that." I take a deep breath, deciding to appease him because I know my job could be on the line. "I'll apply."

"Great. Proposals are due next week." He checks his watch, getting to his feet with a groan. "And I'm officially fucking late."

"Not a good look, doctor."

"Get fucked, *doctor*," he laughs, turning around and heading for the door.

I watch him waltz toward the path before he spots Imogen, waving as he heads right for her.

"Shit."

Quickly, I pull the remote out of my pocket and make triple sure I've turned it off. The collar of my shirt feels too tight all of a sudden, but from here at least, Imogen seems totally fine. In fact, she's all smiles as Frankie stands in front of her. I guzzle the rest of my coffee and grab my phone to distract myself, finding two missed text messages.

> IMOGEN: What do you think you're doing, cowboy?

IMOGEN: You like to play dirty, huh?

I glance back up to see the two of them still in casual conversation, but Frankie quickly slides his phone into his pocket, gesturing toward campus before heading back down the path. Once he's gone, Imogen turns her attention back to me, her eyes steely. She closes her laptop and slides it into her backpack before standing up and shrugging her jacket over her shoulders.

At first, I think she's going to leave me high and dry, but to my surprise she saunters right into the café and makes a beeline for me. My throat becomes a desert as she approaches, and I scan the shop to make sure nobody's looking at us. The baristas are all busy filling orders and everyone else is engrossed in their own little worlds.

"Dr. Burke, could I have a word with you?"

"Have a seat."

I smirk and click the button on the remote just to watch her jaw tick. Her eyes are piercing, but this is way too much fun. I never really thought I had a competitive side but it turns out, when the reward is watching a gorgeous woman on the brink of a climax, I can be pretty ruthless.

"I was thinking we could go someplace more private."

I lean over, my body pulsing with adrenaline. I have no idea what I'm doing so I just let instinct take over.

"And I said *sit*," I growl.

"What the fuck do you think you're doing?" She hisses, sliding into her seat.

I turn the vibrator up another couple steps and savor the sight.

"Just enjoying my coffee." I grin. "You're pretty when you blush, darlin'."

"I'm gonna—"

"You're gonna what?" I tilt my head playfully. "This is what you wanted, isn't it?"

Her entire body tenses and she struggles to control her breathing as someone walks by. Luckily for her they're so focused on their phone that they don't even notice.

God bless technology.

"So, how's the grading coming along?" I ask with a smirk. "Anything giving you trouble?"

"You're really enjoying this, aren't you?" She fires back, holding her voice steady.

"Of course I am, it's a game. Don't you enjoy playing games?"

Her eyes close for a moment, a smile flickering across her face. I think I've been doing okay, but this could go south at any moment.

"I bet you're soaked through those slutty little panties. I bet you're so wet I could just bend you over this table and fuck you without even warming you up first."

I turn the vibrator off, grab my coffee, and get to my feet.

"Stick around after class this afternoon. I need to give you the rubric for the midterm."

Her body slumps with a mix of relief and disappointment as I head out the door, casually waving at her with the remote before sliding it back into my pocket.

I think I won that round.

CHAPTER TWENTY-FIVE

sex on fire

IMOGEN

ROMAN: Don't wear panties to my class.

I flip my phone over. Do you know how hard it is to focus on a discussion when all a man is doing is texting you pure filth?

The worst part is that I can't even sneak into his office for a quickie. Frankie wants to see me after class to talk about my work, work that I care enough about to put my life on hold for. Academia isn't so much a job as it is a vocation, so I knew I was giving up a lot going into the PhD program. Everything else comes second.

I should be excited to sit down and talk about the academic aspects of kink and subcultures, all with a man whose work I deeply admire, but the closer the meeting gets the more anxiety I feel. Have I done enough? Am I ready for this? It's hard to say after spending all my time thinking about Roman.

I curse under my breath as one of my classmates brings up a point about Bourdieu that I realize never made its way into my paper. I try to follow along and make notes, but the urge to text him back is over-whelming.

IMOGEN: You're a fucking menace.

> ROMAN: You started it, my dear.

> IMOGEN: It seems to me, Dr. Burke, that you might not know who you're messing with.

"Imogen?" Abi asks. "Thoughts?"

Shit.

What was the last thing someone said that I can use as a talking point?

"Sorry, I got distracted," I laugh, feeling myself turning slightly red as I set my phone down.

"Bourdieu presents the idea that our freedoms lie in multiple places: between social and class constraints that determine our personal tastes, our style of dress, or even the jokes that we laugh at, providing the space for us to have choice or preference. Do you have any thoughts on that?"

Jesus, *do* I have thoughts on that?

Okay, I just have to focus, I did this reading after all. To be fair, I did some of it at a house party where I was smoking a joint, but I'd hoped that I retained... *something*.

"Well, I think there are lots of rules that tend to guide us. Everything from high-stakes stuff like following the law to low-stakes, like what kind of music we listen to. And even when it comes to school or jobs, we have class restrictions, geographic restrictions, and financial restrictions that shape our decision making."

Abi looks... disappointed.

"So the takeaway is we're not really free."

"I... don't think we are. Maybe?"

I'm sure it's a rudimentary understanding of the reading, and I feel like an idiot for not saying something profound or interesting. My mind has a tendency to wander, to find something more exciting than sitting around talking about theory... even if I *like* theory, and as much as I want to show that I'm capable of analyzing this material, I still feel like I'm miles behind my cohort.

This whole secret friends with benefits thing I've got going on with Roman isn't helping the situation. I'm finishing my assignments, I'm doing the readings, but the problem is that I don't know if I'm actually retaining anything with something so weighty looming over me.

"Okay," Abi says with a soft sigh. "We're out of time. I'll get your papers back to you next week and you can start to piece together your final assignment on a theory of your choosing."

Everyone starts to pack up as Abi shoots me a smile from the front of the room. Shame stings the back of my throat and I flip my phone over on the desk; I should have turned the damn thing off and paid attention.

"Good work today. I'm looking forward to your paper."

My heart skips a beat and I can't help but perk up at the compliment. I try not to rely on academic approval, but when you come from a family of professors it's like fuel.

"Yeah? I felt a little shaky at certain points. The material's just so dense. I hope I didn't sound... like I was just repeating the readings."

I scoop up my things and follow her out of the classroom.

There's something about Abi that always puts me at ease. I've only really known her in this capacity for a few weeks, and already she's the coolest professor I've ever had.

"That's the point of these discussions, and it's how we get the readings into our head. The most I ask is that you guys do your best to think through the questions that are being posed in the material. We're not here to get it all right, we're here to build an understanding of these frameworks so that you can use them as jumping-off points for your dissertations."

I'm not here to get it all right, but I want to. I know theory is a grind—hell, I know this whole thing is a grind, but sometimes, when I'm not immediately good at something, it starts to eat away at me.

"Thanks Dr. King, I appreciate it."

Luckily, or maybe unluckily, I have something to take my mind off of it.

Abi waves at me and heads for the elevator as I turn toward Frankie's office. It's just a few feet from Roman's, whose door, I can't help but notice, is open. I dip into the bathroom, quickly blocking the stall door with my body while I slide my panties off and tuck them into my jacket pocket.

The plan is to drop these onto his desk and watch him freak out while I slink off to meet with Frankie. I'm grinning like an idiot as I march toward his office, but when I get there, it's empty. His laptop is closed, but there's an open book and a steaming cup of coffee on his desk. Must have just missed him.

"Damn."

I really wanted to see his face, but this will have to do.

I slip over to his desk and try one of the drawers. The top one is locked, but another opens with ease. I quickly drop the panties in and slide it shut, the book on his desk catching my eye before I think to peel away.

I recognize the cover immediately, it's *Stigma: Notes on the Management of a Spoiled Identity* by Erving Goffman. I read him obsessively during my master's degree. The pages are fully annotated in what I'm sure is Roman's sprawling cursive. I can barely read it, but it looks way more elegant than my own chicken scratch. I lean down, trying to see if he's written anything illuminating in the margins. I'm excited to see his interpretation of my favorite sociologist. If they'd let me read nothing *but* Goffman, grad school would be a breeze.

Mid-way through a sentence I hear footsteps, rushing for the door as my heart pounds in my chest. Before I can quite make it, I slam right into his rock solid body. Roman's hair's a little messier, like he's been absent-mindedly running his fingers through it; the smell of his cologne and the intensity of his gaze as he looks down at me makes me giddy.

"To what do I owe the pleasure?"

"I, uh— I..." Out of the corner of my eye, I see someone walking past and clear my throat. "I have those papers graded. Put 'em on your desk."

Roman's lips curl into a devilish grin.

"Anything else?"

I slip past him as quickly as I can, dodging into the hallway.

"Nope! I'll see you in a bit!"

"Remember to stick around after class today," he says, lazily glancing over his shoulder just far enough to show off that damn smile.

I scurry down the hall before my fantasies of him bending me over his desk can take root in my mind, shaking them off as I approach Frankie's office. As the head of the department, and the person in charge of my future, I need to have a good relationship with him, but it helps that he also just seems like a good guy.

Hiding all of this from him has kind of started to make me feel sick.

"Dr. Hughes?" I knock on the door. "You wanted to see me?"

He looks up, a golden curl falling across his face as he greets me.

"Come on in— and I thought I told you to call me Frankie," he laughs. "The Doctor thing is too professional."

His office has a huge window with a bookshelf next to it that looks like it's about to burst. Some potted plants line another shelf just above his desk, along with sports memorabilia, some framed journal articles, and photographs. I shut the door and sit down as Frankie closes his laptop, turning his chair to face me.

"So? How's it been? I know this is our first official meeting, but I figured I'd let you get settled in before we really got to talking about your project."

"It's been good," I reply, keeping my hands clasped in my lap. "Great, actually. It's an adjustment from NYU, but it's been a nice change of pace."

Frankie isn't intimidating, but I respect him and his work. I've been reading his stuff since my master's degree, and his writing takes up at least a third of my bibliography. He approaches kink with empathy and understanding rather than viewing it as something deviant.

"Glad to hear you're adjusting." Frankie wheels his chair a little closer to me. "Listen, there's a big conference coming up in Aspen. And I mean *big*. There's going to be publishers there, huge names in academia, and so it's a great chance to network. I was wondering if you'd want to submit your dissertation idea as a paper. You could present it, and—"

"Yes!" I'm already on my feet, my hands balled into fists while I'm shaking with excitement. "Fuck yes! I'm so in! I mean— Sorry, that was unprofessional."

This is the shit I've been dreaming about since I started grad school. I've watched from the sidelines as my dad and my brother presented at academic conferences, and now I get the chance to do it myself?

There's no way I could say no.

This is my chance to really prove to myself that I can do this.

But then panic starts to set in.

I pitched something extremely vague for my dissertation topic: Stigma in Kink Spaces Among Working Professionals. It's something I became interested in solely based on one hookup. I dommed for a banking executive. A real button-up guy in his day to day life, but behind closed doors? He fully submitted to me. Afterward, we spent a long time talking over drinks and I got the sense that he'd compartmentalized the person he was in the club and the person he was at work.

"You okay?" Frankie asks, showing off his kind smile.

"Yeah, uh... you know, the thing I pitched it was... vague. It was mostly to get me in here, it doesn't have a lot of, I don't know..."

A pitch is easy, but a presentation? That requires a theoretical framework, methodology, ethics, sample size... and since we were only allocated two pages for our application, I spent a lot of time on my research question and literature review and not all that other important stuff.

"That's fine," he assures me, raising his hand. "Your topic is stigma and kink, right?"

I nod.

He slaps a notebook down on his desk, grabbing his pen and twirling it between his fingers at an impressive speed. It makes me wonder if he used to be a drummer or something.

"All we have to do is narrow it down then. Any ideas?"

I'm great under pressure, and I *can* be quick on my feet, but right now, it's hard to think clearly. I have to push through the brain fog from class, and doubly Roman's distractions. Then again, isn't my relationship with Roman exactly what I've been writing about? The way we met on the app, the pseudonyms, the filtered pictures, fake names only...

Before I can stop myself, the words are pouring out of my mouth.

"What about kink as a highly stigmatized part of identity, all through the lens of social media and Goffman's work on identity management?"

Thank you, Roman Burke, for coming through at the eleventh hour. As usual.

Frankie nods, scribbling something down as my phone buzzes in my jacket pocket. I pull it out to see a text from Roman. It's a picture of my panties between his teeth.

> ROMAN: I'm looking for my present. Am I hot or cold?

"Imogen? Did you hear me?" Frankie asks.

"What? Sorry." My cheeks burn as I quickly put my phone away. "I'm all ears."

"Methodology. Data collection. Ethics— that's going to be a big one. I need all of these fleshed out really well for the pitch, okay? You have a three page limit, not including a bibliography." I pull out my notebook and start jotting things down as he goes. "Proposals are due next week. Can you get one to me in the next couple of days so I can look it over and give feedback?"

Sure, let's throw this on top of keeping a secret fuck buddy and all the other shit I have to do. If I'm lucky enough to make it through my PhD, this is going to be the rest of my life.

"No problem!"

"Great! Just remember that I've got your back on this."

I get to my feet and shake his hand. Despite the complete emotional overload that's right around the corner, I know I can do it. All I have to do is knock this thing out of the park.

"Thanks, Frankie."

My phone buzzes in my pocket again as I walk out the door. Roman's been bratty *and* distracting today, which means he's winning.

We can't have that.

CHAPTER TWENTY-SIX

king of my heart

ROMAN

Imogen and her little yellow sundress are making it very hard to focus on finishing this lecture. My eyes are immediately drawn to her playful smirk, but when she uncrosses her legs, I get the slightest glimpse of her bare pussy.

Christ.

I clear my throat, realizing I've stopped in the middle of the lecture and return to check my notes. I'm sweating bullets underneath my shirt, and the only saving grace is that it's a very dark navy.

That's when I see my phone light up.

> IMOGEN: When everyone's gone, will you fuck me on that table?

> IMOGEN: Please, Professor?

I think I may have forgotten how to breathe.

> IMOGEN: You might want to pick your jaw up off the floor, first.

I know I deserve this for the stunt I pulled at the coffee shop, and there's a part of me that loves it, but she's really not making my job easy. I grab my water bottle and down the entire thing in a few gulps.

"Does anyone have any questions about anything I've covered so far? I know this stuff is dense."

I'm praying somebody can lob me a softball that can help to get us back on track. Instead, all I get is another message.

> IMOGEN: You're pretty when you blush, cowboy.

Sunlight shines through the stained glass, making her glow in a soft kaleidoscope of pink, coral, and aquamarine.

I want to end class early, bend her over this table, and devour her from behind.

"Dr. Burke? I have a question."

Finally, someone to save me from this nightmare.

"Yes!" I bark, a little too enthusiastically. "Sorry, you guys know how excited I can get about questions. Go ahead."

"Foucault says that punishment produces positive effects. Am— am I reading that right?"

My phone lights up and I can't keep my eyes from darting down to it.

> IMOGEN: Do you think punishment would benefit me, Doctor?

I'm finding It difficult to get my brain into the right gear when all of Imogen's texts are burning into the back of my eyes.

"Yes," I reply, locking my phone. "We have to think of *punishment*, not as just some repressive force, which it is— but also as something that's..."

There are so many ways I could punish her. Right now, I'm considering gagging her with my cock until tears stream down her face.

"Dr. Burke?"

"Yeah," I rasp. "Sorry. Proponents of punishment say that it benefits society because it can reduce crime and deviance, but it also subjugates people and asserts power, as well as control over populations. That's a big positive for the state, right? But Foucault argues that punishment has shifted from these giant spectacles of public torture and executions to something quieter. It's not about the state punishing more, it's about punishing better. We *want* to be good citizens, we *want* to obey, we want to be *productive* citizens. Why do you think that is?"

The student glances down at her laptop, scrolling through her notes.

"Because subjugation is embedded into us?"

"Exactly! So, the book isn't really about prisons and punishment, it's about power, and how it flows through every institution that touches our lives. Does that help?"

"I think so, yeah. Thanks."

It must be 3:20, because suddenly everyone's packing up. Thank god.

"Alright, we'll pick back up next week. I want you all to keep plugging away at Foucault. I know he's tough, but look at the supplementary materials on the course website. I put some podcasts up there, and some videos as well."

Some students are already halfway out the door as I begin gathering my things, answering a few questions as I go. Imogen has a small crowd around her, chatting about the paper and handling it all with a radiant smile.

She's pure goddamn sunshine.

I wonder what I did to deserve someone like her... and then I pull that thought *all* the way back, because she's not really mine. We're just fooling around.

"Imogen, can you stay behind?" I ask, waiting until the last of the students are almost out the door. "I want to go over some things with you."

"Sure, Dr. Burke."

We go about our respective tasks until the door finally closes, leaving us both standing in silence, staring at each other.

Waiting.

I can hear the blood roaring in my ears, anticipation sinking its claws into the back of my neck. I only last a few moments before I snatch her by the waist and pull her to me, devouring her in a hungry kiss. She gets me back with equal ferociousness as I pin her against the table; my mind swims with thoughts of her soft lips, strawberry lipgloss, and that fucking tongue that not so long ago was so expertly swirling around my cock.

"What the hell were you thinking sending me that shit?" I bite down on her earlobe, sucking until the sweetest sound pours from her mouth. "Hmm? Answer me."

My hands are everywhere, gliding up her thighs and sliding back around to grip her ass as hard as I can, all while she's grinding on my knee. She looks like a woman possessed, eyes gleaming as she grins with a supreme confidence.

"You loved every second of it, cowboy."

My cock is already desperate to be touched, but I'm going to see how long I can hold out.

"Turn around and put your hands on the table."

"Yes, Professor."

Fuck.

It sounds so good coming from those gorgeous lips. I grab her arm, twisting it behind her back and pushing her against the table. She yelps and glances over her shoulder, but it's only a moment before she's flashing me another cocky smile.

"I take it you like being called that, *Professor*."

I lower myself to my knees, my cock aching.

"As long as it's coming from you, darlin', it all sounds like music to my ears. Now spread your legs and flip your skirt up. I wanna see all of you."

I start to trail my lips up the back of one thigh, gently nipping at it. She wiggles her plump little ass right in my face and I reach up and smack it hard enough to make her moan.

Suddenly, I catch the faintest sound of voices outside and I freeze. I can't tell if they're coming closer, or simply passing by, but either way there's only one thought in my head now: this is so fucking dangerous.

If a student walked in, it would all be over.

My heart slams against my chest and my stomach is in knots, but before I can rationalize my way into stopping, Imogen takes control of the situation.

"Someone could walk in, Dr. Burke."

She heard them too, but there's absolutely no fear in her eyes. Just excitement.

"If they did, all they'd see is you bent over this table, moaning like a little slut."

She gasps, dragging her fingernails along the top of the table as I spread her cheeks and spit on her asshole.

"Do you like being called that, *slut?*"

"Yes, Professor," she whines.

This woman brings out something depraved in me, and I'm really starting to enjoy who I become when I'm with her. I've never been this dominant with a partner, and I'm flying by the seat of my pants, but it's more than just the feeling of something novel. I feel secure in a way I've rarely ever felt before.

Confident.

"Keep your eyes on the door, we don't want anyone interrupting my meal."

Her giggle makes me smile, butterflies stirring up my stomach. I have to admit, it's been a long time since I talked this dirty to someone.

I glide my fingers along her pussy lips, using just enough pressure to torment her without giving too much.

"I didn't get to taste all of you last time," I murmur, sliding one finger inside of her and pumping it slowly, in and out.

"Dirty boy," she rasps.

I press down against her G-spot, her legs quivering as she turns her head to face me. Before she can react I reach out and smack her ass hard enough to leave a palm print on her pristine skin.

"I *said* eyes on the door."

"Yes, sir."

Her breath hitches and she crushes another whimper as I slowly pull my finger out of her. I lick her all the way from her clit to her tight little asshole, focusing on making delicate circles with the tip of my tongue. Imogen responds with the most ragged, feral sound I've heard come out of her.

"You like that?"

"Holy fuck!" She grunts, her hips rocking against my face. "Don't stop! Please don't fucking stop!"

I return to her pussy, flicking her clit faster as I relish the way it throbs against my tongue. She tastes sharp and sweet all at once, and her little moans and whines only make my heart pound faster and faster. My cock's been straining, begging to be touched since I started, but I keep my hands on her. I can wait.

I *will* wait.

"Yes!" She cries. "Fuck, just like that! Please, please—"

I pull away and give her ass another rough slap, Imogen pounding her fist against the table, and I hear a deep growl rumble through her as I get to my feet. She's glaring at me over her shoulder, those warm eyes suddenly hardened and cold.

"You fucking—"

"Talk back to me again and you won't come for the rest of the week," I reply, unzipping my jeans and glancing at the door a final time before gliding my cock between her pussy lips.

"Please, Professor!" She begs, her voice soft and demure. "I'm sorry, I'll be such a good girl."

Deep down inside I want someone to hear us, to hear her screaming for me. As terrified as I am to get caught, the idea's begun to make me more excited than it probably should.

"You're the one who started this, darlin'. I'm just giving you a real taste of your own medicine. Now where are the—"

"No condoms," she grunts. "Fuck me bare."

The words take a second to land.

"Bare?"

"That's what I said." She turns around, hopping up onto the table. "That's what I want."

"You— you want—"

"I want all of you. No barriers." She spreads her legs, her smile full of confidence, but I can still see a flicker of vulnerability in her eyes. I feel like she's been thinking about this for a while. "I've tested negative, I'm on birth control, and I haven't been with anyone else in nearly half a year."

My throat is so fucking dry and my head spins.

"Longer for me."

She grabs my wrist and pulls me toward her, winding her legs around my waist.

"Then fuck me like I'm yours, Roman."

I guess things might be a little less casual than I thought.

Our kiss is feverish, the perfect prelude before I thrust into her with a punishing amount of force. I watch as her head rocks back, and enjoy the show as a moan springs from the depths of her throat. I feel my entire body sing her praises as my nerves light up one after the other; my hands glide up her waist and she cups her breasts, teasing her pierced nipples as we set a manic and desperate rhythm.

"Fuck, Roman!" She screams as I lean over, taking her nipple in my mouth and biting down hard.

I press my thighs into the table and push my palms into the rough wood to get more friction. My hips crash against hers over and over and over again, hard enough to leave bruises, but judging by the look on her face, she doesn't want me to stop. In fact, she looks so frenzied I think she might even kill me if I did.

My balls ache, my cock throbbing inside of her as I teeter right on the edge, but I have to make her come first. I pull back and lick my thumb, pressing it down on her clit and working it in quick and intense circles. She has one hand clamped over her mouth to keep from making too much noise, but I don't give a fuck if someone walks in anymore.

My vision goes fuzzy around the edges as I come, but I can still see her lavender hair shimmering in the refracted sunlight all the way to the end. She's angelic, sweat glistening on her skin, her cheeks the prettiest shade of pink I've ever seen, and as my body works through the dying embers of my orgasm, I lay myself down next to her.

"I want to take you away for the weekend. No secrets, no sneaking around. Just the two of us."

I feel a pang of regret the second the words spill out of me, yearning to take them back. Maybe it's too much, too intense for her this quickly. We're friends with benefits. We play mini golf, we fuck, and that's it.

She gazes over at me, her eyes gleaming with something between confusion and interest. Is it pity? Of course it is. She's going to say no, and I'm going to have to pretend like she didn't didn't break my goddamn heart.

But Imogen just smiles, showing off that little crooked tooth.

"I'd follow you anywhere, cowboy."

CHAPTER TWENTY-SEVEN
it's complicated
IMOGEN

THURSDAY NIGHT
PIPER AND JAY'S APARTMENT

"A whole weekend together, huh?" Piper asks, passing me a joint while balancing a massive glass of chardonnay on her knee.

"Yeah," I reply with a chuckle. "Why, is that crazy?"

We've been sitting on her patio, watching the sunset for half an hour or so while I work on my conference application. The weed feels like it might actually be helping with the theory portion, but how it's going to read tomorrow is anyone's guess. My brain feels... bigger, though.

Is it supposed to feel bigger? West coast weed is something else.

"I mean, it's less crazy than sleeping with him while risking your place in your program, *and* his job all at once." She pauses, tapping her nails tentatively against her glass. "But I guess that's not really my business."

"Sounds like you just made it your business," I fire back.

She grins.

"You did say you guys were casual though, what's changed?"

"Nothing, we still are," I reply. "That's what we agreed on; it just makes the most sense."

Piper snorts into her wine and I arch a brow, looking up from my laptop.

"What?"

"A weekend at a ranch isn't casual, babe. That's a couples' thing."

Is it? It's been a hell of a long time since I dated someone.

I was surprised when Roman asked me to go away for the weekend, but it was a no brainer. A whole weekend in the fresh air with a hot older man? I wanted to tell him I'd pack my bags and we could leave that night, but unfortunately the reality of a packed schedule hit back pretty quickly.

Since then he's been texting me pictures of the ranch every day, and each time I get a new one, my excitement grows. Wide open spaces, endless trees, and *so* many horses. For someone like me, who's lived in cities my entire life, it looks so serene and peaceful.

"Earth to Iggy!" She snaps her fingers in my face. "I'm right, aren't I?"

I glower at her. Why does she have to make this into something it's not?

"You don't have to be a couple to do stuff like this. It's just fun."

"Fine, whatever you say," she sighs. "But when did this start back up? I thought you guys were going to be all professional and shit."

"After Jay got punched in the face. When I started walking home from the party, I realized that I didn't have my keys, and..."

"Roman swooped in like a knight in shining armor and saved you?"

"Well, more like meandered in looking confused while walking his dog."

I have to admit, even though I *don't* want to talk about how I feel about Roman, it's nice to gossip about something positive. Usually, I'm just telling her how bad my hookups are, or she's helping me swipe through guys on KinkFinder.

"You wanna know what I think?"

"No," I reply. "But you're gonna tell me anyway, aren't you?"

Piper doesn't miss a fucking beat, barreling past my half-hearted dismissal.

"I think you like him. Much more than you've liked your other hookups."

"Look, he's no-strings-attached, and either of us can walk away any time we want. Besides, how come you're the one giving *me* relationship advice? You're with a guy for six months and all of the sudden you're Dr. Phil?"

"First of all, that dude can't even call himself a doctor anymore," Piper chuckles. "And second, Jay and I may have only been dating for half a year, but emotionally we've been together from the moment we started loathing each other, way back in our forensic psychology class. Our love is built on a beautiful foundation of mutual dislike; it's a truly powerful thing!"

"If I remember correctly *I'm* the one who suggested we go to that party where you made out with him. Sounds like you might owe me."

"*Hate*-made-out with him," Piper corrects, her finger raised to the air in defiance.

"Yeah, because adding a superlative really changes the meaning of the sentence."

"Hate isn't a superlative, it's..." She thinks for a second and frowns. "An adverb? Make out is the action, so the verb... and hate is modifying— does any of this sound right, or am I just really high?"

I take a big gulp of my wine and shrug my shoulders.

"I don't know, dude. I got a C in English. I just toss big words down on paper and hope they make sense."

Piper sighs and stretches out her long, tanned legs.

"Whatever, I give up. My brain fucking hurts from grading anyway."

"How's the program going?" I ask, happy to shift the subject to anything but my serious-not-serious relationship.

"Good. I submitted a paper to a journal– oh, and Jay got an invite to a conference in Orange County. I think I'm gonna tag along with him."

Piper smiles and I see that look in her eyes, that look that tells me this thing with her and Jay might just be forever.

"And how's the whole living situation going?"

"It's good. Really good." She beams, blush creeping into her cheeks. "Kind of didn't expect it to be this good."

"What do you mean?"

"I don't know, I guess I was worried that we moved so fast it was gonna fall apart, but... I really love him. I know he's an idiot sometimes, but he's *my* idiot, you know?"

"I'm happy for you, Pipes."

I remember meeting her after class, listening to her obsess over how much she couldn't stand the guy. She wanted to punch him in the face, and honestly, if it ever came down to it, my money would be on Piper. Jay looks tough with all his tattoos and muscles, but he'd be down in a second.

"Don't worry Iggy, you'll get your own idiot someday." Suddenly, her face lights up in mock-excitement, emphatically putting her hand on my leg. "Oh my god, maybe you already found him!"

"Roman's not an idiot."

His indecisiveness is irritating, sure, but it's more than just being an idiot. Besides, there's no way I've just stumbled into...

"I think him playing *will we, won't we* for weeks on end might push him into the idiot category."

"Or just being a man, right?"

She snickers and bumps her shoulder against mine.

Maybe *I'm* the idiot thinking this was going to be casual.

I know this is dangerous. It *feels* dangerous, but what do you do when a person starts to consume your every thought? The whole thing is filthy and forbidden, a never ending supply of dopamine hidden in an unmarked paper bag.

"Look, all I'm saying is I get the sense that there actually are some strings attached to Mr. No Strings."

Roman and I have similar demons. He's been alone for so long, struggling with how to move forward, and I feel like I've thrown a wrench into all that. I walk around like I'm healed, but inside I'm terrified to really connect. Somewhere along the way I stopped seeing love as balm, and started to see it as just another potential source of pain.

"I don't know," I sigh, taking a final swig of wine. "Why couldn't this be simple?"

I get home from Piper's around 10:00pm to find Logan sprawled out on the couch. He's got his phone in his hand, scrolling through some app or other as the TV sits on idle.

"You planning on staring at the login screen all night?"

"Oh, oops!" He laughs. "I got distracted texting Frankie about something, which led to me searching up a George Herbert Mead paper so I could win an argument with him. Now I'm ten Wikipedia articles deep reading about–" He grabs his glasses off the coffee table. "The history of the Wisconsin Central Railway Company, apparently."

I'm only half listening. A big part of my brain is still stuck on what Piper and I talked about. *Am* I falling for Roman? No, that's impossible. We barely know each other; I think I know his dick better than I know him as a person. What I can't deny is that whenever he texts me my whole body buzzes, and I can never get my grubby hands on my phone fast enough to reply. He's like a shot of whiskey straight to my brain.

Logan tilts his head, staring at me with a curious expression.

"Are you offended by the Wisconsin Central Railway Company or something?"

"What? No," I scoff. "I can safely say I have no strong opinions on the subject. Anyway, I'm not ready to hit the hay yet, you wanna watch something?"

Logan beams, springing out of his seat.

"Stay right there, I'll make popcorn! You want a drink?"

"Just soda water," I tell him as I pull out my phone and check for texts.

"Lime? Lemon?"

Nothing.

"Lime, please."

He side-steps the couch, barely avoiding a toe-related disaster, and sprints for the kitchen. I'm exhausted, but I like watching movies with Logan. Besides, if I start ignoring him and rushing straight to my room every night to text Roman, he might start to pry.

> IMOGEN: What do I bring for horseback riding? And is it actual horseback riding or sexy horseback riding?

"What do you wanna watch?" Logan shouts from the kitchen.

> ROMAN: What's sexy horseback riding?

> IMOGEN: I don't know, I just realized that could be interpreted in some really fucked up ways.

206

> ROMAN: Oh, definitely. I'll call the FBI. Launch a full scale investigation into the shit you look up online.

"Hey!" A piece of popcorn hits me square in the forehead. "Are you even listening to me?"

I blush, a little embarrassed that I got so swept up in a couple of text messages.

"Pick anything you want," I reply, flashing him a sugary smile. "I'm cool with whatever as long as it's scary."

Logan's eyes flick down to my phone and I lock it.

"What's so interesting on there?"

"Thirst traps of hot guys. You wouldn't be interested."

"Whoa, whoa, whoa," he chuckles, sitting back down beside me on the couch. "Depends on who we're talking about. Maybe it's Burt Reynolds."

I stare at him in disbelief.

"Who would make thirst traps of Burt Reynolds?"

"First of all, he was hot shit back in the day." Logan retorts, clearly prepared to defend himself as he scrolls through Netflix. "Second of all, *I* would absolutely make thirst traps of Burt Reynolds. If I knew how."

"You're such a shithead."

"Yeah but you love me."

"Okay, sure, fine. What about Fright Night?"

I point at the TV, in the hopes of dragging him away from the topic at hand.

"Ooh, old one or new one?"

He's immediately looking on with rapt attention, like it's some sort of test.

"Ugh, you know how I feel about the new one, Stephen Geoffreys as Evil Ed was *the pinnacle* of weird. Old one, every day of the week."

My phone lights up just as Logan hits play, and I can't resist checking it one more time before we're too deep into sexy Jerry Dandrige's evil vampire plot.

"Is that another thirst trap?"

I shove him to the other end of the couch.

"Pay attention to the movie, dingus."

> ROMAN: Bring thick leggings for riding, comfortable shoes, a sweater, and anything else your pretty heart desires.

We'll need a blindfold. I can definitely bring that.

"I forgot to tell you, Piper and Jay rented an AirBnB in the Cascade... Hills or something?" I'm coming up with all this entirely on the fly, which is pretty impressive considering I often forget my *actual* plans about 5 minutes after I make them. "We're just going to grade papers, drink wine and shit like that, but I wanted to let you know I won't be around this weekend."

"Sounds like a good time," Logan replies, eyes glued to the screen as Roddy McDowell does his best Vincent Price impression.

I let out a sigh of relief, tossing some popcorn into my mouth to calm my squirming stomach. Not a single part of me feels good about lying to my brother, and so brazenly too, but it's not *that* big of a lie.

"I'm glad we did this. The whole you-moving-in thing."

I smile, despite it all.

"Me too."

CHAPTER TWENTY-EIGHT

cowboy like me

IMOGEN

THE CASCADE FOOTHILLS

"I can't believe you brought the hat," I grumble.

Even behind his sunglasses, I can see the little mischievous glint in his eyes. He's so proud that he held out on me with the cowboy hat for almost the whole drive, choosing to bust it out only five minutes before we arrived at the ranch. It's not even enough time for me to give him road head.

"Gotta keep the sun outta my eyes."

"You're literally wearing sunglasses."

He's dressed in a green and blue plaid button-up and a pair of Wranglers that really accentuate his ass. And we can't forget the cowboy boots, and now, the *fucking* cowboy hat. It's all black with a dark brown leather band and a wide brim. He looks like he should be chewing tobacco and calling me sugar.

"I just wanted to see you sweat when you saw a real cowboy," he purrs. "You *did* sweat when I pulled this thing out, right?"

"No comment," I mutter, staring straight ahead.

We pull up to the ranch and I'm immediately struck by the view: gentle, rolling hills and trails disappearing into lush trees surrounding a small house, with some horses grazing in the grass off to the side. It's so beautiful that I can't help snapping a picture to send Piper.

> IMOGEN: [Image attached] Getting laid and going horseback riding.

> PIPES: 20 bucks says you're gonna fall off that thing.

I snort, and Roman glances over at me.

"What?"

"Piper thinks I'm gonna fall off the horse."

"That's why I'll be there with you, to make sure that doesn't happen."

I flash him a faux-puzzled expression.

"Wait, *I thought* you were here to get laid."

He leans over, slipping his fingers under my chin and tilting it up just a bit. I can smell the mint from his toothpaste mixing with the spicy scent of his cologne as his mouth hovers close to mine.

"You're a mouthy little thing today, aren't you?"

"Want to shut me up?"

"Not at all. It's just that every time you talk, I start thinking about those pretty lips doing something real indecent."

He claims my mouth in a soft yet fiery kiss before quickly pulling away again.

"What's gotten into you?" I ask.

"Freedom."

Before I can respond, he's grabbing a bag and letting Mitzy out of the car, only leaving me wanting more. We follow Mitzy while she trots ahead, up the driveway toward the large blue ranch house, then suddenly I hear a shrill whistle from beside me.

"Hey, Carter!"

After a few seconds the front door swings open and a man in his late 60s steps out. He's got short, curly gray hair, dark brown skin, and kind eyes, dressed in a light blue button-up and black jeans.

The moment he sees Roman his face breaks out in a smile.

"Roman Burke," he sighs, jogging down the stairs. "How the hell are ya?"

Roman takes off his sunglasses and hooks them into his shirt. There's a confidence in his stride as he approaches the man, and the two of them share a warm embrace amidst laughter.

"It's good to see you, kid."

"Kid?" Roman scoffs. "We're both getting on in our years, old timer."

"I think I've got a few years on you yet," Carter chuckles, his eyes falling on me. "This must be the gorgeous young lady you were telling me about on the phone. Carter Williams. Pleasure to meet you."

"Imogen Flynn."

Carter's handshake is firm, his eyes twinkling as he studies me. I wonder how much Roman told him.

"The kid here and I go way back. I've known him since he was about as tall as Mitzy. He used to sneak into the pen with all the bulls... almost gave his momma a heart attack." Carter crouches down, giving Mitzy a scratch behind her ears. "Missed this old girl, too, of course."

"Is it still okay for her to run around?"

"Oh, absolutely! She can be as big a menace as she wants. Even picked up a couple of big ol' bones for her to chew on."

Roman shakes his head, grinning as Mitzy trots up the front steps and into the house, making herself at home.

"I heard it's your first time riding," Carter tells me. "I picked out a special horse just for you— oh, and Roman? Cash is all ready for you. Told him you were coming."

"Perfect. How is the old man, anyway?"

"A stubborn asshole just like his owner."

We drop off our bags and Carter leads to the stables, where to my surprise Roman reaches for my hand, his fingers linking with mine. He looks so calm, like all the tension he's been carrying has just melted away, wrapping his arm around my waist as the old ranch hand gestures to one of the stalls. A gorgeous horse with a speckled brown and white coat pokes its head out.

"This is Polly." Carter strolls right up to the animal, giving her a gentle pat. "She's the calmest, most relaxed old lady I know. Nothing bothers her. I always give new riders the calmest horses. They're more forgiving of mistakes."

"Mistakes?" I ask nervously, a thousand terrible scenarios flashing through my mind.

Carter leans over to me, his eyes bright and his mouth curled into a dazzling smile.

"You're likely to bump them when you start riding, make errors turning, maybe forget the best way to do things. Polly here won't mind one bit, she's always happy as a clam. Worse comes to worse, she loves apple slices. You wanna really win her over, that's how. We'll give you some snacks to take with you."

"Go on." Roman rubs my back. "You can pet her."

I take a timid step forward but stop mid-way. She looks sweet, but she's... big.

"She's not gonna bite you," Roman assures me.

I've never been this close to a horse before, except for one time. Logan and I rode in one of those horse-drawn carriages for my 21st birthday, but that was different. We weren't actually *on* those horses, and we were so hammered we wouldn't have been afraid even if we were about to be trampled to death.

"Are you sure?" I squeak. "I was googling pictures of horse teeth in the car, and they're— are you laughing?"

Carter and Roman's shoulders are shaking.

"Man, you didn't tell me she was funny too."

"Hey, I'm doing my best out here!" I bark, a smile creeping across my face despite trying my best to look serious.

"Trust me, really, she's not gonna take your hand off," Carter reassures me, opening the stall door for us to step inside. "Polly's a big ol' sweetheart."

I take another step.

"Where do I pet her?"

"Here, I can show you."

Roman steps forward, wrapping his fingers around my wrist and guiding my hand up to Polly's neck. I start lightly at first to make sure she's comfortable before I get a little more intense, and she lets out a gentle sound of affirmation.

She's so soft.

"That means she likes you."

I can't help but giggle, continuing to alternate between gentle strokes of my hand and the more intense scratches she seems to really love.

"Atta girl," he purrs.

"Are you talking to her, or to me?"

Roman leans in close, his lips brushing against my ear.

"It's always you, darlin'."

I'm trying not to blush too hard, but this more flirtatious and playful edge isn't making it easy. I want to hit him with my own line, something to make him as flustered as me, but before I can come up with anything he's already placed an old brush in my hand.

"What's this for?"

"Keeps her from getting saddle sores and it'll help the two of you bond. She could use some pampering."

He grasps my wrist gently, and guides me in brushing Polly's coat.

"I'm all about pampering," I chuckle. "We're gonna get along well."

Polly radiates calm, and for the first time in a while, my mind feels quiet. I'm not thinking about the possibility of getting caught, about what this trip means for the both of us, or about my application to the conference. I'm just... existing.

It's nice.

I brush the horse slowly, taking my time to smooth down her coat bit by bit, but when I move to head behind her, Roman quickly stops me.

"Never walk behind 'em. Doesn't matter how tame they are, better safe than sorry."

"Right." My cheeks burn with embarrassment. "Sorry."

Once I'm finished, Roman teaches me how to secure her bridle. He goes slowly, making sure that I'm following every step and I watch with fascination as he secures her saddle and her bit.

"Now we've just gotta get you on her," he says with a smirk. "But we'll do that when we get outside."

I nod, psyching myself up as Carter takes a step forward and motions to another stable.

"Roman, you wanna get reacquainted with Cash?"

"You bet. Can't wait to see my boy."

We head out of the stable and I tug on Roman's sleeve. He's mentioned a family horse before.

"Is Cash yours?"

"He was my dad's, technically, but I took care of him and rode him the most."

Carter opens another stall door and I'm greeted by the sight of an enormous black stallion, with a coat that reminds me of the night sky.

"Holy shit he's like two of me tall!"

I take a step back, watching Roman nuzzle up against Cash. He sinks against his horse like no time has passed at all, completely comfortable next to the massive creature. He grabs a brush and starts to glide it through the horse's coat, placing kisses on his neck.

"Missed you, baby boy."

The natural crease between his brows has all but disappeared.

"These are for you." I hear something thunk down beside me and look over to see Carter with a pair of worn black riding boots on the ground. "Should fit."

"What's wrong with my sneakers?"

"You're gonna need ankle support," he announces, gesturing at the boots. "Put 'em on."

I sit down on a small stool and slide off my shoes, stashing them in the corner while Carter helps me into my boots.

"Now you look like a pro."

Carter fetches Polly, gently guiding her to the middle of the enclosure. There's already a small set of stairs set up, and he walks me through how to mount a horse correctly. She's as calm as can be, even after I drop the reins a few times trying to figure out how to grip them. It takes a while, but I feel like I'm getting somewhere as I put my foot in her stirrup, angling my knee in the direction of Polly's face as instructed.

"Okay, good. Now, put your palm right in the middle of the saddle and straighten your leg."

I take my time, pivoting slightly and making sure my hand is *really* on the saddle before fully committing. My nerves take a while to adjust to the fact that I'm going to be riding an animal who could, at any moment, decide she doesn't want me on her damn back anymore and buck me off.

"Now, push up, and swing your other leg over, and— that's it!" Carter exclaims as I manage to get it all in one clumsy motion.

My heart pounds as Roman beams up at me, walking over to pat my leg before giving Polly a good scratch on the neck.

"Atta girl."

"Now this time I *know* you're talking to her," I chuckle.

He shoots me a wink before the two men begin to walk me through actually moving on the horse. I'm a little unsteady to begin with, and it definitely takes some brain power to make sure that I'm going through all the right steps: look at where I'm planning to go, squeeze my butt first, then my thighs, then my calves. When Polly finally starts walking I can feel at least half the tension bleed out of my body all at once.

"Holy shit! I'm riding a fucking horse!"

Roman snaps a picture, grinning from ear to ear.

"You're doing great!" Carter calls, reassuring me despite how unsteady I'm still feeling.

We spend a lot of the next hour or so going over stopping, starting, and steering, and I end up doing more than a few laps around the enclosure with Polly. She's patient and sweet, and before long I feel like I'm really getting the hang of this.

"Hey, I'm pretty— oh shit." I'm trying to steer toward them, but I mix up which leg I'm pushing against Polly and wind up turning away from them. "Okay, I *was* pretty good at this! Come on, girl."

I correct my technique, and after a few seconds, manage to turn to face the two of them.

"See? We did it eventually, right Polly?"

Roman watches proudly, his plaid shirt riding up a little while he leans against the fence, and I get a look at the soft trail of dark hair that disappears underneath the waistband of his jeans.

He motions back to the stables with a quick flick of his head.

"I'll go get the old man."

"What do you mean, you're already here!" I tease.

"Keep up the backtalk, darlin'. We'll see where it gets you."

I can feel every inch of my skin grow hot under my clothes, Roman tossing me a flirtatious look before disappearing inside.

Carter chuckles to himself as he double-checks to make sure everything is secure.

"The kid seems pretty damn smitten. It's been a long time since I've seen him like this."

Before I can manage a reply I hear Roman guiding Cash out of the stable, and watch him set up and mount the massive horse in one fluid motion.

"You ready to ride, little miss lippy?" He pats his saddlebag. "Got apples, a blanket, and some snacks and drinks just for us."

"Of course!" I exclaim, stroking Polly's neck. "We got this, right, Polly?"

"Take the low road," Carter shouts as he grabs the gate for us. "Less hills for the newbie. I'll get the guest house ready for you in the meantime."

"Thanks, Carter. We'll see you in a bit."

Roman turns Cash toward the path and I follow, beside and slightly behind.

"You good, darlin'? I don't have to tie you to the saddle to keep you on that horse, do I?"

"No," I laugh. "But if you've got rope, I'm sure we can make good use of it."

CHAPTER TWENTY-NINE
the alchemy
ROMAN

I used to bring Christa up here. She would paint the horses from a little spot on the patio, and we'd make coffee and pack a lunch and head up to the hills for the afternoon. I was worried being up here would cause more pain, but seeing Carter and Cash has only brought back good memories.

After she died, there was just too much pain associated with this place that it was hard to make the trek up, and I forgot how much I missed it. The fresh air, the horses, the cool breeze brushing past my face, it all takes me back to her, and a time in my life where I felt like anything was possible.

Imogen's laughter echoes through the trees, the sun behind her creating an angelic glow; being here with someone new makes me feel the way I used to, before grief carved its name into my bones.

"Didn't Carter say no hills?" She asks, a slightly panicked edge to her voice.

It helps that Polly is gentle and Imogen is calm, because Cash would be a different story. He's a bit of a wild card, even with me, and that's after knowing me his entire life.

"Just the price of privacy," I chuckle.

We haven't seen a single soul since we started riding; the only sounds around us are the wind brushing through the trees, and hooves thumping gently against the dirt. The air is so clean up here, I find myself invigorated with every breath.

We ride a good chunk of the way in silence, Imogen taking in the surroundings for the first time while I reminisce. When we reach the top of the hill I lead her to a small clearing surrounded by lush green trees, overlooking the area.

"Holy shit," she murmurs. "Is this all Carter's property?"

The scene is idyllic, horses grazing over gentle rolling hills for what must be miles in each direction, with barely a manmade structure in sight.

"It's all broken up. Different ranches, run by different folks. It's beautiful though, isn't it?"

"Yeah." She loosens her grip on the reins and pulls out her phone, snapping a picture of the view, and another quick one of me as I stare out at the vast landscape below us.

"Fuck, you look sexy in this picture," she says under her breath.

Imogen admires her work for another moment or two before sliding her phone back into her leggings, looking at the ground with a strained expression. It's only after a minute that I realize she's struggling to figure out a way down off her horse.

"What are you doing?"

"Carter taught me how to get on the horse, but he didn't say anything about getting down."

I chuckle, shaking my head.

"Seems like a good spot for a picnic anyway. I think Polly and Cash could use some grub."

I hop off my horse and Imogen immediately tries to mirror me, grabbing Polly's saddle and nearly pulling it all the way to the side. I snatch her by the waist as quickly as I can to keep her from falling off, not to mention taking the whole damn saddle with her.

"I got ya, darlin'."

I make sure Polly's calm before helping Imogen down, her hair a mess and her eyes already wild with expectation. She wraps her arms around the back of my neck and plants a heated kiss on my lips, my breath hitching as I kiss her back.

"My hero."

And here I thought keeping things casual would make things easier.

"C'mon. Let's get them tied up and fed first."

"You got enough rope for you too, cowboy?"

"More than enough," I murmur, my body alight with anticipation.

I teach her how to tie a good knot that'll hold even if Polly decides she wants to wander down the hill. It's a clove hitch that my dad taught me when I was a kid. I've tied this knot so many times, I could do it in my sleep. Make one loop around the branch near the end of the rope, and then a second loop just above the first. Finally, slide the free end into the second loop and pull it tight.

"Polly's got a tendency to wander, so we wanna get her nice and secured," I say, fastening a thick knot before quickly undoing it again. "Here, you try."

She takes the rope from me and follows the same steps, managing to tie the exact same knot with ease.

"Were you in girl scouts or something?"

"No," she laughs. "I learned it from a dom. You do pick up some useful skills."

My cheeks warm and I nod, watching her hands expertly tighten the knot and wondering what exactly she has in store for me. I've been so focused on whether or not this was right or wrong, about what either of us might lose if I actually pursued her, I haven't really been living in the present.

But this is exactly where I want to be.

I move on to tie up Cash, grabbing an apple and a pocket knife from his saddlebag when I'm done.

"Here, give her some of these," I mutter, slicing the apple up into smaller pieces and handing them off to Imogen. "Make sure you keep your fingers away from her teeth. She's usually pretty gentle, but if I remember right she gets a little overzealous when apples are on the line."

"Got it," Imogen replies, her face a mix of excitement and nerves.

Cash only eats a few of his apple slices before turning his nose up at the rest of them. Imogen and Polly, on the other hand, are already bonding; my girl's a regular Snow White.

I unhook the bag from Cash's saddle and pull out a blanket, along with a small bottle of champagne, two plastic cups, more fruit, cheese, and two sandwiches on homemade bread.

"I'm absolutely certain you said *snacks* in the car." Imogen chuckles, sitting down beside me. "This is a full meal!"

"It's not even close to what I can whip up in the kitchen." I pop the cork on the champagne bottle, pouring us two glasses. "You want roasted turkey and bacon on rye, or on sourdough?"

Her eyes get bigger.

"Sourdough!"

I grin.

"Good choice."

I pass it over and Imogen unwraps her sandwich, holding it up with a gasp.

"This is almost as big as my fucking head!"

She made a joke that all she eats at home when Logan's away is waffles and chocolate bars. I decided if she's going to be with me, she's going to eat well, so I snuck some vegetables in there, and tied it all together with a honey mustard vinaigrette made from scratch.

She takes a big bite, resting her free hand on my thigh. She looks ridiculous, with some sauce smeared on her face, but it's so damn cute I almost regret wiping it away. I lick my thumb clean, her cheeks pink as she cuddles up close and rests her head on my shoulder. It's so peaceful, all I can hear is the wind brushing past the trees and the sound of the horses' soft whinnies.

"I can't get over how beautiful it is," she murmurs.

"Yeah, I've missed it."

It's so nice to have someone to share it with again.

"So, you used to live out here?"

I shake my head, sipping my drink.

"My dad knew Carter from back in their bull riding days. When he died, there was no one to take care of Cash. So, I called up Carter and told him I'd pay him anything he wanted if he'd board the old man for me. I paid a shitload of money to have him driven here all the way from Montana, too."

"How much?"

"Lots. Some people pay a few thousand a month to board a horse."

She coughs, her shoulders shaking with laughter.

"That's a New York apartment!" She checks herself. "Well, a shitty one."

"I know." I look over at Cash, smiling as I watch him scrape the ground with his hoof. "But he's family. It's kind of like I have a piece of my dad back whenever I get to hang out with him."

Imogen gazes up at me, a strand of hair blowing into her face.

"You're really sweet, Roman."

"I'm just doing my job when it comes to Cash. Carter's ranch has got lots of space, he can run around with other horses... It's my responsibility to make sure he's taken care of, and at least he's free out here."

"It's still sweet." She sets the rest of her sandwich down and cups my cheek. "You know, I keep thinking about our mini golf date and how sweet you were, even back then."

"You made it awfully easy for a guy to open up."

"Well that's a relief, because you make it easy for me, too." She pauses. "I kind of adore you."

My mouth is dry, and my heart is pounding. This all feels so Hallmark, but I love it. Stepping out of my comfort zone and really embracing all of this has made me realize just how much more I want than I initially thought.

"I adore you too." I smile. "This is so cheesy."

"I like cheesy," she murmurs as her lips press against mine.

I slide my hand around her waist to pull her on top of me, starting to worry friends with benefits might not be enough.

Imogen climbs into my lap, straddling me as she deepens the kiss. My heart pounds and a warm tingle rushes down my spine as she grinds down on my cock. Between her warmth and the sun's, I can't really tell which makes me feel more alive.

I think it's her.

My hands glide up her waist, cupping her breasts while she rolls her hips and presses down onto me. Her back arches, and she moans. I know exactly what I want, and while I love the power I have over her in these moments, when I tear my mouth away from hers I'm aching to give it all away.

"Tie me to that tree."

"What about our lunch?"

"Just think of it as working up an appetite."

She flashes me a playful little smirk.

"Yes, sir."

Imogen climbs off of me and I immediately start packing our sandwiches back up, shoving them into the bag to keep a certain wandering horse from chowing down. By the time I get to my feet she's already got a spool of rope lazily hanging off her hand, sauntering toward me with a sultry sway. She places a hand on my chest, staring up at me as I sweat, my eyes fixed on the rope in her hand. Everything about her exudes confidence.

"Ever had your cock worshiped?" She asks.

"No, but it sounds... fun?"

"I think I owe you, you know, for leaving you hanging in your office the other day."

Imogen's hand drifts down to my cock, squeezing me through my jeans until I let out a groan.

"Be a good boy and pick a tree for me to tie you to."

I take my hat off, gently placing it on top of her head as she flashes me a puzzled expression.

"What's this for?"

"That means you're in charge, darlin'."

CHAPTER THIRTY

ROMAN

CASCADE FOOTHILLS

"Too tight?" She asks, her fingers brushing against mine as she tests the ropes.

Imogen has always reminded me of a dessert, and I've definitely been enjoying savoring her like one.

"I asked you a question," she purrs. "Are you comfortable?"

We've moved off the trail and into a more secluded part of the forest, but close enough that I can still hear the horses if they get spooked.

"Yes, Mistress."

She's got me tied to a tree, standing straight up and totally unable to move, but at least no one will find us here.

"Good boy."

This has been one of my biggest fantasies since my twenties, and I've been pushing it down for years, thinking no one would ever go for it. It was just something that sat in the back of my brain; something to think about in the shower. In the past, the woman in my fantasy was faceless, but now, all I see is her.

Imogen steps in front of me and pulls out a long silk blindfold.

"Ready?"

She looks exquisite, all that lavender hair flowing down over her shoulders. When the light hits it, I swear it glitters.

"Yes, Mistress."

She places the cloth over my eyes and I dip my head, letting her secure it with a firm knot in the back. I feel her grasp my chin and she kisses me, her lips tasting like sweet champagne. A moment later I feel her teeth against my ear, warm breath fanning my skin.

"You look so fucking hot like this," she breathes. "All mine."

The hairs on the back of my neck stand up straight as Imogen pops the buttons on my shirt, working swiftly as she makes her way down. Cool air brushes against my skin, my heart thundering as her fingernails lightly graze my chest.

"You don't have to be quiet for me, cowboy. I want to hear every *single* sound you make. Can you moan for me?" She whispers.

"Y— yes, Mistress."

"That's a good boy."

Everything feels amplified— I can hear every rush of breath and every rustle of the wind through the trees. This is exactly the kind of release I've been craving. To completely submit to someone like this, to trust them so implicitly... it makes me feel fucking powerful.

"Fuck, you're almost busting out of these jeans." She grabs my cock through my pants, squeezing until she pulls a whimper out from the depths of my chest. "Is this all for me?"

The jingle of my belt buckle makes me squirm.

"Oh, baby, look at you," she coos. "You're all excited and I haven't even started yet."

The texture of her voice is almost the same as it was the night she first hit me with that belt.

"You're such a tease."

She sinks her nails into my thigh, making me hiss.

"Talk back to me again and maybe I'll leave you like this. Can you picture it? What would it be like sitting out here alone for *hours*, cowboy?"

My heart pounds and my stomach turns in knots as I imagine her following through on the threat.

"I think I preferred it when you called me a slut." I grin, knowing it'll get her riled up. "Isn't that what you said, darlin'?"

I can hear the gentle *whoosh* the leather makes against denim as she slides my belt off, followed by the dull thunk as it hits the ground. Blood pounds in my ears, an almost deafening sound, as her fingers work the buttons on my pants. I need to calm myself down, make sure I don't lose myself too quickly. I want to *hear* her choking on my cock and talking dirty to me, not just suddenly come to my senses and have it all be over.

I tug a little at my binds as Imogen pulls my zipper down, compelled to run my hands over her body no matter how futile it is to try. Her fingers wrap around the base of my cock, and I groan with a mix of pain and anticipation as my head rocks right back into the tree.

"*Fuck.*"

"Careful now," she giggles, giving me a long, slow stroke. "You're so big, I don't know *how* you're gonna fit all the way down my throat."

I hate to be that guy, but this shit works on me every single time.

She slides her tongue along my shaft, teasing the most sensitive part of my cock, just below the head. Each swipe of her tongue is methodical, like she's savoring a lollipop— and it's all just to make me squirm. Thank god I have these ropes to hold me up, or this would be pretty goddamn embarrassing.

Imogen wraps her lips around my head and she gives me a few gentle sucks before releasing me with a pop. Electricity shoots down my spine as my eyes go wide behind the blindfold. I want to see everything she's doing to me, picturing it isn't enough.

"How long have you been planning this?" I ask, my voice shaking almost as badly as my legs.

"Hmm..." She clicks her tongue, swirling her finger around the tip of my cock. "That's a *good* question."

Damn, she's good at tormenting me, and I want to see just how far she can take it. She likes bratty. She likes power play. I can be good at both.

"Then answer it."

I hiss as she slaps my cock, the stinging sensation lingering for a moment.

"I should have gagged you– actually..."

All I feel is cool air around my body at her sudden absence, hearing leaves rustle with each of her steps. Suddenly, a piece of fabric is shoved between my teeth, and my mouth waters at the lingering taste of her. The pathetic whimper that spills from deep inside surprises even me, and her cruel chuckle returns with a vengeance as she delicately grazes her nails along my shaft.

"You mouth off again and I'm going to edge you until you fucking cry, do you understand me?"

Her voice is a lightning strike, setting my entire body ablaze, and I tremble as her lips ghost over mine. I wish I could see the look in her eyes right now. I try to speak, to tell her I understand, and that I'd do *anything* if only she'd touch me again, but I forget there's a pair of lace panties stuffed between my teeth.

"Nod your head like a good boy. You want to be a good boy, don't you?"

I obey, and Imogen rewards my silent nod with a sweet, lingering kiss.

"Now, to answer your question before you so rudely interrupted." She spits on my cock, swirling her tongue around the crown. "I've been thinking about this since you played that naughty little trick on me with the vibrator. *But* I decided I would be gracious."

A growl erupts from my chest and Imogen giggles, sinking her teeth into my thigh. I want to spit these panties out and moan for her, but I'm afraid she really *will* leave me tied to this tree if I do. At least until she decides to come back for more.

The next thing I know, she's taking me *all* the way down her throat, the tip of her nose bumping my pubic bone. I smile, hearing her choke and sputter as her head bobs up and down, letting me get comfortable with the pace as that warm tingling sensation continues to build.

I hit the back of her throat and a whine escapes me, muffled and soft. I'm trying to slow down, to control myself. I'm panting, my breath coming in too quickly. Too hard. Pressure builds and builds. I'm trying *not* to come, but my heart is beating so fast I think I won't have much of a say in the matter.

And it all keeps building.

Until I'm shaking.

All I can hear is the sound of her choking on my dick.

All I feel is softness and heat as I'm about to shoot straight down her throat.

And then she slips away, removing her hands.

Her mouth.

Everything.

The shock of it all makes me shudder, and I involuntarily smack my head against the tree, tears gathering at the corners of my eyes as the sharp stabbing in my skull only sort of covers up my desperation.

Then the ropes loosen and she rips her panties out of my mouth.

"Wh—"

The blindfold comes off just as quickly, the afternoon sun assaulting my eyes, and I have to blink for a few seconds to get rid of the little white spots. I look down to see the rope at my feet, following its trail for a few moments before finding her. She's completely naked save for my hat that's sitting slightly askew on her head, the other end of the rope dangled lazily in her hand.

She stares me down like I'm a fresh meal.

I don't think my heart rate has slowed in at least ten minutes, and there's no way that's changing any time soon.

"I thought you said you'd be gracious."

"And I can *change my mind* anytime I want." She tilts her head, her eyes gleaming with a playful cruelty. "If you want to come, you have to work for it."

"What?"

"Did I suck your brains right out of your dick?" She asks, her voice whetted with a mocking edge. "I *said* if you want to come, you have to work for it."

I tilt my head, still a bit perplexed, but she's already closed the gap between us, looping the rope around my neck.

"This..." She ties a knot before picking the rest up off the ground. "Is your leash, and if you want to be a good boy, you'll get down on your knees and come when you're called."

She bites her lip, her cheeks bright pink.

"*Are* you a good boy?"

I sink right into the role, nodding silently, but as I go to pull my pants up, Imogen shakes her head.

"Nuh-uh. I want you on your hands and knees, just the way you are right now." She gives the leash a firm tug, making me stumble. "Crawling to me."

I drop down, hitting the cool ground with a thud. A devilish smile eclipses her face and she crooks her finger, letting the rope slacken as she backs up into a tree. She reaches down, playing with her pussy.

"This is what you want, isn't it?"

"Yes."

I'm so turned on I'd bark for her if she asked me to.

"Then *come*."

She gives the rope another tug and I lurch forward, my eyes on her and only her as I crawl through broken sticks and leaves that cling to my palms. My fingers sink into the soil, my pants sitting around my knees, making me feel totally exposed. This is fucking *humiliating*; a year ago, I'd be questioning my own sanity, and yet now all I want to do is please her.

I want to be her good boy.

"That's it," she moans, slowly strumming her clit. "You belong on your knees."

When I make it to her, I immediately sit up on my haunches, placing my hands on her thighs. The action earns me a slap in the face.

"Bad boy." She clicks her tongue. "I didn't say you could touch."

My head spins and all I can focus on is how it all feels. The ache inside me grows more intense, and I have to start battling the urge to get to my feet and take what I want.

"I need you bad, darlin'."

She raises a brow, grinning from ear to ear.

"Keep talking."

"You're so goddamn beautiful." I sit up a little higher, my nails sinking into her skin, and she sucks in a breath as I reach her pussy. "Please, Mistress, let me fuck you. Let me please you. Let me make you come."

Just the thought of the taste of her makes me drool.

Her lips part and I test the waters, leaning into her pussy and giving her clit a gentle flick with the tip of my tongue. Her hips roll forward, but before I can go in again, she tugs upward on the leash.

"On your feet," she commands.

I stand and she slides a coy finger under my chin.

"Now, fuck me until I break."

She wraps her legs around my waist as I lift her up, pushing into her with one slow, delicious thrust. I'm desperate to watch her fall apart while I fuck her, squeezing her throat with each slam of my hips against hers. Her eyelids flutter, sweat gathering on her forehead as her eyes roll back and her body shudders with pleasure.

I grin at the thought of giving her a taste of her own medicine.

"Should I pull out right now? Deny you the way you've denied me?"

"No!" Her voice is hoarse and broken, like it's been dragged through glass. "Nononono! I'll be so fucking good. I promise I promise! *Please*, baby."

I'm shaking like a fucking leaf, struggling to hold onto this position of power I've barely earned. Imogen's fingernails dig into my biceps, and the pain is so exquisite I want her to draw blood.

"You're pretty when you're desperate," I purr.

"Oh, God!"

"God's not gonna make you come," I growl. "Say my name, darlin'."

She screams it out, her voice bouncing off the trees.

"Tell me what you want."

A thin sheen of sweat glistens on her face and she smiles.

"Fill me up. I want to feel you dripping out of me for days."

I groan, burying my face in her shoulder. The idea sends me reeling and I slam into her, dizzy at the thought of watching my cum dripping down her thighs.

"You want all of it?"

"Yes," she whimpers. "Please, Roman."

Her voice breaks, her body twitching as she reaches her peak.

"Roman, I'm so close!"

Her nails sink into the back of my neck, locking me into this position. I feel like I'm being pulled apart at the seams, and even though I want to stay buried in her like this forever, I can't stave off my climax much longer. Maybe it's time to push things a little further, indulging in a fantasy I've only entertained a handful of times.

"You want my baby?"

I lift my head and her eyes burn into mine, her lip curling into a wicked grin.

"Fucking give it to me, cowboy."

And then suddenly I'm coming, my climax ripping through me like a hot knife through butter. I cry out in ecstasy all while the vibrations of

Imogen's moans ripple through me. Sweat and saliva coat my skin and my thrusts start to slow down as my climax fades into the afterglow.

I hold her tight, running my fingers through her hair as our combined heart rates start to come down. Even though I know it was just a fantasy, that she's on the pill and neither of us was being serious, the thought stirred something in me. As we breathe together, the breeze cooling our skin, it nags at the back of my mind, quickly blossoming into a stark realization.

I don't want casual.

I don't want friends with benefits.

I want every little piece of her.

I want it all.

CHAPTER THIRTY-ONE

wanna be yours

IMOGEN

CASCADE FOOTHILLS

"Taste this."

Roman is holding out a spoon with a little bit of homemade spaghetti sauce. It smells divine, made up of fresh garlic, onions, and assorted herbs that he picked from the garden out back. This place has horses, fresh air, and a fucking *garden*. It's paradise, and it's a shame we have to go home on Sunday. It really has been wonderfully peaceful here.

I lean over and try it, instantly blown away by the tang of the tomatoes, the perfect amount of salt, and a little bit of cayenne for heat. This man fucks like a God and cooks like a Michelin star chef. I don't think there's anything he *can't* do at this point.

"Holy shit. That's—"

Mitzy whines at our feet and Roman chuckles, shaking his head.

"Nope. Not for dogs."

"Maybe she could get a treat instead."

"She's had enough treats, Imogen," he laughs.

"Aww, you're so mean!" I crouch down and kiss her adorable little face as she wags her tail. "How can you deny her?"

"Well, *someone* gave her half a croissant this morning."

231

I sigh, staring into her soulful eyes.

"I would give her all the money in my bank account if she asked for it. Isn't that right, Mitz?"

"I'm sure she'd just eat it," Roman snorts.

I give Mitzy a couple of slices of cucumber to tide her over before returning to prep for the salad. Roman is dealing with the gnocchi, hand rolling it himself; his shirt sleeves are pulled back past his elbows, and I watch the muscles in his forearm flex from the corner of my eye as he works. The fine dusting of flour on the cutting board reminds me of our night in the pantry, my cheeks burning as I try to focus on chopping.

"Have you started your application for the conference?" I ask him.

"I'm about halfway through, what about you?"

"I'm... making headway."

"Well, you wanna hang out on the couch and watch Chopped while we finish them up after dinner?"

I beam and raise my eyebrows.

"You watch Chopped?"

"It's my favorite show," he replies, filling up a pot with water to boil.

"Oh, me too! Piper and I used to watch it while we graded papers. I always secretly wanted to be on it, but I kind of suck at cooking."

He takes a look at the veggies I've sliced up and gives me an approving nod.

"I think you're doing just fine, darlin'."

I always appreciate academic validation, but Roman's is even better. Plus, sometimes it comes with sex as a bonus.

"Okay, so what's your pitch for the conference?"

My anxiety around submitting this thing is massive. Frankie's already given me pretty good feedback on some things that need improvement, but my fear is paralyzing. What if I get rejected? What if I submit the wrong file? Once, I was applying for an office job and submitted an itinerary for a trip Piper and I were going on that included the words *bring dildos.*

Logan said that wasn't grounds for joining the witness protection program. He also told me never to say the word *dildo* in front of him ever again.

"It's a lot more personal than I originally intended, but it's something I've been noodling with for a long time." Roman pauses to clear his throat, and I get a whiff of fresh garlic and cayenne as he flips the chicken over in the pan. "It's about people's perceptions around bereavement and suicide. You know, how everyone treats you like you're glass that's about to shatter? I was supposed to work on it with your brother, but I got his blessing to finish it on my own."

"I just assumed he'd be partnering up with Abi for something, but I guess not."

"Yeah, well..." Roman frowns, scrunching up his face for a moment. "Never mind, it's nothing."

"Do you know something I don't know?"

"Nope."

He clearly wants to change the subject, but if anyone's going to have secret details on their potential relationship, it's got to be Roman. Besides, I've gotten pretty good at getting this man to open up.

"Oh, come on," I laugh. "You're his best friend! You guys talk about stuff! They're totally boning, aren't they?"

Okay, maybe I could've been a bit more subtle.

"It's against university policy to fraternize with colleagues in your own department," he murmurs. "And trust me, I've tried poking that bear. If there *is* anything going on, Logan's not about to spill the beans."

Damn. Maybe he doesn't know anything.

"Okay, so nothing concrete, but do you have any theories?"

"Well, I'm not about to get him in trouble," he chuckles. "And this is all just my assumptions, alright?"

"Of course, it's just a theory."

He nods.

"Your brother was definitely chasing Abi a couple years ago, and while I don't know if that ever really died down, they were *awfully* close at her birthday party back in August. Until someone sees evidence of any kind of fraternization, it's just speculation, but I told him to be careful just the same."

"So, if they *were* sleeping together, hypothetically, what happens?"

Roman blows out a breath.

"They would be subject to a disciplinary hearing, and one of them would have to transfer to another department, or leave the university in the worst case."

We stare at each other for a moment before Roman turns away, fiddling nervously with the burner.

"I guess this is the part where we talk about what we do if *we* get caught," I murmur.

"Yeah," he whispers. "Yeah, I've been thinking about that."

I try to play it cool as I dump the chopped-up veggies into the salad bowl and give it a mix.

"Imogen, look at me."

His voice is gentle, but there's an urgent undercurrent to it that makes my skin prickle.

"I *adore* you. You're fiercely intelligent, you make me laugh, you taught me some of the *raunchiest* shit in bed— sorry, I don't know if that's a—"

"It's a compliment," I laugh. "It's a good compliment."

He smiles.

"I feel so good around you."

All I have to do is say that I don't want to be just friends who fuck. I want to blurt it out: that I want something more, something I haven't had in years, something I've been too afraid to admit.

That I'm falling in love with him.

My head is a mess, swirling around that phrase over and over and playing out all the ways he could react to it. Most of them are bad.

He brushes his thumb across my cheek with a tilt of his head.

"Why are you crying?"

"Because I adore you too," I laugh. "And I don't know what to do about that."

"If we get caught, nothing's changing between us."

I'm not so sure it's true, but I'm willing to believe the lie if only for my own sanity. Roman Burke breaking my heart might just make me swear off men forever.

I'll become a Nun.

"I've also been thinking that... I want to be more than just friends with benefits. I want you. Completely."

He's saying everything I was thinking on Piper's patio the other night, putting everything on the line in a way that I've been too afraid to. I don't want to stop seeing him, I don't want anyone else. There hasn't even been a serious *thought* of anyone else since we met.

I swallow hard, about to hurl myself into the abyss.

I hope it's worth it.

"I think I've wanted more since we first met, back when you were still Henry."

"It's my middle name," he laughs.

"Damn, I guess I fucked up. My middle name's Gwendolyn. I just pulled Jade out of my ass."

He snorts, leaning down to kiss me.

"God, I think you're the most gorgeous fuckin' thing I've seen in years."

I wrap my arms around his neck as he kisses me again and again, pushing me into the counter. Both of us are out of breath by the time he tears his mouth away, and I grip the collar of his shirt.

"Fuck me."

"After dinner." He grins. "You can hold out for a little longer, can't you?"

"You know, being all hot and emotional and then withholding your penis is a federal offense."

"You sure about that?"

"Yup. Washington Criminal Code. Look it up."

"Let me guess. Section 69?"

I snort, giving him a gentle shove.

"You're such a tease."

He closes the gap between us, kissing the tip of my nose.

"I'll let you cuff me later, darlin'."

Roman gently pats my ass before motioning to the two untouched bell peppers sitting next to my knife. I love how easily we fall into this playfulness.

"C'mon. Finish chopping those, and I'll teach you how to plate all of this."

I turn and pick the knife back up again, grabbing a bell pepper for the salad. Before I can move to slice it in half, Roman presses his body against mine, wrapping his fingers around my wrist.

"Here, I'll show you an easier way."

I don't know the first thing about how to cut veggies, I just sort of do it, so I'm happy to get a cooking lesson from Roman, at least so long as he keeps standing this close to me.

"Yes, Chef."

He lets out the tiniest grunt that he probably thinks I can't hear as he presses his body into mine, practically caging me in.

"Don't start calling me that."

"Why? It clearly turns you on."

He dips his head, playfully flicking my ear with the tip of his tongue.

"Just be a good girl and do as you're told."

Roman kisses my temple and straightens, grabbing the pepper and placing it on the cutting board.

"Okay, are you ready for your first lesson? Pepper slicing 101."

"Ready!" I chirp. It could be about anything and I'd be just as excited.

"You wanna cut the top and bottom off..."

He guides my hand, sparks shooting up my arm as we delicately slice off the bottom of the pepper first.

"Just like that, make sure not to take off too much."

I didn't realize that chopping vegetables could make you this sweaty, but then again, most people aren't being pressed into the counter while they're trying to work.

Roman holds on to my wrist, his other hand on my waist, gently gliding up and down. It's like he's purposely trying to distract me, but I manage to keep my focus and slice the other half of the pepper.

"Perfect." His voice is low and gravelly, causing goosebumps to form on my arms.

He helps me push the remnants aside with the blade of the knife.

"If you're going to be this sexy, I don't know how successful I'm going to be at cutting the rest of this thing."

I wish he'd just bend me over this counter and take what he clearly wants, but it looks like he wants to drag this out a little longer.

"I promise not to steer you wrong, darlin'. Now you wanna stand it up and cut down the side of the pepper so you can open it."

I do as I'm told, making a long vertical slice, and Roman nods in approval.

"See, this makes it easier to cut off the white parts and the center. Then, you slice it into long, thin pieces."

I roll it out, cutting away all the stuff we don't need as I sink into the smell of Roman's cologne, wrapped up in the warmth of his body. It's so rare that I get to spend this kind of time with another person or allow this much intimacy into my life.

I finish slicing up the pepper, tossing it into the salad bowl while Roman moves on to teaching me how to make a homemade vinaigrette.

"It's just olive oil, balsamic, a little bit of honey, salt, and pepper."

He doesn't even measure, he just goes for it. I smile, watching him whisk it up before grabbing a little tasting spoon and offering some to me. It's perfect, sweet and tangy with just the right amount of pepper.

Once the salad is mixed, he moves on to the steps of how to plate everything, up to and including grabbing a clean cloth to wipe away any sauce that gets on the edge of the dish. It's so beautiful I almost don't want to eat it, but he insists.

"I want to see if it tastes as good as it looks."

He uncorks the wine that's already sitting at the table, pouring us each a generous glass as we settle into our seats. The sun is setting, and we have a beautiful view of the ranch from our place by the window. Outside, I spot Polly grazing in the field.

"Oh, look! That's my girl!"

Roman chuckles.

"You wanna take her and Cash for another ride tomorrow morning before we head out?"

"Sounds great. At least if we can get those applications sent off tonight."

I cut into my chicken and take a bite, groaning at the perfect juicy flavor.

"My compliments to the hottest chef in the world."

Roman shakes his head, looking surprisingly bashful.

"Hey, you did a lot of the work too, you should be congratulating yourself."

"Mmm... I think you can congratulate me later when you eat me out on the patio."

He chokes on his wine, his eyes wide as he sets the glass down, all while I calmly nibble at my pasta.

"That's payback for your sexy cooking lesson."

He snorts, taking another sip to recover as we dig in. It's quiet as we eat, and I keep finding my gaze wandering back to him. His brows are knit together and he's chewing his meal like he's grading his own cooking, looking for flaws. If there are any, I can't taste them.

Other than the waffles we had back at his apartment, this is the first meal we've had as a couple.

At least I think we're a couple.

"So, can I ask you something?"

"Of course."

I pause, taking another sip of wine for courage.

"When you said you wanted to be more than friends with benefits, does that mean..."

Roman stares at me, leaning back in his chair. He looks truly and entirely confident, maybe for the first time since I've known him, like he's made a decision after a hell of a lot of internal debate.

"It means I'm asking you to be my girlfriend."

"You want me to be your girlfriend?"

"God, it sounds so high school when you say it back like that, but..." He laughs, shaking his head. "Do *you* want that? To be together, for real?"

We're risking everything, hoping that we'll make it through to the other side unscathed. I know the other shoe could drop at any minute, and when it does, it's going to hurt.

Bad.

It might just ruin everything the two of us have going right now, but...

"Yes."

The word feels so right leaving my tongue, like it's the only thing I was made to say. Roman beams, raising his glass, the two of us clinking them together in a little toast just to us.

"I adore you, darlin'."

I can't believe this is what I was so afraid of, what I avoided for so long. But with him, it just feels right.

"I adore you, too, cowboy."

CHAPTER THIRTY-TWO
the albatross
IMOGEN

TWO DAYS LATER

"What do you feel like watching?" I ask, scrolling through the horror movie section on Netflix. "Everything either sucks or we've seen it before."

I've spent so much time with Roman that I've really missed our little ritual of watching a horror movie together a few times a week, but Logan is on his phone, his brow furrowed in concentration, and clearly not listening to me. I grab a piece of popcorn from the bowl, tossing it at him, and he sneers.

"Too busy texting Abi to listen to your *dear* sister?"

"Actually, I'm submitting a book pitch to a publisher," he replies, digging the popcorn out of his hair and popping it straight into his mouth.

"What's the book about?"

"Dad."

His voice is so soft, sweetness and adoration cut right into it.

I think the reason why Logan is as successful as he is in academia is because he's emotionally accessible. People find him warm, charming, and relatable. They empathize with him and his research because it comes from such a profoundly personal place. Even in his stiffest writing, he

239

weaves in stories about our dad. He's never been shy of his biases, something we argue about all the time in academia.

Are we being objective enough?

When you're studying society and human beings, I don't think objectivity is possible. Logan always taught me that people are experts in their own lives, and that we all live with our own unique truths and experiences.

That includes researchers.

"Oh, what about Evil Dead?" He asks, shoving his phone into his pocket.

"Original or remake?"

"Dude, remake sucks," he laughs. "Put the original on."

I scroll through and pull it up, hitting play and cracking open my beer as the two of us put our feet up on the coffee table. Only a few minutes in and my phone chimes in my pocket. I try to ignore it, but Logan's clearly noticed.

"Need to get that? We can pause the movie."

"Nah. It's just Piper."

It's Roman. We've been texting a lot since the ranch, and things have gotten more intense. The problem is, I can't just come out and tell my brother that I'm dating his best friend. He'd flip out.

Logan chews on his lip, fiddling with the buttons on his cardigan when my phone goes off again. This time, I reach into my pocket, angling my body away from him.

> ROMAN: There's a cute little spot called Guardian Point. Teenagers used to go there to make out in the 80s, but I was thinking we could head out there tomorrow and have a picnic under the stars. I'll cook us up something special.

I've never dated a guy who was this much of a romantic.

> IMOGEN: Pick me up at 6:00?

> ROMAN: You got it, darlin'.

I slide my phone back into the pocket of my hoodie and sigh.

"How's Piper?" Logan asks, his eyes still glued to the screen.

He's been weird since I got back. It's like he's doing a great impression of my goofy-ass brother, but with a little bit of distance he doesn't usually bring to the table.

"She's fine," I reply, digging into the bowl of popcorn.

I assumed something happened with his work, or maybe with Abi, but I have no way of really knowing.

"Had some time to catch up over the weekend?" Logan asks, a bit more of an edge creeping into his voice.

I turn to him, eyes already narrowed.

"Yeah. It was nice. Dude, what is your deal?"

"Nothing," Logan replies. "Except that I saw Piper and Jay at the Hi-Dive on Saturday night."

I can feel my stomach drop as I stare straight ahead at the screen, barely taking in what I'm seeing. My mind is racing, struggling to find the right thread in the braid I've woven.

"Why lie to me?" Logan asks.

Shame turns to anger, my go-to defense mechanism.

"Why do you care? I'm an adult. Where I go, and what I do—"

"Look, I get that, but you don't have to keep things from me. What could be so bad that you feel like you have to lie about going somewhere with your friends?"

I want to tell him the truth. He'll freak out, but if I explain it, he might understand. But I can't. I'd risk more than just my relationship with my brother. If this whole thing is blown wide open, Roman could lose everything.

"It's nothing," I insist, fighting the urge to get up and run out of the house. "I just— look, I know you're my brother but that doesn't give you the right to know every single thing about my life."

Logan snorts, shaking his head.

"You're being such a fucking child."

"And you're trying to be dad!"

The second the words leave my lips, I feel a pang of regret.

Fucking stupid.

"That's an asshole move and you know it," he growls.

But he doesn't get up and walk away. I've got that Flynn temper— my dad's temper— and the tendency to blurt things out that I shouldn't. It's either part of my ADHD, or I'm just an asshole. Logan used to be like this too, but I guess he's learned to control it over the years.

"I'm sorry," I murmur, watching nervously as he grabs the remote and turns the volume down on the TV.

He shifts his body, staring at me with piercing eyes, and it takes me a few seconds before I can actually return his gaze.

"I really am sorry, Logan. I shouldn't have—"

"Look, Iggy. I get it, okay? And you're right, you are an adult. It's not my job to be your parent, but you're also my sister. Of course I'm curious about your life."

The two of us have always been close, save for the chunk of time after dad died where neither of us really knew how to cope. Even back during my failed teenage rebellion phase I could count on Logan to pick me up from a sketchy party or a crappy date. He's always been there for me.

I think that's why holding this secret back is killing me.

Logan puts his hand on my shoulder.

"We don't get a hell of a lot of time on this earth, and capitalism—"

"Oh, god, Logan please don't go all Karl Marx on me while we're having a moment," I laugh.

"No, I'm being real! The system's designed to keep us apart with 9-5 jobs and all the stupid busywork shit we have to do in our lives. We don't get a lot of time to tell people that we love them, and I love you, Ig."

"I love you too," I whisper.

He smiles, a little sadly.

"So why did you lie to me?"

I have to come up with something, anything, but it can't be the truth. I'm not having that conversation right now. Maybe I can sculpt a version of it though, something that'll ease my conscience a little.

"Okay," I sigh. "The truth is, I'm seeing someone. He's in the kink scene– we both are."

It's only a lie of omission.

My brother's eyebrows disappear into his mess of hair and he fiddles nervously with the watch on his wrist. Dad's Rolex that he got after teaching for 20 years.

"*That's* what you felt the need to hide from me?" He asks, voice sharp like he still wants to fight.

I clear my throat, pausing for a second to craft the rest of the scenario. Whatever story I invent, I have to be able to stick with.

"I hid him because he's really special, and this is really important to me. We spent the weekend together, went ho— we went hiking together. It all happened so fast, Logan. I just didn't want to start telling you about him and have it all blow up in my face."

He's quiet for a long time and I wonder if he even believes me. Maybe the story's not that convincing? At least not the way I'm telling it with so little detail. Should I give him more information?

Simple explanations are rarely simple for me. Piper says I overshare, and right now, I can feel the urge to add in some flavor. How tall this imaginary guy is, what he does for a living, what we ate, what we did all weekend... Besides sex, that is. My brother does not need to hear about that.

"Is that safe?" He finally asks. "You know, being away from home with a guy you don't know?"

"I do know him," I laugh. "I'm dating him."

Might as well tell part of the truth, right?

"So he's good to you?"

"Yes. Do you wanna run a background check on him?"

"No, I assume you've already done that," he retorts, biting back a smile. "I'm just confused. You're seeing someone and you seem to like them enough to be pursuing a relationship, but you didn't want to tell me?"

"You're doing it again," I warn. "You're doing dad's thing."

He rolls his eyes.

"Iggy, I'm not trying to be him."

"You are, though! A little, at least. You started stepping in for him when he got sicker, and you never completely stopped."

I really felt that shift in him. He became more protective of me, always wanting to spend more time together, even if it was just phone calls or FaceTime. Logan's grief is an open wound that he shares with everyone around him; I could never do the same because I felt like I was burdening people. I never wanted to be treated like glass, but I didn't realize the kind of anguish I was swallowing by not talking about it.

"Okay, fine. I didn't tell you the truth because I was worried you'd judge me about being involved with kink and–"

"Hey, I'm not gonna judge. The other day I had to listen to Frankie talk about fisting while I was trying to eat an eclair."

"That's not the best dessert choice for that conversation."

"That's what I told him!"

His smile is warm, eyes twinkling.

"You don't have to be ashamed of that part of your life," he assures me.

I clear my throat, preparing myself to reveal a little bit more of the truth than I initially expected.

"It's not just that. Things are getting serious with Henry..." The name just slips out, but I keep talking. Maybe he'll forget. "It's been a long time since I've felt this comfortable letting someone into my life and I think there's a part of me that feels like I'm going to mess that up."

"Mess it up how?"

Suddenly, all of these insecurities that I've been holding on to for years start to bubble to the surface, perfectly timed as a character in the movie lets out a blood-curdling scream. Logan reaches for the remote, shutting the TV off and forcing me to look at him. He's got the kind of look on his face that makes you want to crack your entire heart open. It's annoyingly effective.

"People leave relationships all the time, Logan, and I'm afraid I'll push him away." I sniffle and take a breath to steady myself. "I think sometimes it's easier to be alone, but this guy broke through every single wall I put up like they were nothing."

He doesn't say anything, instead reaching over and grasping my wrist, giving it a light squeeze as a tear trickles down my cheek.

"I know you're still dealing with all that grief, Iggy; it's scary, and it's hard, and it makes you want to isolate, but the thing that gets you through it is connecting with people. That's what did it for me, even when it hurt. You just have to remember that all we do is grow, change, and move forward. Sometimes moving forward means moving on."

When I sat down today, I wasn't expecting a therapy session from Dr. Logan Flynn. He might be in the wrong line of work.

"Grief will eat you alive if you go at it alone. I know you never really opened up after what happened."

I didn't because life goes on. Even when your world is falling apart, and it feels like nothing will ever be the same, you still have to get up in the morning. You still have to pay your bills. You can't tell everyone you're not fine, even if all you want to do is scream, grabbing your own pain by the throat and begging for it to stop.

Because you can only say you're not fine for so long before people start to leave.

"I didn't want to..." I stare at the ceiling, trying to give myself something solid to latch onto. "I was worried that—I didn't want to be selfish, you know? Dad made his choice, and it was the right choice with his prognosis, but even while we were holding his hand and he was slipping away, there was a part of me that wanted to scream at him to keep fighting. Then, when it was all said and done, I just felt– I don't know... abandoned? *Fuck*, that's so selfish."

"No, it's not," Logan whispers. "I remember when he called and told me about the cancer, I hit the floor. I couldn't breathe. I couldn't think. I felt this urge to run to him and ask him for help. You know, get advice from my dad, right? That's what you do. It didn't matter that it was happening to *him*, it's all I could think to do."

I nod, my chin quivering as I relive my own phone call with him.

He asked me if I was sitting down.

I wasn't. I was hunting for something on my desk, rambling aimlessly, and when he said the words, they didn't quite register.

Glioblastoma.

Terminal.

The diagnosis sounded like it was from language I'd never heard before, and by the time the words sunk in, I was already drowning.

Terminal? No. Not *my* dad. Not my dad who stood 6'3" and almost 200lbs of muscle. Not my dad who battled monsters in my closet when I was a kid, and checked under my bed to make sure it was safe to sleep. He was strong, and he was smart. He could command a packed room while somehow making you feel like you were the only person in it.

Cancer wouldn't take someone like that.

I was in denial right up until the nurse who helped him pass handed him the medication to swallow. All of my grief got tangled up in my throat and all I could choke out was, 'I love you' while my heart was begging him to stay. I didn't get to say all the things I wanted to.

I sniffle as Logan pulls me in for a big hug.

"I wish I'd handled all of this better," I confess through the tears.

"There's no handbook for this shit. You're doing the best you can."

"Doesn't feel like it," I laugh. "I can't even have a normal relationship. It's just easier to keep people at arm's length."

It *was* easier.

Before I met Roman.

"Well, you can't keep me away," Logan replies. "I'll annoy you forever."

CHAPTER THIRTY-THREE

IMOGEN

"You told him about me, huh?"

Roman chuckles as we lie on the hood of his car, staring up at the inky blue sky.

It's so clear out here, and the stars look like little diamonds scattered in a dark sea. I think I've spotted Orion's belt about 500 times, but each time Roman tells me I'm not anywhere close to it.

"Sort of." I turn to him with a wince. "Do you think he's gonna figure it out?"

"Well, he and Frankie already know I'm seeing someone, but they have no idea who it is."

Music pours out of the car stereo. At the start of the ride he insisted on a playlist that I quickly dubbed 'divorced dad rock.' It's a lot of Bryan Adams, Springsteen... stuff I grew up listening to on long road trips with my parents.

"We really should have coordinated lies."

"Hey, you could have texted me," he laughs.

"He sprang it on me and I had to come up with something that was at least a little bit credible." That uncomfortable feeling starts to grow in my gut. "I hate lying to him."

"I do too," Roman mutters. "I don't wanna hurt him."

In my heart of hearts, I don't think Logan would be that upset. Shocked, maybe, but it's not like he would disown me. I know my brother pretty well, and even if the news was hard for him to swallow, it wouldn't take him too long to come around.

Roman gnaws on his fingernail as we sit in silence for a while, and my eyes fall on the little bow and arrow tattooed on his knuckles that I keep forgetting to ask him about.

"Are you a Sagittarius?"

"How'd you guess?"

I reach over and trace the bow and arrow with my fingertips. Roman laughs.

"Oh, yeah. I just needed something to fill the space and the artist suggested my zodiac." He turns to me. "What's your sign?"

"Leo."

"I'm not going to pretend I know what that means," he laughs. "Gotta admit, I only know the names."

"Don't worry, I won't be checking to analyze our relationship prospects."

This is my favorite part of a relationship, the part where you're still figuring each other out. I hope we keep surprising each other, finding out what makes the other person tick along the way.

He smiles, staring up at the stars as I nuzzle into his chest.

"I love learning more about you," he murmurs.

"You do?"

"Of course! Like, tell me something you're passionate about. Something I don't already know."

I used to be so confident in my identity, but now that it's all wrapped up in school, I'm not really sure of my passions outside of it.

"I don't really know."

He looks down at me and grins.

"You've gotta have something."

"I mean, it's kind of a hard question! I like horror movies, because of my dad, and uh... reading, I guess? I like romance books. I like to read about people falling in love, the kind that won't be able to live without each other."

Before he can keep digging, I decide to flip the tables on him.

"What about you? Any passions outside of educating the masses?"

"Definitely cooking. After Christa died, I thought about traveling the world like Anthony Bourdain."

I could absolutely picture Roman with an obscure YouTube channel, traveling to different places and trying new cuisine while he gushes about it. Every time he talks about food his eyes light up. You can taste the passion in the dishes he makes. Nothing is half-assed.

"So, are you over academia then?"

He smiles, but there's a hint of bitterness to his expression, like someone reflecting on their past and all the turns they've ever taken.

"It takes a lot out of a person," he murmurs. "I know cooking does, too, but it's also exacting and... it's the kind of thing I could lose myself in."

Makes sense. He had a lot to run from.

And again, we're silent for a while, one song on the playlist fading into the next. I recognize it immediately, *Fast Car* by Tracy Chapman, but I'm clearly not the only one. Roman slides off the hood, leaning into the driver's side and turning up the volume.

"You know what else I'm passionate about?" He asks, walking toward me. "Dancing."

"Dancing?" I laugh.

"Hell yeah. You wanna dance with me?"

"Here?"

"Yeah. Why not?"

"You ride horses, you cook, you have a huge dick, and now you're telling me you dance?"

"To be fair, I never said I danced *well*, but the rest is all true."

He throws me a wink, holding out his hand. I can't resist him like this, with his mussed hair and playful expression.

"C'mon, darlin'."

I let him take me in his arms and rest my head on his chest, listening to his heartbeat. He smells so good, and the feeling of his arms around me is even better. It's not even about the sex, not only about it at least, I just love hanging out with him. It's been a really long time since I've felt like this about someone.

But that's what makes me terrified.

Ninety percent of relationships that begin before the age of 30 end prematurely. Fifty percent of marriages end in divorce; that number goes up to sixty-seven percent for second marriages, and seventy-four percent for third marriages. Everything that exists, everything that ever will be, has an expiration date.

Is that why love always feel so insurmountable, and so fucking complicated? I'm drowning in it, tossed into a raging river without a life raft and the only thing I have to hold on to is him.

Is that even love, or a panic attack?

I'm crying into Roman's shirt, clinging to him as hard as I fucking can as the realization hits me like an avalanche. I tried so hard not to love him, but he makes it so easy. He understands what I've been through on a profound level, and even though our pain differs at certain points, we're walking the same complicated path. He brings the support I've needed for years and never bothered to reach out for.

I always thought I would just push through it, like I've pushed through everything in my life, but grief can't be bulldozed. It has to be cared for and tended to. It's a permanent change in the landscape, and I can never go back to the way things used to be.

"Hey," Roman whispers, cupping my face in his hands. "What's the matter?"

The thought of saying the words scares me more than agreeing to a full-blown relationship with this man. It means that when the truth comes out, and things begin to fall apart, I'm afraid my heart is going to fucking shatter.

"Talk to me, darlin'. What's going on?"

"I think I'm—" I sputter and sniffle. "I think I'm falling in love—"

"I know," he whispers, pulling me in as close as he can.

A laugh bubbles up from my throat as I look up at his own red-rimmed eyes. He seems so fragile, and suddenly I'm terrified of breaking him. My body is screaming to back out of this, to shut up and tell him I didn't mean it, but the look on his face keeps me rooted to the ground.

"You know?"

I don't mean for my words to sound so pathetic, but I'm hanging on by a thread right now, and it's all I can do to keep myself together.

"Yeah." His voice is soft and soothing. "I love you, Imogen. I've been in love with you for a while, and I know you love me too."

The flood of relief that washes through me is quickly overpowered by fear. I can't even catch a break from my own anxiety for a second.

"Roman, I'm afraid that the deeper we get into this, the more it's going to hurt when..." I trail off, my breath catching in my chest as I hold back a sob.

"When what?"

"When everyone finds out."

He rocks me gently from side to side.

"Whatever happens and whoever finds out, nothing between us is going to change. I won't give you up."

"How can you promise that?" I ask, my voice trembling. "That nothing's going to change?"

He can say all of these lovely things, but when push comes to shove, will it even be something he can control?

"I don't know for sure what will happen, I just know there has to be some kind of solution, and that we'll find it. Together."

After we got back from the ranch, when we decided to jump into this with both feet, I started looking into those potential solutions. There wasn't much help on the university website. Of course they wouldn't have a whole page devoted to what to do if you're fucking a professor, but after digging around online and reading some personal accounts, I found that most people in our position either split up, get fired, or quit.

"How long have you known you loved me?"

"A while, I think," he says softly. "I was so fucking scared. I was scared you'd reject me, and I was scared that this was all happening too fast and it was getting out of control, but... I couldn't stop feeling what I was feeling."

"It's annoying, right?"

Roman's laugh is so warm it's like crawling underneath a duvet at the end of a long day.

"Stay with me tonight. I'll make you pancakes and pack you lunch in the morning."

"We'll have to swing by my place. I'll tell Logan I'm going to see my *boyfriend*."

"Alright, perfect. And I'll hide in the bushes like a creep."

"Aww, you're my favorite creep," I giggle.

I kiss him on the cheek, full of relief that the world didn't fall apart. We didn't fall apart.

"We're going to be okay," he assures me. "You know that, right?"

We pack up our stuff, toss out our trash, and get back into the car. As he turns the engine over, I absentmindedly check my phone, noticing an email notification from the university.

Dear Imogen Flynn,
We are pleased to inform you that your application to the Aspen Sociology Conference next month has been accepted.

I start screaming with excitement, not even bothering with the rest of the email. I just keep reading the word accepted over and over again. This is everything I've been working toward. I busted my ass on that application and it paid off.

But as quickly as my joy overwhelmed me, a sobering realization creeps in.

I can't even call my dad.

It's a cruel thought that instantly makes my eyes sting.

"What's wrong?" Roman asks.

"I got into the conference," I whisper, showing him the email.

I can almost hear my dad cheering for me, just like he did when I got into NYU. He was so excited, he took me out for ice cream to celebrate and told me how proud he was. We listened to Tom Petty and talked for hours.

"What's wrong, then?"

I burst into tears, covering my face with both hands as Roman wraps his arms around me.

"I wish he was here," I weep into his chest, struggling to get the words out. "My dad."

"Maybe he is," Roman whispers, brushing a hand against my cheek.

"If you say something cheesy that makes me cry again, I'm walking home."

That feeling of grief, something I assumed we shared, has always been so sharp and painful to me, but it's clear that Roman's managed to find some level of comfort in it I've never been able to grasp.

"Do you remember when I told you about the eulogy I read for Christa? About how people never really leave, their energy just spreads out into the universe?"

Roman smiles.

"He's here, Imogen, and I know he'd be damn proud of you."

CHAPTER THIRTY-FOUR

delicate

ROMAN

ASPEN COLORADO

DAY ONE OF THE ASPEN SOCIOLOGICAL CONFERENCE

Cross country skiing is hell.

Cross country skiing after I've eaten ten tacos is even worse.

My legs hurt, my hip hurts, and my back is killing me. I want to shove Logan's face into some yellow snow for this, but I keep pushing forward out of spite instead.

"You know, this isn't so bad," Imogen grunts. "I'm starting to get the hang of it."

"I don't know," I sigh. "It feels more like a big long fucking *walk* than skiing."

"What's the problem?" Logan asks, gesturing to the scenery. "Look at all of this! If we were going downhill, we'd just be zooming past all of it!"

"You mean falling past it."

Abi chuckles, holding up her camera in front of the group and snapping a photo. I'm pretty sure I've never looked angrier in a picture before, but she's beaming.

Today was the first full day at the conference. Logan presented in the morning, and Abi in the afternoon, with both Imogen and my presentations relegated to the next day. The four of us got in late last night, but it turned out the hotel we expected to be staying at was overbooked, so we were taken to a large four-bedroom cabin about 15 minutes from the resort. By snowmobile, of course.

Logan, of course, wanted to ski back tonight. Just a quick trip, he said. Now I'm stuck in a snow suit that makes me look like the goddamn Michelin Man, locked in a purgatory of never-ending cross country skiing. It was pretty fun at first, but now the sound of ice crunching beneath our poles is starting to drive me crazy.

That said, as much as my knees and legs hate Logan right now, I have to admit the setting is gorgeous. Lush trees and soft white powder surround us, and you can see little cabins with their windows lit up in the distance.

Everything looks so cozy and tranquil.

"So, where's this lookout you wanted to see?" I ask, pausing next to our fearless leader.

Logan points up ahead with his pole, gesturing vaguely into the distance.

"Guy at the conference said that's a great spot, right near that clearing there. Claimed you can see the entire resort."

We head toward a small group of trees, Abi and Logan in front while Imogen and I trail behind. She's still a little unsteady and awkward with her ski poles, so I rest my hand on her back to keep her from accidentally tripping over them.

"Thanks," she laughs, her cheeks pink.

Imogen's been so focused on preparing for her presentation for the last month that we haven't had much time to spend together, mostly just texting or FaceTiming when we can. Needless to say, I've been itching for some physical contact.

When we thought we were getting a hotel, we had all these elaborate plans to sneak around, maybe even have dinner somewhere private. But with her room just above mine in a tiny cabin, it's been hard for us to have any physical contact. Last night, we talked on the phone until we both fell asleep. Today, we couldn't stop texting each other, even when we were in the same room.

It's been hell trying to keep my hands off of her. When we were walking to get lunch, I almost reached out for her out of habit.

"Oh! I see it!" Logan's excited yelp brings me right back to the present. "Just up there!"

We glide through the snow for another few minutes before finally making it to the clearing that Logan was talking about. I look up at the sky in all of its vastness to see a beautiful shade of lavender, bleeding into the pink and orange swirl of clouds. It's the color of Imogen's hair, as if it was painted into the sky with gigantic brush strokes.

We take a bit of time, everyone snapping pictures of the sunset before Logan puts his hands on his hips, staring at us through massive ski goggles. He looks like a mad scientist as he takes off his hat, shaking out his shaggy hair.

"You guys wanna head back?"

"*God* yes!" Imogen calls out. "I need a fucking bottle of wine and some Advil. My legs are killing me."

"You actually shouldn't mix Ibuprofen with alcohol," Logan cuts in. "It's bad for—"

"The last time I checked, you were a doctor of *philosophy*, dude."

"It doesn't mean I don't know how to read the back of the bottle, dipshit."

Logan laughs, giving his sister a shove, and she yelps, stumbling back into me. I grab her by the waist, letting out a nervous chuckle as she turns around. I can't tell if it's just the winter chill that's making her cheeks flame or if it's me.

"Are you okay?" I remove my hands the second she nods, glancing over at Logan with a scowl. "Be nice to your sister, jackass."

"She started it!" He turns to Imogen, flexing his bicep. "Sorry, just getting too buff in the gym, I guess."

"You look like Gumby's anemic cousin," she spits, flipping him off.

I hear the sound of a camera shutter from off to the side, and turn to find Abi beaming.

"Aww! Look at that! It's like you're a little family! I'm printing this and putting it in my office."

Logan puts his hat back on, grinning from ear to ear.

"Alright, sibling-abuse out of the way, you fuckers wanna get drunk and play the board games I found in that creepy old basement?"

"Sure," Abi replies. "So long as you promise they're not haunted."

Logan laughs as we start to trek in the direction of the cabin.

"Haunted?"

"Yeah, like Evil Dead."

"That was the Necronomicon in the basement," Logan chuckles. "I thought you knew your horror movies!"

"That all sounds great, but before we get into evil board games, how about I cook something up?" I ask, shooting Imogen a knowing look. "Logan shouldn't be losing on an empty stomach, after all."

Logan lets out a dismissive snort, smacking me gently with one of his poles as he passes me.

"*Wow!* Okay, I see how it is, Burke. I'll kick your ass any time, any day."

"Bring it on, pipe cleaner."

The cabin is beautiful, with four bedrooms and two bathrooms split between two floors. The downstairs is all open-concept, with a kitchen, a living room, and a small dining area that I've set up for dinner. It's softly lit with a bit of a rustic feel, the only exception being the ridiculous crystal chandelier hanging from the ceiling.

I feel totally at home in this kitchen, pouring white wine into the pan to deglaze it and make a sauce. I'm cooking chicken breast and roasted vegetables, something simple and warm after being outside for so long. For dessert, I've got some of those mini cinnamon buns that come in a tube. All I need to do is make some more cream cheese icing. They never give you enough in those store bought containers.

Logan tosses the veggies in olive oil and seasoning before taking out a baking tray. Behind us, I can hear Imogen and Abi laughing from the couch, both of them clutching big glasses of red wine. Every so often, I catch Imogen's eye and she tosses me the tiniest flirtatious glance. It feels like the dinner party all over again.

"I'm so glad Frankie got us this cabin," Logan sighs.

"Yeah, turns out it's pretty great."

Except that I would have been just fine eating room service and having a hell of a lot more privacy. Somehow, Imogen and I will have to find a way to make it work, because there's no way I can stay away from her all weekend.

I know myself, and I am not a strong man, not when it comes to her.

"How's your presentation coming?"

"Finished," I reply, glancing over at Logan and panicking as he lifts the bottle of olive oil like he's going to pour it directly on the pan. "Hey, hey! Parchment paper."

"The oil will make sure it won't stick," he replies.

"Yeah, and then that shit's gonna be swimming in grease," I fire back. "Parchment paper, Flynn."

"Abi! Roman's bullying me!" Logan calls over his shoulder.

I roll my eyes.

"Abi, do you even need me to list the dozen things he's done wrong, or...?"

"I believe the chef!" Abi calls back, her laughter ringing through the cabin.

Logan frowns, muttering to himself under his breath, but grabs the parchment paper and spreads it out on the tray anyway.

"So, did you enjoy the first day?" He asks.

"Yeah, it's been, uh... it's good. Informative."

It's not really a lie, even if I've spent more time in the presentations texting Imogen than actually paying attention to the material. That big brain of mine doesn't stand a chance when we're in the same room. I'm surprised I can even focus on cooking.

"Yeah? Because you've been on your phone. A lot." He tries to ruffle my hair but I smack him away. "Oh my god, is it the girlfriend?"

I exhale, glancing out the window at the snow falling in thick white flakes.

"I need to add some butter," I tell him. "Make a cream sauce."

"Look, you're distracted right now," he laughs.

I shake my head, walking to the fridge to grab a big block of butter.

"Look, it's not like I wanted to be here," I tell him. "Frankie put me up to it."

"Oh, I know," Logan replies. "Because I asked him to."

I raise a brow in irritation, but Logan only shrugs in response.

"You're up for review, Roman! You haven't published anything in a while and the clock is ticking. This shows that you're engaged with your work, at the very least."

I want to tell him that I've been checked out for so long that the thought of failing a review doesn't scare me anymore.

"You're meddling."

"Of course I am! Because I give a shit!"

Logan grins, clapping me on the shoulder.

"What's going on? Besides the obvious, I mean."

I stare at him, blinking as the butter melts in the pan.

"What's the obvious?"

"I mean Christa, and everything you've been dealing with."

Logan talks about my grief like it's a fresh wound and not the dark cloud that's been looming over me for the last few years. He'd have no way of knowing that I've managed to start moving past it, to some small extent at least.

"I don't know," I sigh. "I guess I'm just working my way back to the person I used to be."

Even if he doesn't really exist anymore. Not in the same way.

"You know you can talk to me, right?" Logan asks. "I've been worried about you since you came back from sabbatical. It feels like your heart isn't in it anymore."

"It is," I retort. "I love teaching, but you know how exhausting this job gets. All the red tape and bureaucratic bullshit we have to deal with. It's not just a job, it's... draining."

And I think it's the reason why Christa felt like she couldn't talk to me about everything that was going on inside her head. I was married to her, sure, but my work was ever present. Because that's what was drilled into me from graduate school: above all else, my research was the most important.

But now that old identity is starting to fracture, and the more Imogen helps me to rediscover the pieces of me that I've locked away, the more I realize that I want something else. I want simplicity, I want passion, I want her.

"You know, sometimes I feel like I'm just moving on autopilot in this job."

"And how long have you felt that way?"

"Since she died." My voice is tight as Logan loads the veggies into the oven. "Is that normal?"

"I think grief is different for everyone. I was just talking to Iggy the other day about this guy she's seeing, and how she hasn't been letting anyone in because she's afraid she'll lose them."

Part of me wants to ask what she said about me, but that would open up an entire can of bullshit that would ruin the weekend.

"There's no handbook for how to get through this shit– not really, anyway. We all cope in different ways and if you have to numb yourself out for a while, then that's something you have to do, but it doesn't stop me from being worried about you."

"You don't have to worry," I assure him. "I'll be okay. Just gotta get back on the horse."

Logan flashes me a small smile, and I can tell he doesn't believe me, but that's fine. He doesn't need to.

"Hey!" Abi calls from her spot on the couch. "How long until dinner's ready?"

"Yeah, we're starving!" Imogen echoes after her.

"Fifteen minutes, ladies! Logan, be a doll and refill their wine."

"When did I become the butler?" He scoffs.

"When you argued with me about the vegetables," I reply, elbowing him in the ribs. "Go on. Those ladies are dying of dehydration and you're just standing there."

Imogen grins at her brother, shaking her wine glass.

"Come on, Jeeves. Don't be stingy with your pours, either!"

"I take it back," Logan grumbles. "This whole group cabin thing was a terrible idea."

I smile as he grabs the wine bottle and saunters toward the girls, pouring them both generous glasses. Amidst the laughter and the playful ribbings, I catch Imogen's attention for just a moment, the loving look in her eyes setting my heart on fire all over again before she quickly looks away.

"I don't know," I mutter to myself, quietly plating the dish. "Maybe it's not so bad after all."

CHAPTER THIRTY-FIVE

ROMAN

It's a couple hours after dinner and we're locked into a ruthless game of Monopoly, drinking prosecco out of tiny mugs in front of a crackling fire. I don't know how many bottles we've torn through, but it feels like I haven't stopped laughing for ten minutes. I've been so isolated for so many years, I forgot how much fun I can have if I just let my guard down.

Logan's been trying to buy my properties off of me, his proposed deals getting shittier by the minute, but I'm paying more attention to Imogen, all pink-cheeked and bright eyed in her giant NYU sweater. As I watch her giggle at one of Abi's jokes, I just can't help myself, reaching into my pocket and pulling out my phone.

> ROMAN: I need you.

I send the text without even considering the fact that her phone is right in front of her, face up on the table for everyone to see. Clearly I've had one too many drinks.

Imogen's eyes flick toward her phone and she turns it over with lightning speed, just as Abi gets to her feet.

"I'm going to get our big real estate mogul some water, he needs hydration."

"I have hydration!" Logan wails, lifting his mug of wine. "I'm good!"

"You *are not!*" Abi laughs, heading for the cupboards.

Logan rolls his eyes and goes back to hunting through his properties, frowning as he counts his cards.

"I thought I had more than this."

"You've been selling them, pal," I laugh. "You traded me one for a bottle of wine, remember?"

Abi places a big glass of ice water in front of him, patting him on the shoulder.

"Drink up, Doc."

He stares up at her, pure adoration etched into his features.

"You know what you are, Doctor King?"

"What?" She giggles.

"You're the *goddamn King* of the Doctors!"

Abi ruffles his hair, messing it up even more than it already is.

"You need to slow down, Flynn."

"I can't slow down," he slurs. "I'm about to pull off the best real estate deal in the history of... history!"

"Oh, really?" Abi laughs. "Let's see it, then! Show the class."

He leans over the table, knocking over some of the game pieces as he points at me.

"I'll give you the keys to my car if I can have Park Place." The moment I start laughing, he pulls his keys out of his pocket, jingling them in my face. "Roman, are you listening? You could be the proud new owner of *my* Jaguar."

One of his eyes is drooping and he can barely keep focused on me, much less point in my direction. I scoff and sip my drink as the girls exchange an eye roll at Logan's expense.

"You know, for an Irishman, you're really shit at handling your liquor," I chuckle.

"That's not true," Logan slurs. "Abi, tell him how many beers I had in Seattle."

"Four," Abi replies, stone-faced.

"You hear that Burke, four!" He bellows, smacking his hand on the table.

Logan's always been a wild drunk— not violent or anything, just incredibly talkative and easily excitable.

Like a puppy.

And then he usually passes out.

Also like a puppy.

"Now, car for Park Place. C'mon, Burke. Don't bitch out on me in my hour of need."

"Logan, don't do something you're gonna regret in the morning!" Imogen groans, flinging a card at him. "Here, you can have Baltic Avenue if you leave Roman alone."

We clink glasses and Logan snorts, pointing at the two of us.

"I don't like that you're friends," he mumbles, the words barely coherent. "I can't have two of you tag teaming me."

I look over to see Abi staring at us with a gleam in her eyes, like she's trying to figure something out. I do my best to ignore it, keeping my attention on Logan.

"Well, it's hard not to when you get hammered off of three glasses of wine."

It's only another half hour or so before we're in the final stages of the game.

Imogen's swimming in cash from people landing on her hotels, even after gifting her brother another property or two to keep him solvent.

Abi's laughing at everything while she miscounts money, wondering out loud why she's missing five hundred dollars every couple minutes.

Logan's broke and mortgaging houses, still insistent that he can win the game until he lands in jail one final time, slumping over and letting out a defeated groan.

"I hate this fucking game! It's haunted by the basement curse!"

"No, you're just so drunk you can barely think." Abi scoops up the dice and rolls for her turn, landing on one of my properties with a grimace as she forks over twenty-five bucks. "What do you guys wanna do tomorrow?"

"There's that party," Logan mumbles, lifting his head.

Great. Another event where I have to keep my hands to myself.

"Party?" Abi asks. "I don't remember anything about a party."

"Yeah, some kinda… networking thing for the faculties." Logan finishes the last of his drink. "I can't remember the details, but it's open bar."

"Open bar? Really?" Abi asks. "That's generous for a conference."

"Well, it makes it easier for a bunch of socially awkward nerds to talk to people."

"Speaking for yourself there, dude?"

Imogen snickers as I roll the dice, landing on Chance.

"Hey, at least my nerdiness wasn't genetic," Logan fires back. "You wore orthotics and coke bottle glasses until tenth grade."

"I'm going to smother you in your sleep," she growls.

"Okay, okay!" Abi waves her arms. "That's enough fighting! You guys wanna go to this super-cool new party tomorrow?"

"I don't know," I murmur, flipping over the Chance card.

Go to jail.

"Yes!" Logan bellows. "Welcome to the slammer, Burke! We can be cellmates!"

"Let's not make that a reality, shall we?"

"Yeah, good point. You snore, I'd shank you in a second," Logan snickers.

"Oh, please, you wouldn't last *half a second* in a fight with me."

He flips me the bird, and suddenly I can feel Imogen's hand on my shoulder.

"Brutal, cowboy."

I bristle at the name, my heart pounding.

"What did you call him?" Logan snorts.

Abi perks up and that look in her eyes makes me nervous.

"Was it cowboy?" She laughs.

Imogen's cheeks turn bright pink and she lets out a nervous chuckle, removing her hand as my body stiffens. Now we're even when it comes to fuckups.

"Uh, Roman and I were talking one day after class and he said he used to ride horses, so... I started calling him cowboy. In class. It's just a dumb joke we have."

She laughs, a little too loudly.

Abi's eyes volley between the two of us, her suspicion clearly evident now, but I stay quiet. She doesn't have much proof, and what she does have, I can write off as friendly banter between colleagues. As far as anyone knows that's all it is.

"I forgot about your whole growing up on a ranch thing," Logan mutters, laying his head down on the gameboard.

"Well, I don't talk about it that much. It was a long time ago."

"So, did you, like, work on the ranch?" Abi asks. "How come I've never heard about this before?"

I roll my eyes, my nerves fried from the possibility that this little nickname could be our undoing.

"My dad was a bull rider and my uncle was a rodeo clown. They toured together for years, but they always came back to our ranch in Montana. That's where I grew up."

"A bull rider?! How did I not know about this?" Abi laughs.

"Roman's very secretive about his rodeo-clown ancestry." Logan's eyes go wide with a sudden realization. "If I run down to the basement and get some rope, can you lasso something?"

"Yeah, you," I fire back, kicking him gently under the table. "I'll drag your ass all the way to your room. It's the only way you'll get a good night's sleep."

Logan makes a face at me as Imogen rolls the dice.

"How come you ended up going into academia then?" She asks. "It seems like you really took to life on the ranch."

I've never really figured out the answer to this question. I was always good in school, where the rest of my family never made it beyond a tenth grade education. To be fair, they didn't need to. They were smart as hell at what they did: raising animals, keeping the ranch running, and making sure we always had money in the bank and food on the table.

"I don't know," I sigh. "I think part of me always wanted to see what the world was like beyond the ranch, even from a young age. When I told my dad I got into a PhD program, he was so proud; said I'd be the first doctor in the family. I think he always sort of knew I would never stay in Montana."

"Wow," Abi sighs. "I thought me being a secret Canadian was cool, this is so much better."

"You're Canadian?" Imogen gasps, making a big show of covering her mouth in surprise.

"Yeah." She nods, sipping her wine. "I grew up in Ontario. I actually, uh... I met Logan at a conference in Toronto before I got the job at EBU."

She blushes, shaking her head.

"Sorry, whose turn was it?"

"Uh, Roman's, I think," Imogen replies, sliding me the dice.

We go around the board a few more times, the conversation fading bit by bit until I decide I've had enough. I need them to go to bed so that I can get my hands on Imogen. It's been hell not being able to touch her all damn day.

"Well, I'm ready to call it," I sigh. "Is there a big loser sign I'm supposed to wear or something?"

Logan tosses his cards down, nodding while trying not to pass out.

"Nah, I forgot to make one for you." He yawns, stretching his long arms over his head. "I'm gonna go to bed."

"Same," Abi agrees.

She starts to pack up and I reach for her hand.

"Don't worry about it, I've got this. Go to bed. And take him with you."

Abi heads for the stairs, catching Logan just before he trips and gives himself a concussion.

"Come on, drunky. Let's go."

Imogen and I begin cleaning up the game, and tossing out our empty bottles as Logan and Abi disappear upstairs. I hear a bedroom door shut and take the leap, dropping the money in my hand and moving in for a kiss. I can hear Abi and Logan laughing upstairs as Imogen rubs her nose against mine.

"Tonight?"

I'm exhausted, but I'd be an idiot not to take advantage of the fact that our bunkmates are not only sleeping upstairs, but probably too wasted to even notice what we're doing down here.

"Wait until they're asleep and then slip back down here. You're in charge."

CHAPTER THIRTY-SIX

volcano

IMOGEN

Well, my desire for a good dicking has finally overpowered my ravenous need for academic validation. I should be thinking about my presentation tomorrow, but right now, all I can stare at is the clock, counting down the minutes until I get to fuck that gorgeous man.

I squeeze my thighs together and grab my phone to text him for what has to be the hundredth time. I never used to be this clingy, but I guess love changes you.

> IMOGEN: Can I fuck you now?

> ROMAN: Ten more minutes. Pretend to go to the kitchen first, get a drink of water.

> IMOGEN: Chill out, Columbo. We're not planning the perfect murder.

> ROMAN: We still have to be discreet, and Columbo didn't plan murders, he solved them. Show Peter Falk some respect.

I groan, rolling onto my back with my phone clutched firmly in my hand. It's no different than us sneaking around the university, but now that we're in such close quarters, the tension has mounted to the point where I feel like I'm choking on it.

> IMOGEN: I've got something special for you tonight, cowboy.

I see three dots appear and then disappear a few times.

> ROMAN: As long as it doesn't wake anyone up, I'm game.

Sighing, I pull up the picture Abi took of us this afternoon when we were skiing. Fuck, I've got it so bad it's disgusting. It feels like this is the first time I'm falling in love. *Really* falling in love. The kind of shit you see in movies. I glance up at the clock again. It's been an hour. Logan and Abi have to be asleep by now.

"Fuck this," I growl, tossing the blankets off of me.

I grab two spools of rope, some lube, and a vibrating cock ring out of my bag. Then, I change into a pair of lacy black underwear, before shrugging on a silk robe and nothing else. I leave my phone on the bed and stick my head out the door, glancing around. It's pitch black and all that surrounds me is a crushing silence, accompanied by the lightest rattling of the wind against the windows.

I creep past Logan's room, pressing my ear against the door to listen for any sign that he's awake. Nothing. Good. I slip down the hall toward the staircase, only stopping in my tracks when I see Abi's bedroom door wide open. I feel my blood freeze. There's no way I can make it past without her seeing me. I stand stock-still for a minute, and then another, straining for any sound to let me know if it's safe to pass. But there's nothing. So I creep a little closer, and closer still, finally getting up the courage to peek inside.

It's... empty?

My eyes dart toward Logan's room and back again, a grin creeping onto my lips.

Oh my god, I knew it.

Now I just have to remember to tell Roman when this is all over.

I sneak down the stairs until I reach the kitchen, and run the sink for a few seconds to complete the ruse. When I turn around he's already standing in the doorway in nothing but a pair of charcoal sweatpants, his eyes falling on the rope that's dangling from my fingers.

Roman silently beckons me to follow him to his room. It's a cozy space with a large bed and minimal furnishings. His laptop sits lonely on the desk, his luggage resting neatly against the wall. Everything in here smells like him— his cologne, his sweat— even the sheets that are rumpled from a restless night.

I set everything down on the dresser and slip off my robe, Roman's lips parting as he stares at me like a man half-starved and taking a step toward me.

I step back with a taunting look on my face.

I want him to work for it a little.

"I'm in charge tonight, cowboy. Remember?"

"Of course I do."

There's so much confidence in his voice. I want to draw this out, but it's taking a hell of a lot of self-control not to leap onto him and fuck him right on the floor.

"I want to have some fun with you before I ride that big cock." I gesture to his desk, my voice just barely above a whisper. "Take your pants off and bring that chair over here."

I can see the full body shiver rushing through him, knowing every moment is a struggle for him not to grab me and slam me up against the wall. Roman kicks off his sweats, grabbing the chair and dragging it toward the desk. He sits down, placing his hands on his thighs and waits for instructions.

I'm getting turned on just watching his dick throb.

"What a good boy you are."

I pluck the cord of rope from the dresser and begin to wrap it around him, securing his hands behind the chair to immediately remove any sense of control he's managed to hold on to. As I tighten the knot, I lean down, brushing my lips against his ear.

"Do you remember the coffee shop? What you did to me?"

I can almost feel the hairs on the back of his neck stand on end as he shifts his weight around, testing his bindings.

"How could I forget?" He purrs. "You were such a desperate little slut, squirming in your seat the entire time."

I grasp his hair, forcing his head back.

"And now you're *my* desperate little slut, cowboy."

I walk to the dresser, grabbing the lube and cock ring and getting on my knees. He watches with rapt attention as I squeeze some lube out onto his cock, and he lets out an excited whimper as I spread it with *long* strokes.

"Oh my *god*."

"Shhh. We're supposed to be quiet, remember? Besides, I haven't even started yet."

I slide the ring over the head of his cock, holding it there for a moment. It's kind of shaped like one of those shitty costume-jewelry rings, but with a rectangle at the top instead of a cheap gem. Honestly, it looks kind of ridiculous, but looks aren't everything. I roll it down to the base, clicking a little button on the side to start the vibrations, and wait for him to adjust to the new sensation.

"Is it uncomfortable at all?" I ask, stroking his thighs.

"No," he groans. "Feels nice."

"Good. Strawberry's the word if you want me to stop, okay?"

He nods.

"Now, you're going to keep your eyes on me while I see what this thing can do, and don't you *dare* look away. I want to see what it looks like when you're right on the edge."

With a devilish grin I press the button again, toggling to more intense vibrations. It's not loud enough to get us caught, but when Roman's mouth drops open, I'm worried *he* might make up the difference.

"Just relax, cowboy." I flick the tip of his cock with my tongue. "I've got you."

I wrap my lips around him, sucking in gentle pulses until I can feel his legs begin to shake. The vibration against my mouth is strange at first, but after a while, I start to get used to it. Roman's breathing is shaky and his body rigid, and my panties are soaked just watching him get overcome with desire.

Before things go too far I release him, licking my fingers and gliding them along his perineum as he rocks back and forth, trying desperately to fuck my mouth.

"What do you usually jerk off to?" I ask.

"Porn."

"Be more specific," I giggle, tilting my head quizzically.

"There's this one— ah, *fuck*," he groans as I squeeze his cock.

"Concentrate," I purr. "Eyes on me."

I see sweat gathering on his forehead as he swallows. He's trying his hardest not to come right now.

"I couldn't see her face, but she used him like a toy. And the way she came..."

His hips buck, and I take the opportunity to turn up the vibrations even further.

"I want you to use me like that," he grunts. "I want your hand around my throat. I want to come so deep inside you that it's dripping out for days."

I need him. It's like a hunger that I can't satiate any way besides crawling on top of him, and fucking him until I'm in pieces.

"You would want that, you fucking slut."

His voice is nearly breaking beneath the weight of his desire, but he never takes his eyes off of me.

"Please, darlin'."

He lets out another raspy moan as I get to my feet and begin to straddle him, grinding my pussy against his shaft. My body is desperate, rolling over him like a wave as we breathe together, electricity crawling up inside me until it's sitting at the back of my neck and wrapped around my throat.

"I'm gonna come if you don't s– stop."

"You don't do a damn thing without my permission."

In that moment, I can feel what must be every muscle in his body clench like a fist, but I refuse to let up. I continue to torment him, every roll of my hips bleeding into pure fucking ecstasy. Just when I feel like I might fall apart, I stop, carefully climbing off of him while trying to hide my shaking legs.

He can't know how close I was.

He's trying so hard to fight his body's natural impulses.

"We can't have you coming before you've filled me up, can we?"

I turn off the toy to give him a little bit of relief, and his body slumps and he looks like he could cry.

Good.

I move behind him, slowly undoing the knot I made at the back of the chair.

"I think I'll give you a reward."

"What kind of reward?" He rasps.

"It's no fun if I tell you. Maybe we'll play another game."

As I free him from his bindings, he gets to his feet.

"Wha–"

In one swift motion, he grabs me by the waist and tosses me onto the bed.

"No more fucking games," he growls, grabbing my panties and tearing them right off of me.

I gasp as his eyes meet with mine, a wicked grin spreading over his face.

"Pretty good, huh?"

He glides his mouth down my body, wet hot kisses littering my skin until he reaches the inside of my thigh and bites down hard. I clamp one hand over my mouth, struggling to keep as quiet as I can while he soothes the newly formed bite-mark with his tongue.

He pushes my legs wide apart as he groans into my cunt, lapping at my clit. The feeling of his stubble against my thighs, the heat from his lips and the way his tongue swirls around my swollen bud makes me feel like I'm going to dissolve into the fucking mattress.

Roman always makes sure I'm taken care of. I saw it that first night, his eagerness to please— not just for his own pleasure, but mine. The sex was good back then, but it's evolved into something so much better. I think there must be something about sex when you're in love— really in love, and it's an unspoken connection that I've only ever shared with him.

One that I only ever *want* to share with him.

He slides two fingers inside me, pressing up against my G-spot and stroking until I'm a squirming mess.

"Faster," I beg. "Please– oh, *fuck*."

I love the way he seems to have committed every inch of my body to memory, knowing exactly where to touch and lick me. He even knows how to graze my clit with his teeth, just a *little*, to send me into a frenzy.

I've got one hand gripping his hair for dear life while I tease my nipples with the other, twisting at my piercings until I'm teetering on the edge between pleasure and pain. I lift my head, spotting Roman grinding his hips against the mattress. His perfect ass flexes and the muscles in his back ripple. Just the sight of him makes me want to explode.

"Come for me," he moans, burying his face in my cunt one final time.

I squeeze my eyes shut, grabbing a pillow as I obey, and shoving it onto my face so hard it's smothering.

But I don't care. Logan *cannot* hear this.

Roman fucks me all the way through it before slowly sliding his fingers out, leaving me feeling hollow inside. I can feel him pull the pillow away from my face, and I open my eyes to his beautiful smile as he dips his head down for a kiss.

"Ride me."

We scramble to swap positions, his voice so deep it makes me shiver. He sits up, back against the headboard as he turns the cock ring back on. I climb on top of him, gripping his shoulder and easing myself down slowly. And there's that stretching sensation, that beautiful, burning pain that takes just a few moments to get used to until it melts into pure bliss.

"Take your time, sweet thing."

Roman rests both hands on my hips, slowly guiding me the rest of the way down until I've taken all of him, and I'm rewarded with soft kisses all the way along my jaw.

"That's a good girl."

I sit still for a moment, relishing the feeling, but it's not long before I find myself rocking my hips again. Warmth and pressure builds as my clit grinds against the cock ring, still swollen and sensitive, but I know there's still a little ways to go before my body reaches its limit.

Roman watches me, lips parted and curled into a little half smile. I smile back, trying not to whimper when the head of his cock hits the spot that makes my toes curl. My breath hitches as he grabs my wrist, placing my hand on his chest, right above his heart. It's pounding just as hard as mine is.

"From the second I saw you, I knew I wouldn't be able to get you out of my head," he whispers.

For some reason, the words make me tear up.

Because it's him, this man I planned to avoid.

A man who was damaged and broken, just like me.

And a man who's found the courage to begin to heal.

"I love you, darlin'."

My climax builds and builds until all other thoughts and sounds are drowned out around me. I don't know how hard I'm fucking him, I just know there's no way I'm keeping my voice down anymore.

Roman's arms wrap around me, pressing my body tightly against his, and when I topple over the edge, I have to bite down on his shoulder again just to keep myself still. He grunts and begins to buck up into me, fucking me even harder as he chases his own release.

"I love you too," I whimper as little aftershocks of my climax ripple through me.

Roman guides my body, one hand underneath my ass, keeping up the pace until I hear him groan, his cock flexing as he comes.

The two of us match our haggard breaths as we come back down to earth, laying together as he strokes my hair.

"Stay for a while?"

And I do. I stay there, pressed against him, kissing each and every little mark I've made on his body. I'd stay forever if I could, needing no one and nothing else.

No matter the risks.

CHAPTER THIRTY-SEVEN

running up that hill

IMOGEN

My laptop is sitting on the podium, my presentation on the big screen, demanding everyone's attention— and the best part? There are people in the audience, waiting for *me* to speak.

This is it, it's my big fucking moment.

I was up at the crack of dawn; I prepped my notes, picked a cute outfit, and spent half the morning fighting Logan for the bathroom because I needed to do my hair. Despite his hangover, he was in pretty good spirits, even helping Roman make pancakes before we headed over to the conference center.

I'm shaking, the lavender pantsuit I picked out already starting to suffocate me.

Why did I choose vintage polyester?

I reach into a pocket and pull out my inhaler, taking a puff and holding my breath. The last thing I need to do is give myself an asthma attack, like the day I presented my master's thesis. I wound myself up so tight that my lungs decided to turn on me, and my professor had to take me to the hospital. I was so embarrassed I never wanted to show my face on campus again.

My phone buzzes.

ROMAN: Kick some ass and take no prisoners up there.

He finished his presentation earlier in the day and he's sitting in the audience now. He seemed so casual about it before he got onstage, but when he was up there it was almost robotic. It was like his heart wasn't really in it.

I hadn't thought about it before, but he's probably done so many of these that this must be just part of the job for him by now. I've read through his publication history: he's written over thirty papers, co-edited five books, and given tons of talks, but all that stopped after he lost his wife. It makes sense. Grief can take so much from you, your passions, your hobbies, your routines. Some people throw themselves into their work, others just go numb, or sink into a deep depression.

About a year after my dad died, I was coming out of the subway and got hit with a massive whiff of the exact same cologne he was wearing when he passed. I thought I was having a panic attack; it felt like I was reliving his death all over again. Turns out smell is one of our most powerful senses when it comes to memory.

"You can do this," Logan tells me, pulling me from my thoughts with a gentle shake. "I believe you."

"You mean you believe *in* me," I laugh.

Logan blinks, brows knit together. Despite the long shower and painkillers, he looks like he's going to puke up the pancakes he ate this morning.

"Isn't that what I said?"

"Dude, you are *hung over*," I chuckle, patting him on the shoulder.

His eyes are rimmed red, sweat constantly beading on his brow no matter how many times he wipes it away. I feel like I should be able to see the alcohol fumes wafting off of him.

"Yeah, really? Those Advil were like throwing pennies at an armored truck, but I'm here. I'm going to be here for you the whole time. Right here."

"Unless he's gotta throw up," Abi chimes in. "Then he'll be somewhere else, hopefully."

Logan ignores her, giving me a hug before the host begins to announce my presentation. I can barely process what he's saying, pulling my phone out of my pocket out of sheer habit.

Three missed texts that have all come in within the last couple of minutes.

PIPES: YOU'RE GONNA FUCKING KILL IT!

JAY: YOOOOO! Iggy! You got this!

MOM: I'm so proud of you, drink water, don't pass out, and remember to celebrate YOU. Shine bright, baby girl. Your dad would be SO proud of you right now. I know he's watching.

Before I can even think of replying to any of them, the host calls my name. Applause rings out and I step onto the stage, my heart in my throat. To a lot of attendees, this is just another lecture; something routine that they do every few months. But to me, it's a huge stepping stone.

I just have to get over the anxiety first.

"Hey, Iggy!" Logan shouts out from backstage. "Shine bright, kiddo!"

I have fifteen minutes to demonstrate what I know and what I plan to do with my dissertation. Even if I fumble words or have technical difficulties, it'll be fine. I know this paper inside and out.

My hands are cold, yet incredibly sweaty at the same time. Needles prick my throat. I glance down to see a bottle of water tucked beneath the podium, and I snatch it up before looking out at a sea of faces I don't recognize. As I scan the crowd, I spot Roman up front and I smile back nervously.

"Hi—" the mic whines a little and I take a step back, chuckling. "Look, I've been up here for five seconds and I'm already causing technical difficulties."

The little wave of laughter makes everything a bit easier, my anxiety beginning to melt away. The only thing that would make this better would be seeing my dad front and center.

I clear my throat, willing myself not to get misty eyed.

"My name is Imogen Flynn, I'm a PhD student at Emerald Bay University." I take a sip of water, steadying myself. "I'd actually like to start this presentation with a question: What do you think you know about kink or BDSM?"

I grab the remote, clicking to the slide with a big question mark and a pair of leather cuffs on it. It gets a few giggles but a surprising number of people raise their hands, and I pick a few out of the audience one by one.

"Whips," someone suggests.

There's another ripple of laughter and I click the remote and the word appears on the slide.

"Another one," I call, pointing to someone else.

"Bondage."

I click the remote again, the word popping up on the big screen behind me.

"Good one. This is like a kinky little game show."

That gets more giggles from the crowd as I take a few more suggestions.

Ropes, torture, sadism... all the standard responses I've come to expect doing this work.

"Most of the things you named can absolutely factor into kink, but the core of it is trust." I clear my throat, tapping my pocket to make sure my inhaler didn't fall out. "This paper is going to explore identity management, how people balance who they are in the kink space with who they are in their professional lives. I'll be speaking to participants with high profile and public facing jobs about the judgment they face, the ways in which they obscure their identity in online spaces, and how they walk the line between kink and their personal or professional lifestyles."

I sink into the presentation, alternating between discussing facts and using small anecdotes from other papers and theses I've written. I've been working in this area since my bachelor's degree, so I know the literature well. I don't think I stumble or forget anything, but even if I did, who gives a shit? It doesn't have to be perfect, but it should be fun. Today, I'm giving myself some grace.

I go over every detail of my project, spending a little extra time on my methodology and ethics sections, going through the finer details and what I hope to accomplish. I watch as people check their phones, slip in and out to take calls, or go to the bathroom, but not Roman.

He doesn't look away for a second.

When I get to the end of the presentation, I want nothing more than to run straight into his arms. Knowing I can't is a lot more heartbreaking than I'd care to admit. I field a few questions about methodology and ethics, which I handle with relative ease, before a hand goes up: a young woman with long blonde hair in a pink blazer.

"I'm just curious about what led you to this research topic?"

I glance off to the side and see Logan giving me the thumbs up. When I first expressed this interest as a thesis, I told him I had a friend who was involved in the scene. It wasn't necessarily untrue, but I wasn't ready to reveal just how personal it all was to me.

"I've been involved in kink for a couple of years now and I've always been interested in how people manage their identities— including me. Kink was a way to deal with a personal tragedy in my life. It gave me the space and freedom to tap into those emotions and work through them. It's a delicate balance, and I'm curious about how others approach it."

The woman nods, seemingly satisfied with my answer, and I glance around, catching another hand in the air. I recognize Dr. Simon Wallace, a man who taught a couple of my courses at NYU. He was the kind of professor who said that nobody would get an A in his class, and I could never forget the tiny round glasses that frame his large dark eyes.

"Stigma tends to be viewed, theoretically, as the outcome of a series of interpersonal encounters and attitudes. Do you think that people's attitudes toward sex and kink have become more open in recent years, and if so, how are you going to account for that in your work?"

It's clearly a softball question, especially from a professor who made two people cry when I was in his class, but there's no way I'm complaining.

"This audience just proved that their immediate responses to kink are primarily stereotypes surrounding BDSM, all of which can contribute to stigma. I'm hoping to look at people who are into things like consensual non-consent, a total power exchange, pet play, dumbification, all of these things that conjure specific negative images for people who aren't experienced in the scene."

"Thank you."

There's a pang of discomfort in my belly as his eyes glide up and down my body. I blow out a breath, shaking it off before moving on to take a few more questions. When my time is finally up, I exit the stage to respectable applause, and Logan is there to greet me.

"You fucking *killed it* out there!" He laughs, pulling me in for a big hug.

My body slumps with relief against his, all of my anxiety and adrenaline rushing out of me at the same time.

"It was surprisingly easy once I got into it."

"You handled those questions well," Abi chimes in.

"Very well," Roman says, beaming as he strides toward us. "You're a natural."

I have to ball my hands up into fists to keep from reaching for him, and judging by the look in his eye, he's thinking the same thing. I want him to take me in his arms and kiss me, but instead all I can say is...

"Thanks, Dr. Burke."

"Okay, we need to celebrate!" Logan exclaims. "Lunch is on me, and then tonight, we're doing that fundraiser."

Shit, I forgot about that. Another few hours where Roman and I have to keep our hands off each other.

"Oh! Before I forget, Iggy, I want to introduce you to some people who work for Oxford University Press."

"Wait... How fancy is this party?" Roman asks.

"Fancy enough for you to be wearing dress pants, cowboy," Logan quips, elbowing him in the ribs. "And no plaid shirts, you'll bring shame to the university!"

"You really wanna drink more after last night, Logan?" Abi asks.

"Hell no," he replies. "But I don't wanna stay cooped up in a cabin playing Monopoly again— and the three of *you* can get hammered and then *I* can listen to you puke all night while I'm cozy in my bed."

Logan leads us out of the conference room and down a long hallway toward the lounge. He and Abi quickly pull a little ways ahead, and I feel Roman snatch my wrist from behind, tugging me back into a small enclave just out of sight.

He gently pushes me up against the wall, grasping my chin and tipping my head up, those gorgeous eyes dancing over my face. It's killing me that we have to do this in secret. That he can't just grab me and lift me off the ground in front of everyone. This whole thing was fun at first, sneaking around and not taking things seriously, but after I told him I loved him, things got more intense.

Suddenly it all mattered so much more.

Suddenly there was so much more to lose.

"Hi," I whisper.

"Hey."

"This is risky, you know."

"I don't care. All that confidence made you look so goddamn sexy."

He nuzzles against me, the scent of his cologne bringing me back to last night in his room. I can still see the faint marks that the ropes left on his wrists.

"If you were teaching a class, I'd show up 15 minutes early and leave 15 minutes late just so I could spend some more time with you."

My whole face gets hot and I shove him away, trying to turn my head, but Roman holds it in place.

"So cheesy, Dr. Burke."

He smiles.

"You just bring something out in me, darlin'."

He presses his lips to mine and my heart races. If Logan doubles back and finds us, this is all over. That's the thing that terrifies me the most.

"Come on." He flicks his head toward the lounge. "Let's go before they get suspicious."

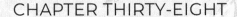

CHAPTER THIRTY-EIGHT

no surprises

ROMAN

I don't know what's worse, seeing her in that little black dress or not being able to bend her over the bar and spank that perfect ass until she's screaming my name.

I've had my fingers clenched around my whisky glass all night while Logan's been parading Imogen around, introducing her to academics to have conversations she's not even half-invested in.

"On a scale of one to ten, how much do you hate this?" Abi asks with a smirk.

"I'm about... a solid six." I take a sip of my drink. "What about you?"

"A three. Although if that was beer in Logan's hand and *not* a glass of seltzer, I'd probably be at a nine."

"He was that bad last night, huh?"

"He got up at least four times to throw up, kept waking me—" She catches herself, her cheeks red as she shakes her head. "I was afraid he'd aspirate or something. I just... I couldn't sleep knowing he was alone in the next room."

She stares at me, something like shame burning on her face.

"You're a good friend." I reach over and give her shoulder a squeeze. "He really does get a little rowdy sometimes, doesn't he?"

"I just don't want me taking care of him to be seen as something it's not." She looks down into her glass and sighs. "We really are just friends."

"Well, if you need someone to talk to about it, I'm not the best at giving advice but I am good at listening. Especially when it's one of my best pals."

"You mean bff," Abi corrects me.

"What the hell are you talking about?"

"Best friend forever."

"I'm not saying that," I grumble, finally spotting Imogen across the room.

"Language evolves, Roman."

"Yeah, but I don't."

Imogen's standing with a group of people, one of whom I recognize as a guy who asked some questions during her presentation. Instead of focusing on what she's trying to say now, though, he's not-so-subtly staring at her tits.

I can feel the grip on my glass tighten. It's so hard to stay focused. I want to be here for Abi, but this guy's so brazen it's pissing me off.

I glance around, hoping Logan will be able to bail her out, only to find him on the other side of the room, wrapped up in another conversation. And then the guy puts his hand on her forearm and motions toward the door. My chest tightens as I choke down my quickly growing anger. Imogen's obviously uncomfortable, shaking her head and forcing a smile while staying rooted in place.

Son of a bitch.

"Hey, um... this is kind of a weird question, but were you awake last night?" Abi asks.

My pulse skyrockets, my hands suddenly clammy as I take a generous sip of my drink. We were careful, and we were quiet.

Right?

"For a bit, yeah," I reply, spewing out the first lie I can think of. "Ig– Imogen and I were cleaning up the game and... I gave her some pointers for her presentation– not that she needed it–" I cut myself off as Abi stares up at me. "Why do you ask?"

"That must have been what I heard," she whispers, gnawing on her thumb nail. "The cabin's just so quiet– I, uh... guess I'm not used to it.

Anyway, I'm gonna go and see if I can pry Logan away from socializing for a bit."

She knows. She has to know. She wouldn't be asking this if she didn't. We haven't been careful enough. I want to say something to convince her otherwise, but I'm afraid if I open my mouth, the truth might come out.

Abi floats toward Logan while I drain my glass, keeping my eyes fixed on Imogen. Her shoulders drift up toward her ears, glancing around while he talks, still smiling politely so as not to upset him. I set my glass down on the table behind me, striding toward them. I hate men like this. The least he could do is be a fucking gentleman and stop staring at her like she's a piece of meat.

"Miss Flynn." I put my hand on her shoulder. "The concierge just called and said there's an issue with your credit card."

Her eyes are filled with relief, her lips parting just a little as she lets out an awkward laugh.

"Oh! I must have given them the wrong—"

"I was hoping we could finish our discussion back in the lounge," the man interjects, sliding his thumb back and forth along her forearm.

He's not even looking at me, he's just staring at her tits again. God, I hate his weasely face. Imogen clears her throat, gently pulling her arm away from his grip, flashing him a polite but forced smile.

"Sorry, another time, maybe."

She slips past me and mouths a *thank you* before moving through the crowd toward the back exit. I plan to follow shortly after her, but then the guy mumbles something that locks me in place.

"What was that?"

I want to hear what this asshole has to say for himself.

"You're a goddamn cockblock," he growls.

My eyes dart around the room, trying to see what I can get away with. Logan and Abi are at the bar, engrossed in a conversation with a small group of people. No one else around is paying the two of us any mind.

I grab him by the arm as hard as I can, squeezing a painful hiss right out of him.

"I ever see you touch a woman like that without her permission again, I'll snap this arm *right off.*"

284

His eyes are wide with fear, but only for a split second before they narrow into slits.

"She came on to *me*," he snarls.

I give him a hard shove, making my way toward the exit where Imogen's been waiting. Without saying a word I take her by the hand, leading her away from the party.

"Thanks for that back there," she laughs as we walk down the long hallway. "He wasn't very subtle, and he just kept asking me about domination and—"

She stops mid-thought, glancing behind her.

"Where are we going?"

I don't answer. I just need to get her alone.

"You know, you didn't have to swoop in. I was just about to spill a drink on Dr. Wallace." She giggles, leaning up against me as we continue. "Wait, are you taking me for a jealousy fuck?"

"You're goddamn right I am."

We shouldn't, but I'm too busy seething, thinking about that asshole laying his hands on her. I never really thought of myself as the jealous type, but I guess I haven't had that many opportunities to test that theory.

I shove the door open as we reach the bathroom, pulling her inside. It's empty, good. We don't even need much time.

"I like this new side to you, Dr. Burke," she purrs.

I drag her into a stall, pushing her up against a wall as I come crashing down on her with a searing kiss. I groan, biting down on her bottom lip and sucking until she lets out a whimper. She tastes like expensive champagne and chocolate covered strawberries. My hands act on their own, pushing her skirt up while she works my zipper, adrenaline pouring through my body like cheap wine.

This whole thing is a very fucking bad idea. But I can't stop. I can never stop when it comes to her, and the only thing I regret is that I took so goddamn long to figure that out and stop trying to avoid it.

I drop to my knees and kiss up her thighs, smirking when I see her bare, glistening pussy.

"Bad girl," I breathe.

Imogen giggles, twirling her hair around her finger.

"I had this fantasy that you'd follow me to the bathroom, and I'd be bent over the counter, all ready for you to take me."

She knows exactly what to say to get me going.

"How's this for a compromise?"

I close my lips around her clit and suck, getting back a ragged moan in response.

"Compromise rarely feels this good," she laughs.

This woman makes me feel completely out of control, and I just know I could spend the rest of the night on my knees for her.

I slide two fingers inside of her slowly, curling them as she gives my hair a hard tug, her hips bucking against me. She's getting wetter, and I can feel her squeezing my fingers tight, her short little gasps telling me she's already close.

"Roman! Fuck!"

She's crushing her voice, trying to keep it as low as possible, but she can't stop the high-pitched whines that spill from her throat. Part of me wants to deny her just to keep the game going, but those sinful sounds she's making have me so goddamn hard, I don't think I *could* stop if I wanted to. She snaps her hips one more time as she comes in my mouth.

There's no way I'm letting her relax yet. I want her first orgasm to roll right into her second. The moment I get to my feet, Imogen is already freeing my cock, one leg hooked around my waist as she strokes me.

"You wanna show me who I belong to, Dr. Burke?"

I'm fucking starved for her.

"Do you want me to scream your name? You wanna fuck me so good, I don't remember *Simon?*"

"Fuck, was that his name?" I snarl.

"Uh-huh," she grins.

"What a fucking asshole."

I grab her by the waist, moving her into the perfect spot.

Nothing about this is sweet. I need to wreck her, to feel her come apart at the seams. I need fingernails digging into my skin and her hands around my throat.

But then...

"I'll meet you outside, Abi! Oh, and have you seen Roman? No?"

We both freeze. Imogen puts her hand over her mouth. My dick softens in seconds. I hear the bathroom door open and curse myself for not looking for a lock.

Imogen squeezes her eyes shut. He'll use the bathroom, then he'll leave. It'll be fine. My heart feels like it's about to explode and I'm brimming with anxiety as I hear the tap run, then stop, his sneakers squeaking on the tile. He's heading for the door. It's fine.

Thank God.

And then my phone starts to chime from my pocket, barely loud enough to be noticed.

"Roman?" Logan asks.

But it is enough.

"Sorry, dude. We just couldn't find you. I won't make you talk if you're taking a shit."

I'm terrified, just letting my phone ring. I can't reach it, or I'll drop her.

"Roman, I know it's you. I can see your shoes."

Why is it that fear makes you feel like you're falling even when you're standing up? I'm shaking so badly that my hands are sweating, and one of her legs slips from my grip, her shoe tumbling off of her foot and landing on the floor.

"Oh," Logan laughs. "*That's* why we couldn't find you."

This is it. It's over. Even if he leaves the room, he'll be waiting outside. Even if he goes back to the ballroom, he'd figure out that we were both gone at the same time. Imogen looks like she's going to be sick and I feel like I want to pass out. There's no way for us to get out of this unscathed, but she breaks first, scrambling out of my grip as she tugs down her dress.

"Logan, it's me."

I zip my pants up just as she pushes the door open, bringing us face to face with her brother, slack jawed and wide-eyed as he takes a big step backward.

"Roman, you..."

I can almost see the calculations as he tallies up the lies we've told him. The appetizers I chowed down on feel like they're about to come right back up, and I almost gag.

"You're fucking my sister?!"

287

It's time for me to be a man and face the truth.

Even if it ruins everything.

"Let's talk."

"Yeah," Logan hisses. "Please, I'd love to know what the fuck is going on here."

I clear my throat, ready to make a case, but Imogen steps in front of me.

"Roman and I–"

"How long has this been going on?!"

She winces.

"Since... August."

"August?!" He looks straight past her. "You've been fucking my sister since August and you didn't think to mention it?!"

"And what would you have said?" Imogen snaps. "You'd have flipped out, just like you're doing right now!"

"I'd be a lot less *pissed* than I am right now, that's for sure! So, what, Iggy? You made up this fake boyfriend to cover up for the fact that you're fucking Roman? What else did you lie to me about?"

She stares down at the floor.

"I was afraid of–"

"We didn't know how you would take it," I cut in. "Lying to you was my idea, I want to be clear. I didn't want to ruin your relationship with your sister."

He turns away, running his hand through his hair.

"I can't fucking believe this. You're both idiots for risking Imogen's place at the school, not to mention your fucking *job*, Roman– but you know what I'm really pissed about?" He turns back to us, his gaze vicious. "Do you know what *really* gets under my skin?"

Imogen takes a step back and I wrap an arm around her shoulder, holding her close.

"You both lied to me for months. And you didn't even think twice about it."

We all stand in silence for a while, awkwardly shifting as we stare at each other, struggling to think of the right thing to say. The tension in the room is so thick I'm afraid whatever I might come up with would only make things worse.

"I guess I'll see you at the cabin," Logan mutters, turning on his foot and storming back out into the hall.

Imogen lets out a sob, burying her face in my chest.

I've never felt like a bigger asshole in my life.

CHAPTER THIRTY-NINE
tell it to my heart
ROMAN

The trek back to the cabin feels like the longest journey of my life, but I have to keep reminding myself that this was always going to happen; we were always going to have to have this conversation one way or another. I just wish it didn't go down the way it did. I don't think I'll ever forget the look in his eyes.

The lights are on inside, Imogen shivering underneath my borrowed suit jacket as we trudge up the steps, neither of us saying a word even after we're inside.

My eyes fall on Abi at the kitchen table, looking up at us from her phone.

"Welcome back."

I shove my hands into my pockets, giving her a nod as she flashes us a pained smile. Logan is at the counter grabbing glasses from the cabinet as I'm rooted to the floor, trying to analyze his body language. He's got a clenched jaw, his lips pressed tightly together as he reaches for the whiskey, pulling the cap off with a soft pop.

Normally, that would all combine to be a bad sign, but he's also changed into that stupid pumpkin sweater, his unruly hair sticking out from his hood. If he really wanted to kick my ass, he wouldn't do it in a goofy sweater.

Right?

"Imogen?" Abi asks, standing up from the table. "Why don't we head upstairs? We can watch a movie or something."

"No, it's fine," Logan murmurs, pouring two generous glasses of whiskey before sliding one in my direction. "You two can stay, Roman and I'll talk outside."

Imogen gnaws at her lip before letting out a somewhat frustrated sigh. I can see the anger building in her as she strides toward the stairs and heads into her room, shutting the door loudly behind her.

I try to lighten the mood a little, gesturing at his outfit.

"You wore my favorite sweater."

Logan's face doesn't move, and his eyes don't even light up in acknowledgement. He only hands me one of the glasses before walking to the back porch in silence, not even bothering to hold the door for me. I catch it just before it slams shut and step out just in time to find him easing himself onto one of the couches with a groan. For a moment I consider having the whole conversation right in the doorway, ready to leave at a moment's notice, but when he finally looks up at me I know I can't. It's best if I face this like a damn man.

I take a seat beside him, leaving enough space that neither of us will feel boxed in. The two of us stare out at the snow-covered landscape as the very last dregs of sunlight vanish beneath the horizon.

"So, you're Henry." He shakes his head, chuckling to himself as he sips his drink. "And I am *so* fucking stupid."

"No, you're not." I shift my body to face him. "And just to be clear, I didn't know she was your sister when we met. It was two weeks before the semester started. Hell, I didn't even know she was a student."

"How?"

"How what?"

"How did you meet, genius?"

"Oh, that... you remember the app Frankie told me about? The kink— the dating... one."

Logan takes in a haggard breath.

"Okay yeah, fine. So you didn't know at the start, that's fair. But you still lied to me, man." His fingers clench around his glass. "You both made shit up to my face and didn't even—"

"Think about your feelings? I did. Believe me, we both did. It's why we didn't tell you. This relationship—"

"Roman, you know the power dynamics at play here. There's only one way this can end for the both of you, and I don't want to have to watch my baby sister shut everyone out again when she inevitably loses the thing she's worked so *fucking* hard for!"

"Look, Logan. I'm *sorry* that we lied to you, but we didn't know how you'd take this, and I didn't want to risk Imogen's spot in the program."

"You already have, man. You have to know that. You've both risked everything she's worked for just by seeing each other, and you made it worse every goddamn day you kept it hidden! You had a chance to set boundaries, and you didn't. You had a chance to put her future first, and you didn't. I know you don't give a shit about your job anymore, but don't you care about her?"

"Of course I care about her. I tried to set boundaries—" Logan scoffs and I glare at him, staring him down before he has a chance to cut in. "We both did, at the start. We tried to be professional, Logan, I promise you, but I don't think we even *could* have stopped this even if we wanted."

My dad used to tell me that people come into your life for a reason, to open up new pathways you didn't know existed. Now I can't imagine my life without Imogen in it, and I don't want to go back to the man I was without her.

"She's worked so hard to get here, Roman. She almost flunked out of school, but she turned it all around so that she could follow in our dad's footsteps. This puts all of that, her entire career, at risk."

Laying the truth bare is terrifying, because I know there are holes in my reasoning. Yes, I could have put my foot down. I could have avoided that damn dinner party, or left her to fend for herself when I found her that night, but I didn't. I couldn't. It felt like my dad was right. Imogen was in my life for a reason, and I wanted to chase that for as long as I could.

"We didn't set out to ruin anything. It wasn't some big goddamn plot to betray you and keep secrets." I pause, trying to choose my words carefully. "It was about both of us finding something that was missing in our lives. That's all. And I know you'd love me to take it all back and say I'll never see her again, but that's not gonna happen."

Logan snorts into his drink.

"Jesus, next you're gonna tell me you're in love with her."

"Yeah." I stare at him, stone faced. "I am."

The anger in his eyes softens into mild confusion.

"Woah, wait. You're serious?"

"As a goddamn heart attack. She's the best thing that's happened to me in a long time, and I'll do whatever it takes to keep her at EBU. Look, it's like I said: we might have fucked up, but I'm not going back."

Logan shifts in his seat, his eyes darting around as he processes what I've said.

"She knows you love her?"

"If there's one thing I learned from Christa, it's to say it as often as possible. I'm excited to wake up and see her every day. I love cooking with her, I love listening to her talk, I even love doing mundane shit like watching TV with her." I clear my throat, sipping my drink for some courage as Logan relaxes a little more into the couch. "She's helping me find the pieces of myself I thought I'd lost forever, and I hope I'm doing the same for her."

"It's funny," he murmurs. "Thinking back to when she first mentioned she was seeing someone, I remember her whole face lighting up. I don't think I've seen that softer side of her since before dad died, I just had no idea *you* were the reason."

"My best friend doesn't even remember my full name, huh?" I tease.

Logan laughs, shrugging his shoulders.

"I've spent my whole life being one of the smartest guys in the room, but I gotta admit, your stupid fucking middle name really slipped past my radar, yeah."

"You're getting old, kiddo."

"Nah, you guys hid it pretty well." He swirls his drink in his glass, a small, *almost* proud smile causing his lip to twitch. "I'm actually kind of impressed."

"Yeah, well it doesn't really matter. It was bound to blow up sometime."

The guilt is like a frigid hand on my shoulder, reminding me that we don't have much time left; that everything is about to come crashing down.

"I think what makes me the angriest is that I can't protect her from what's going to happen when the school finds out," Logan murmurs, staring off into the night.

"That's my fault."

I had the chance to put in for her transfer so many times, and I just didn't, and now we'll be at the mercy of the department. What they decide to do to us is completely out of our control. All we can do is minimize the damage.

"So you're going to tell them, right?" He asks, none of his previous venom coating the words.

"Do we even have a choice at this point?"

"Not really. If someone else catches you two... like a student?"

Logan lets out a breath, shaking his head.

It's the band-aid neither of us could manage to rip off. We knew the consequences, but as long as it remained a secret, I could push my fears a little further every day. After a while, I let myself get lost in her, and in the forbidden nature of it all.

It felt so good, but we could only hide for so long.

"I'll email Frankie in the morning."

Logan nods, sinking a little deeper into his seat, his expression sorrowful as he sips at his drink. I didn't think I could feel any guiltier, but now he looks like a puppy someone left by the side of the road.

"Logan, I'm really sorry we lied to you."

"No." He sighs. "That's not why I'm— I feel like a dick. I didn't know you were in love, I thought you guys were just... you know, boning."

"We wanted to tell you."

"No, you didn't," Logan laughs. "You both wanted to see how far you could push this without getting caught."

"Logan—"

"No, that's... I get it. Once you're in love, it's hard to stop it from sinking its hooks into your brain. Makes you crazy. Makes you do wild shit, stuff that makes no sense."

Suddenly he looks a little anxious, like he's opened up too much, scratching the crystal glass with his fingernail.

"I really do love her," I assure him.

"No, man, I know. If you didn't, you wouldn't be out here right now."

I chuckle.

"Yeah, I'm freezing my balls off."

Logan snickers and reaches over, clinking his glass against mine.

"Thanks for telling me the truth."

I don't feel much better about all of this, but I know what I have to do. I'm going to protect her, and I'll worry about myself later.

"I'm just sorry it took so long."

CHAPTER FORTY

as it was

IMOGEN

"Still awake?" Roman asks, his eyes shut tight but just as sleepless as me.

"Yeah," I murmur. "My head won't stop spinning."

"Yeah, neither will mine."

I was asleep when he came up to my room after his talk with Logan, but we've both been awake and restless since. Sharing a bed with him on our last night feels both right and wrong at the same time. There isn't a point of hiding anymore, but with things still unresolved...

"Logan told me that we should come clean with the department," Roman says softly.

I lift my head, my brows pinched together.

"What, why? Is he planning to sell us out?"

"No, it's just a hell of a lot worse if we get caught." He pauses, shifting a little with a groan. "And based on what happened tonight, it's more of a when than an if."

I gnaw at my lip. There's got to be a better way.

"We'll be more careful."

Roman stares at the ceiling.

"We can't hide this anymore. You know that."

My eyes feel heavy, like I'm grasping at sleep and can't quite keep hold of it, but my mind is moving so fast I can barely pin down a thought.

"Maybe I'll quit," Roman whispers.

His voice is surprisingly calm, and perfectly accompanied by his steady breathing.

"What?"

"Once you're in this for long enough, it all starts to swallow you up. I wasn't fully present in my marriage because I was so obsessed with my work. I think it's one of the reasons I felt so responsible for Christa's death." He tries to steady his voice, the topic having an obvious effect on him. "Besides, if I leave, the school can't touch you. You'll get to keep your spot."

"That's not your responsibility."

"Maybe not," Roman replies. "But we've got to do something, and what your brother said to me just stuck in my head all night: the truth will be a lot easier for everyone to swallow. I think we should schedule a meeting with Frankie when we get back."

I look up at him, playing with the delicate gold chain around his neck as he smiles back at me.

"What would you do?" I ask. "If you quit."

"I've always wanted to go to culinary school and open up a restaurant. It's stupid, but it's something I've been... mulling over in the background. There's a school in Seattle. I've had their website bookmarked for a while. I keep staring at the apply now button, but I've been such a chickenshit."

"You're not."

"Yeah?" He asks. "Then how come I couldn't tell your brother the truth?"

I slowly run my fingers through the fine hair on his chest, and his cheeks grow pink.

"Because it's terrifying to put your entire life on the line not knowing what's waiting for you on the other side."

"Are the two of you pulling from the same font of wisdom?" Roman laughs. "Because I'm pretty sure your brother said the same damn thing to me outside."

I grin and press a soft kiss into his chest.

"Logan's the wise one. I start sentences without realizing how I'm going to end them, then even I'm surprised by the shit that comes out of my mouth."

He startles me with a sudden, loud laugh.

"That might be my favorite quality of yours."

"I thought it was my boobs."

"Fair enough, it's your wisdom *and* your boobs."

"I love you, cowboy."

"I love you right back, darlin'."

I lay my head back down on his chest with a sigh.

It's quiet for a long time before I notice his breathing slow, each individual breath becoming much deeper, and when I look up, he's already fast asleep.

"Asleep so quick? I really fucking envy you right now," I whisper.

I already know I'll probably be up all night, but I can't just sit here alone with my thoughts. I need a glass of water, and maybe some fresh air will clear my head. Once a problem crashes into my life, it's easy for it to become an obsession.

Quietly, I slide off the bed, throwing my robe on and heading out toward the kitchen. On the way, my attention is pulled to a soft light emanating from the living room, and I find Logan perched in a chair by the fireplace. He's got a book in his lap, a lock of hair fallen into his face, and dark circles under his eyes.

"Hey, Ig."

"Hey."

"Can't sleep?"

I shake my head.

"You?"

"Nope."

He lifts the book and I chuckle. All I can make out are the words *quantum physics*.

"Are you trying to bore yourself to death?"

"More like into passing out." He closes the book carefully and sets it aside. "I'm sorry I didn't come to talk to you. I was..."

"I get it." I make my way over and sit on the couch across from him. "Logan, I feel awful for lying to you."

"I know you do," he replies. "But you know why I was angry, don't you?"

I nod.

"I guess both of us just didn't know how you'd react."

He takes a deep breath, running his fingers through his hair.

"Well, I'd be shocked, and I'd probably be a little—"

"Pissed?"

"I don't know," he confesses with a hollow laugh. "But I was gonna say confused."

"I didn't want to lie to you. I promise I didn't, but this all happened so fast and then before I knew it we were together, and then... I was in love."

Logan smiles, and I see a little glimpse of my brother's eternal optimism again. He's exhausted, and close to the end of his rope with me, but he's still in there.

"Roman told me."

"I thought he was just some hot guy on an app at the start. I didn't know he was your friend, or that we'd be working together, or *any* of that shit. You should really sign-post your friends and colleagues on social media."

"Oh, yeah, this is *my* fault," he snorts.

"Well, I have to blame someone other than myself," I tease. "Otherwise I'd have to take accountability for once."

I don't really know what else to say that hasn't probably been said between the two of them. Roman didn't give me the full details of what they talked about, but I figured my brother would eventually want to have a heart to heart.

I guess this is it.

"Do you understand why I was so pissed off at first?" Logan asks.

"Tell me."

He takes a breath, and I follow his gaze out the window. Small white flakes of snow tumble down from the sky, probably the perfect image to accompany the silence around us, only broken up by the crackling fireplace.

"Because I know how hard you fought to get here, Iggy. I know that you put the whole thing on the line for Roman— but I was angry, angry that the boundaries weren't firmer, that neither of you put a stop to it back when you could have..."

"Logan—"

"Let me finish first."

He's right. That over-explaining thing I do won't help the situation right now.

"Then he told me that he loves you, and how much you mean to him, and how fiercely he wants to protect you. I didn't expect that, I thought you guys were just..."

"We tried to stay away from each other, but—"

"You're in love," he whispers. "I get it."

I nod, struggling to hold it together, but a tiny sob manages to escape my lips.

"We are. That's why I'm so fucking scared of what's going to happen next."

Logan stands, moving to sit next to me on the couch.

"I can't protect you from what's going to happen when the department finds out. You know that, right?"

Just the thought of it makes me want to throw up. There's nothing left standing between us and complete and total disgrace.

"I know," I sniffle. "God, I fucked everything up."

Logan shakes his head.

"You can't help where your heart leads you."

He's not wrong, but it doesn't change the fact that I don't have a backup plan, and that's the thing that scares me the most. All of that work, all of those accomplishments I've racked up over the years... thrown away because I fell in love. Now there's nothing to do but tell Frankie what I've done and face the consequences. I've never felt so helpless.

"Iggy, you know that no matter what goes down, I've always got your back, right?"

"I know," I sniffle. "So what do you think is going to happen?"

"I don't fully know," he confesses. "But the school is pretty clear on its student-teacher fraternization policies. Roman will be suspended, he won't be able to publish or teach, and you face expulsion."

"Suspended? For how long?"

"I think that part's up to Frankie's discretion," Logan whispers. "Along with what happens to you."

I stare into the fire, trying to anchor myself and keep from spiraling any further.

"Iggy, even with all of this, do you still see a future with Roman? I mean a real future."

I let out a long, haggard breath. I've definitely thought about it, but we've been so focused on keeping our secret that I haven't let my mind wander that far into the future. Besides, if I let myself daydream too much I'll start to get anxious; old anxieties begin to creep up.

All things do is end.

I know that, but...

"I want it to be real," I whisper. "This is the first time I've really connected with someone in a long time." I fiddle with a stray string on my robe. "It felt so natural to ease into having a boyfriend, instead of just having fun with someone I was fucking—"

I stop myself, burying my face in my hands.

"God, you don't need to be hearing this."

"Hey, I'm a chill big brother!"

I'm a little shocked to find myself laughing, but more than a little relieved.

"That is such bullshit! You looked ready to tear Roman's head off tonight."

"I can't deny I was thinking about it, but now I know why: you both have something you wanted to protect. I might have done the same thing in your shoes."

"Do you moonlight as a therapist or something?" I chuckle.

Logan bumps me with his shoulder. Sometimes he really does know what to say.

"Nah, I just give really good advice, and then never listen to it when I need it."

"Well, either way, thanks again for not punching Roman. Or me, now that I think of it."

"What kind of a brute do you take me for?" He snorts.

"You looked really mad, and you've got that Flynn temper."

"I do *not* have a temper."

"Dude, you tried to fight a mascot on Coney Island once."

"Okay, one: that was a drunk frat dude in a T-Rex costume, not a mascot, and two, he wouldn't stop calling you four eyes!"

I snicker, wishing I had even a fraction of my brother's confidence. Maybe if I did I wouldn't have let things get so far out of control.

"Well, it's way beyond late," Logan sighs. "Me and my boring ass book are going to bed. You should too, missy."

"Yeah, I'm just gonna grab some water first."

Logan nods, heading for the stairs, but stopping in place only a few steps up.

"You know I love you, right Ig? No matter what, you're still my dumbass little sister."

I roll my eyes at him, waving him away.

"And you're still my dumbass big brother."

He smiles, heading the rest of the way up and leaving me alone with my thoughts.

"And I love you too," I mutter to the empty room.

My whole life, my big brother has looked out for me, rescued me from stuff that even mom and dad couldn't, but things are different now. He can't save me from what's about to happen back in Emerald Bay.

CHAPTER FORTY-ONE

ROMAN

EMERALD BAY UNIVERSITY
TUESDAY

"Oh my god, Logan's texting me Frankie-updates," Imogen sighs, handing me her phone. "He's such a fucking busybody."

> LOGAN: Frankie's getting donuts.
>
> LOGAN: He's getting coffee now. Saw it on his Instagram story.
>
> LOGAN: Iggy, I feel like I'm gonna puke.

My whole entire body is clenched, and has been since I put my feet on the ground this morning. I'm not really sure if I want to shit my pants or throw up. Maybe both.

"Ask him if his Highness is here yet," I grumble, passing the phone back. "I hate having to wait this shit out, especially knowing the hammer's coming down."

There's no escaping what's about to happen, and no talking my way out of it. I've got it all meticulously mapped out in my head, right down to the screaming match Frankie and I are going to have. He hates being forced to actually act like HR, and that's what's going to piss him off the most.

"Roman, it'll be—"

"Sorry for the wait, you two!"

Frankie walks around the corner, a nervous smile etched on his face.

I turn to Imogen, who's leaning against the wall, her hands curled into tight fists.

"Regardless of what happens, we're getting through this together, okay?"

"I know."

My heart begins to pound, and as Frankie digs his keys out of his pocket the edges of my vision start getting fuzzy.

"How was Aspen?" He asks, his voice a little pinched.

"Good," the two of us reply in unison.

When I emailed him telling him we needed to talk, he didn't say much. My first thought was that maybe Frankie already knows. Maybe we were too brazen at that dinner party and he caught on.

He opens the door, ushering us inside before easing himself into his seat and staring us down. I shut the door behind us, pulling out a chair for Imogen before taking a seat myself.

"So?" He sips his coffee. "What's going on? Did something happen with a student, or..."

A nervous laugh tumbles out of Imogen's mouth, and Frankie's eyes volley back and forth between us. She clears her throat, but I stop her, putting my hand on her shoulder. The truth feels like it's crushing my windpipe, but I have to get through this. I told her I would handle this; I told her that I would protect her.

"Imogen and I are in a... relationship," I mutter, barely loud enough for him to hear. "We have been for a couple of months now."

Frankie looks like someone twice his size just punched him in the gut. I can see each emotion hitting him in quick succession: shock, disbelief, anger.

"You're fucking kidding me," he says after a moment. His tone is measured, but I can hear the anger tucked just beneath the surface. "You've *got* to be fucking kidding me."

Fear rises up in the back of my throat, threatening to choke the life out of me.

"No," Imogen cuts in. "It's true. We met two weeks before classes started, and..."

I've never prayed harder for a natural disaster in my life. Hurricane. Earthquake. A Biblical plague. I'd take anything to escape Frankie's piercing gaze.

"Jesus, it's been that long? And you didn't say a damn—"

"I didn't know!" I snap, but when I see the anger flashing in his eyes, I pull myself back. "That's not— I didn't know she was my TA until— look, we met on that app you told me about. It didn't have anything to do with the university."

Frankie puts his head in his hands, groaning as I stammer on.

"There wasn't a way to figure out anything about each other because we were using fake names, and after we went on a kind of blind date, we, uh..."

I clear my throat, trying to come up with a professional explanation for how a one night stand works to a man who looks like he wants to strangle me.

"Imogen, help me out here."

"We hooked up in Seattle," she finishes for me. "Again, I had no idea he taught at EBU, and he didn't know I was a student. When we ran into each other at the mixer we were both mortified. Roman was adamant we should end things then and there."

Frankie lifts his head, his face red and his expression strained.

"But clearly he didn't follow through on that," he mutters, eyes shifting back to me. "You know I hate being the fucking bad guy. I don't *want* to be the bad guy right now. I want to say that I'm happy for you, and that this is all fine, but I can't *do that!*"

Tension hangs thick in the air, and out of the corner of my eye I can see Imogen's leg anxiously bouncing up and down, all while she stays deathly focused on Frankie.

"We didn't mean to fall in love," she says after a moment. "It wasn't ever the plan."

He closes his eyes, like hearing the word out loud makes him feel even more uncomfortable.

305

"Roman, you're suspended. With or without pay is still up for debate, but you're not to teach or publish until this gets resolved. You'll have a disciplinary hearing in a month. Sooner if I can manage it."

The ax is coming down and all I can do is accept it, but maybe this won't be the worst thing in the world. It could give me a chance to focus on the things that really matter: Imogen, my culinary interests, going out to visit the ranch... all of the things I've been putting off because I was too busy not really living. It's easy to go through life on autopilot, but I didn't realize how much I'd missed in the last four years.

"Imogen, pending investigation you may be removed from the program—"

"Oh, *fuck* that!" I suddenly find myself on my feet, towering over Frankie with my hands clenched into fists. "Don't punish her for this. You're mad at *me*, so take it out on me."

"Roman, I don't have control over university policies, and they clearly state that this is how things have to go." He stares at Imogen, and I can see the regret in his eyes mixed with disappointment. "I'm sorry. I really am."

She sniffles and I lean over, resting my hands on Frankie's desk.

"Frankie, *please* don't do this to her. She's worked so goddamn hard to get here."

He looks like someone has a gun to his head.

"Look, I'm going to try to make sure things are lenient for the two of you, but I don't know how well I can fix this. You really fucked me on this one."

I don't know what I thought would happen, maybe that I could take the fall for the two of us?

"This could ruin everything she's worked for."

I look over at Imogen to see her staring at the floor, teardrops on her forearms.

"What if I just leave?" She murmurs. "Will Roman still have to be suspended?"

"Yes," Frankie replies, his expression grim. "Keeping Roman on right now is a liability issue for the university, so the suspension and review are happening no matter what."

She cares more about me than she does about her spot, and I care more about keeping her here than I do about my own goddamn future.

"It's gonna be okay." I kiss her on the temple, softly running my fingers through her hair. "I'll make damn sure of it."

This all could have been different. Frankie could be congratulating her for her presentation, and discussing how her dissertation is going. Instead we're talking about the end of her career.

"I'm going to have to speak with the Dean and the graduate committee," Frankie continues, all business once again. "I'll be in touch with you both via email."

"Sure," Imogen whispers.

He sighs, leaning back in his chair as I usher Imogen out of the office.

"Wait outside for me, okay?"

She nods, brushing away tears as I shut the door.

Frankie leans back in his chair, shaking his head.

"I can't fucking believe you." He scoffs. "What's worse is that I didn't even see it. You know if you get fired, there's a good chance you won't be able to teach again, right?"

"I know," I murmur.

He stares at me, blinking erratically, like he's still trying to wrap his head around all of this.

"You know? So you just decided it was time to throw your career away?"

"It's like she said," I sigh, shoving my hands in my pockets. "We didn't mean to fall in love."

Frankie rubs his face, his shoulders slumping in defeat.

"I'll cover your class, let them know you're taking a leave of absence, and I'll... I don't fuckin' know, make something up about Imogen I guess."

Frankie sits there in silence, staring past me, and I take my cue to leave. When I step outside, Logan and Abi are already comforting Imogen, their faces somber. Other professors walk by, heading out for their morning classes, some of them shooting us quizzical looks as they pass.

I wrap my arm around Imogen, pulling her close as Logan's eyes meet mine.

"What happened?"

"I'm suspended, possibly fired pending a disciplinary hearing. There's going to be a full internal investigation, and Imogen could lose her spot in the program."

"I, uh... I might transfer to another school. Maybe UW, in Seattle?" She looks like she's still trying to figure a way out of this rat's nest we've made. "Unless this all ends up branding me with some kind of scarlet fucking letter, at least."

Logan's eyes well with tears and I force a smile to keep my own chin from quivering. It's strange to think I was terrified of this man finding out. I was convinced that Logan would hate me— or worse, hate her, but now he's the one in our corner.

"Logan, I'm gonna drive her home."

"Sure. I'll be back there later tonight. Maybe we can all have dinner and..." He chuckles, at a loss for words. "Cry more?"

Imogen laughs, despite the tears in her eyes.

"That sounds good, but I want to clean out my things first. For when this all goes to shit."

"Iggy..." Logan sighs. "It won't—"

"It will." She rubs the back of her neck. "I know it will, but it's okay. I can figure it out."

I motion toward my office with one hand, doing my best impression of someone who still has it all together.

"I've got some boxes. We can pack your things and load them into my car."

Imogen nods, and the two of us set off on our little mission while Logan and Abi linger in the hallway. Silently, we grab some empty boxes, trudging toward the tiny room she shares with some of the other PhD students.

We pack up books, stacks of papers, and even some pictures that Imogen has on her desk. I notice one of them is a photo of her and her dad sitting outside of NYU in the summer. He's got his arm wrapped around her, and I can almost hear her distinctive laugh as she triumphantly holds up her acceptance letter.

"He was so proud of me that day."

Her eyes meet mine, heartbroken and red, and a tear slides down her cheek as she plucks the photo from my hands, placing it into the box along with the rest of her happier memories.

"I'm ready now."

CHAPTER FORTY-TWO

movement

ROMAN

It's strange to think that just a few months ago, I was standing at this very entrance dreading the thought of seeing her. Now, I can't picture my life without her in it.

"My room's just down here."

Her voice is devoid of warmth, almost cracking as each of us carry a box down the stairs. Her bedroom door is open, the smell of her perfume already floating in the air, and when we step inside I can't help but smile.

I walk around, taking everything in. The romance books that line her shelves, the posters on the walls, her makeup scattered on her vanity, and the clothes strewn on the floor. I'm usually a stickler for cleanliness, but this place looks like home.

It's just so... *her.*

She drops the box she was carrying on the floor and turns to face me, tears welling up in her eyes.

"I'm so sorry this happened."

I take a step toward her.

"Why are you apologizing?"

She breathes slowly, in and out, looking like she's searching for the right words before suddenly starting to laugh.

"You know what? I have no fucking clue. I feel like telling the university to go fuck themselves."

Her breath hitches.

A tear trickles down her cheek and I brush it away with my thumb. She looks so small right now, like any further complication could break her.

"I'm not going to apologize for loving you. I don't care who or what tries to tear us apart. I will *always* find my way back to you, darlin'."

I pull her into my arms, cradling her as tightly as I can as she squeezes her eyes shut, pressing herself into my chest.

"What are we going to do?"

"We'll come up with something. We both get paid to think, right?"

She laughs again, but the heartbreak is evident in her eyes when she stares up at me. This is it. Waves of unhealed grief come screaming to the surface, and I close my eyes, bracing for the inevitable; bracing for some version of *this was great while it lasted, but I can't do this anymore.* Maybe even all of the love that we've built can't withstand this.

But instead of delivering a crushing blow, a single kiss takes my breath away. I push her back toward the bed, closing her in until she pulls me down on top of her. This might be the last time we're going to be together for a while, and there isn't a cell in my body willing to forget the way she feels.

I break the kiss and sit back on my haunches, both of us ravenously tearing off each other's clothes.

"I love you," I rasp, pinning her to the bed. "I love you so fucking much it makes me crazy."

At first, I thought she was just a distraction from my grief, but Imogen's given me my spark back.

I ghost my lips down her neck, stopping to nibble and nip at her skin as her light panting fills the room. She whines, back arching as I reach her nipple and bite through the lace of her bra.

"More."

I grind my hips into the mattress, relieving the pressure that's building inside me. I release her nipple, grabbing her flimsy bra in the center and tearing it in half.

"A few more of these might show up at your door tomorrow as an apology... from an anonymous citizen of Emerald Bay, of course."

She laughs, her eyes brighter but still a little sad. If this is the last time we get to touch for a while, I want to make sure it'll be a night she never forgets.

I toss the torn up remnants of the bra aside and let my mouth close around her nipple, sucking and nibbling on it until she squirms. My name spills out from her lips, mingling with tiny whimpers and moans as her fingers run through my hair. My hands glide down her body to play with the waistband on her leggings.

"What time did your brother say he'd be home?"

"He didn't say anything more specific than 'later,' but I think he wants to give us some privacy. We've got time."

"Good. I'm gonna make you scream so loud they can hear it in the next town over."

We could both use this distraction right about now.

I can't get enough of her, slowly peeling her leggings off and taking extra care to kiss each inch of bare skin. I grab her hand as I catch her sliding it down her body, lacing my fingers between hers and holding it in place.

"Let me take care of you."

She bites her lip as I let my breath fan over her cunt, her moan raspy and rich, like warm honey. I spread her pussy lips with my free hand, groaning as my fingers start to glisten. I can feel her clit throbbing as I glide my fingers along her folds, listening to the pretty little sounds she makes for me. I could do this all goddamn day, watching her get wetter from the anticipation alone.

"Roman," she whines. "Please."

I wrap my lips around her swollen clit, shivering at the taste: sharp and sweet. Her sinful cries bounce off the walls as I grind my hips deeper into the mattress; I don't know how long I'm going to last, but I'll make damn sure this woman comes as hard as she can.

Imogen's hips buck as I slide my fingers inside of her, and I have to move with her body to keep up the pace. All I hear is heavy breathing and all I feel are her sharp nails against my scalp as she holds me in place. I groan into her cunt, curling my fingers until she keens and loosens her grip.

"I want those legs to shake, darlin'. You understand me?"

I take the moment to lift my head in triumph, watching her body trembling as she fights for control.

"Yes!" Her hand slams into the mattress. "Fuck!"

I return to the task at hand, devouring her slowly. Savoring her. I want to make her fall to pieces with my mouth and fingers.

"Oh, fuck! Oh, fuck! I'm so close," she rasps as I lap at her. "Don't stop!"

I don't plan on it.

I push right up against her G-spot, wrapping my mouth around her clit one more time. Imogen rewards me with a deep, guttural groan as she comes apart, her body twitching and her hips snapping like they have a mind of their own.

"Roman– I–"

Suddenly, I feel her go rigid and look up to see her back arched, her pierced nipples aimed right at the ceiling as she cries out. I don't stop licking her until she shoves me away, laughing.

"Down, boy," she rasps. "I need a second."

I back off, taking the opportunity to watch her as she comes down. She's bathed in soft light, sweat glistening on her skin as she takes in long, deep breaths. I want to see her like this every single day for the rest of my life.

I push the thought away as quickly as it comes, focusing on the present. We have to get through the bullshit first before we figure out what comes next.

"You wanna keep going?" I ask, my hope a little too present in the tone of my voice.

Imogen props herself up onto her elbows, grinning at me.

"You said you wanted my legs to shake, cowboy. So slip those pants off and get to work."

I nod, climbing off of the bed and shedding my jeans while Imogen roots around in her nightstand. My eyes trace the soft curves of her body and I try to commit every inch to memory just in case this all goes south.

She produces a small purple vibrator, turning it on and grinning from ear to ear.

"This one's my favorite."

She rolls onto her back, groaning as she uses the toy to circle her nipples. I'm practically drooling at the sight, her heels sunk into the blankets and her wet pussy on full display for me. I can't help myself, climbing back onto the bed and nestling between her thighs as I watch her drag the toy up and down her body.

"Turn it up," I order.

She cocks a brow and I smile.

"Turn it up please, Mistress?"

She doesn't miss a beat, resting it firmly against her clit, her back bowing as a satisfied groan floods the room. It just might be my favorite sound in the world.

"I thought I told you to get to work."

I smile, gently grasping her legs and pushing them up so that her calves are resting on my shoulders. Imogen turns the vibrator up a little higher, gasping as I line myself up and slowly thrust inside of her.

"God, I could stay buried inside you forever."

I begin to move slowly, savoring each stroke, pulling all the way out before thrusting all the way back in again. The vibrations are fucking heavenly against my cock, and I can't help myself, prying the vibrator from her hands. I turn it up even higher, holding it against her until she cries out, the sound almost primal. Crimson blooms on her cheeks, bright red splotches that flow all the way down her neck.

"Oh, *fuck*! Harder!"

"What's my name, darlin'?"

"Roman!" She mewls. "Roman!"

I've got one hand gripping her outer thigh while I hold the vibrator in place with the other, watching her tits bounce with each slam of my hips against hers, and I can feel her squeezing my cock like a goddamn vice. Butterflies swirl in my stomach and sweat trickles down my spine as Imogen stretches her hands above her head, giving in fully.

"Now come for me."

It seems to be all the permission she needs, and her back arches as another throaty cry rips through the room. Just a few more strokes; I'm so goddamn close. My stomach clenches and my head buzzes, bliss coursing through me until *finally* I'm toppling over that cliff, coming so hard my eyes involuntarily slam shut.

My heart slams against my ribs, and I suck in a few gulping breaths before looking down at her tear-stained face. I can feel the sweat clinging to the air as I switch the vibrator off and pull out of her. As we both calm down, and the room slowly begins to stop spinning, we find ourselves tangled up in one another once more. Perhaps for the final time.

"I can't help but feel like this is a goodbye," she whispers.

My heart wrenches in my chest, but I can't let her see it.

I can't let my fear of being left behind consume me.

For once, I have to be strong.

"It's not a goodbye," I assure her, stroking her cheek. "We'll figure it all out."

We'll figure it out because we have to.

CHAPTER FORTY-THREE

week one

IMOGEN

"The application's good, darlin. It's clear and concise, and you've got a solid framework."

"You really think so? Every time I re-read it I keep thinking it's getting shittier."

Roman decided pretty quickly that it probably wasn't a good idea for us to go out in public, especially since he's still waiting on his disciplinary hearing, so we've been Facetiming a lot lately to make up for it.

"Trust me, I'd tell you if it was," he chuckles. *"So when's it due?"*

"Next week. I'm so nervous."

"Don't be," He reassures me. *"You're brilliant, and so is your work. Any school would be lucky to have you."*

The wild thing is even the slightly distorted sound of his voice through my headphones turned out to be a much bigger comfort than I expected.

I roll onto my side, staring at him through the screen. He's nestled in bed, his hair and his beard grown out a bit longer than usual, giving him a bit of an unkempt look. But more than that, he looks tired.

God, I'm sure we both do.

I miss seeing him every day, and I wish we could just go back to the way things were. It all seemed so much simpler back then, even while we were keeping our big secret.

"So, how are you holding up? Have you heard anything about the hearing?"

"No, but these things are slow," he sighs. *"They'll probably wait until the holidays are done to rake my ass over the coals."*

I've been a mess lately, staying in my pajamas and carrying my laptop with me everywhere around the house, like a security blanket. I hate waiting, but I feel like I can't start working on other parts of my life when this one is still in fucking shambles.

"It'll be okay, I promise. You'll get into another school, I'll get through my hearing, and we'll start fresh from there."

His smile is hopeful, but some of that usual twinkle in his eye is gone. I can tell he's trying to be strong, but what if things don't work out?

What happens then?

CHAPTER FORTY-FOUR

week two

IMOGEN

> IMOGEN: I submitted a few of my applications today.

> ROMAN: How do you feel?

> IMOGEN: Fucking terrified. What if none of them let me in?

> ROMAN: Then we figure something else out. But, you have to stay positive, okay?

> IMOGEN: Heard anything about the hearing yet?

> ROMAN: Nope. When I know, you'll know.

> IMOGEN: God, this sucks. Are you still coming over? Logan and I are doing movie night.

My brother's been trying to maintain some sense of normalcy around the house, refusing to let me get *too* down in the dumps about all of this. Everything just feels so strange now, but I'm trying to stay focused on the good things.

Stay positive, just like he said.

ROMAN: I wouldn't miss it for the world.

CHAPTER FORTY-FIVE

IMOGEN

> IMOGEN: Hey, are you alive? I haven't heard from you in a few days.

Read: 5:17pm

> IMOGEN: I miss you, cowboy.

Read: 1:10am

CHAPTER FORTY-SIX

week four

IMOGEN

"Any word from Roman?" I ask, passing over a few decorations for the tree. Logan's throwing a little Christmas party this weekend, so he dragged me out of bed to help with the decorating. He even enlisted Piper, Jay, and Abi to lift my spirits, though he claimed it was for party prep. I'm not sure how well it's working, but it is kind of nice not to be both miserable *and* alone.

"Sorry Iggy. I tried texting, tried calling... I even tried going straight to the source and buzzing his apartment. Pretended to be the pizza guy." He shakes his head. "He wouldn't even answer the intercom."

What's driving me crazy is I don't even understand what happened; all I know is one day he just stopped communicating, not just with me but with everyone. It's been torture staring at my phone, just willing him to text or call this whole last week, so much so I'd even be happy with a single stupid emoji at this point.

But as pissed off as I am, I have to admit I can sort of relate.

I've become a shut-in over the past few weeks myself, because I'd much rather be in bed than be around people pitying me. Unfortunately, all I do lately is spend most of my free time going through old texts trying to figure out what I did to push Roman away.

I don't handle rejection well, not below the surface at least. I internalize it and spend forever blaming myself: not good enough, not funny enough, not smart enough, not pretty enough.

Not worthy of sticking around for.

No matter what it was, I had to have done something.

My therapist called it 'rejection sensitive dysphoria', and when it sinks its ugly little teeth into you, it can feel like the world is ending.

"What's the dude's deal anyway?" Jay asks. "Is it really that hard to pick up a phone and send a text? That's the decent thing to do."

"Thanks, Jay."

"I got your back, girl, don't worry."

"I mean... it's complicated," Logan murmurs, immediately drawing Abi's ire.

"No, you don't get to make excuses for him!"

"I'm not trying to make excuses, Abi. He just slips into these massive bouts of depression, and it's hard for him to climb out of them. It doesn't mean I'm not pissed off at him for doing what he's doing, it's just... complicated."

I can tell Logan is doing his best to cover up how helpless he feels, because I've heard some of the voicemails he's left over the past few days. He's been trying to keep his tone measured and cool, to stay supportive to both of us at the same time, but It's clear this whole thing is starting to wear on him.

On the other hand, I'm just dealing with a shitload of my own questions that I don't have the answers to.

Is Roman okay? Are *we* okay?

Will we even be able to make it through this?

And what happens next if we don't?

"Not that anyone *asked* for my opinion," Piper interjects, staring down at us from the top of a ladder. "But Roman probably feels like this is his fault. Iggy's got to change schools and he needs to prepare for what I would assume is a pretty invasive disciplinary hearing. He might feel disconnected, or maybe he doesn't want to burden anyone with his own baggage."

"Depressed or not, nearly two weeks is a long-ass time to go without even saying hi to someone you said you loved," Jay replies, pointing at Piper. "Imagine if I went two whole weeks without talking to you."

Piper smirks, brandishing a candy cane like a knife.

"I'd kick your fucking door down."

I think the old me would have done the same, gone right to Roman's apartment and hit that buzzer until he *had* to let me in, so that he could see what the fuck he was doing to me. Sometimes I think about it to the point where I actually get dressed, and almost even make it to my front door.

But then that anger dissolves into pure, undistilled anxiety.

It's possible that the past month has given him a lot of time to think about us, about the future, and about how it's all going to work out.

Or how it's not.

I feel another rush of tears coming on, my nose stinging as all of my fears claw their way back up to the surface. I gave this man my heart and now he won't even talk to me.

"Maybe all of it's just too hard." My voice breaks as I crouch down, struggling to grab another decoration. "Maybe he doesn't want this anymore, and—"

It's too hard to get the words out.

Great. Now everyone in this room is looking at me like I'm some fragile vase on the brink of tipping over. I liked it better when I didn't feel anything at all.

"I need some air."

I head out back to the patio, greeted by the smell of crisp winter rain. It's pouring, the clouds hanging thick in the sky as the massive trees that surround the backyard sway ever so slightly in the wind. I take a breath, easing myself into one of the small patio chairs barely covered by the awning. Aside from opening a window in my bedroom, I haven't really been outside that much during this whole thing. I don't have anywhere to go, but more importantly I don't want to start crying in the grocery store. Again.

I pull my phone out, hoping beyond hope.

Nothing from Roman.

I really was starting to think things were going to work out here, really started to believe the two of us had something special. Now I want to throw this phone into the bay for all the anxiety and sleepless nights it's given me.

I guess that's what you get for opening up.

What a fucking idiot.

I bristle at the sound of the patio door creaking open, expecting my brother to be checking in on me for the 100th time.

"You didn't think we'd let you sit out here alone, did you?"

Piper is holding a mug of steaming hot tea while Abi clutches a big fuzzy blanket close to her chest.

"Damn, you're not going to let me freeze to death on the porch?" I ask, as she hands me the cup. "Might be the most humane way to go at this point."

Abi drapes a blanket over me as she and Piper drag a couple more chairs over, crowding in the final few inches of dry real estate.

"We figured you might need some girl talk."

"I don't know what to say that hasn't already been said," I mutter. "It feels like he's probably ready to end things. Maybe he just can't find the balls to do it."

Piper's a little lost for words, but Abi's not ready to throw in the towel, looking absolutely determined to make a positive impact on my otherwise terrible day.

"You know, before I came to Emerald Bay, I was engaged," she says softly. "The night of my engagement party, I sent him a picture of the dress I wanted to wear. The text bounced back as undeliverable. I tried again, and the same thing happened. Then, my friend tried..."

"Same thing?" Piper asks.

Abi nods, a scowl taking over her face.

"I had no way of getting a hold of him. I came home to find that he'd packed up his shit. Didn't even leave a note. He went to his mom's place a few hours away. She wouldn't talk to me either."

When I first told Logan and Abi that it had been a week since I'd heard from Roman, she was more upset than he was; much more than I expected her to be.

Now I think I get it.

"Did you ever find out why he did it?"

She shakes her head, chuckling bitterly to herself.

"As far as I know, I'm still blocked on everything. I'd like to tell you that I was the bigger person and made peace with it, but I'm still hurt and angry after two whole years— hell, it's gotta be almost three now."

"I'd burn his fucking house down," Piper mutters under her breath.

"Abi, I don't know if that story made me feel any better. I'm still upset, but now I'm mad at Roman *and* at— what was your ex's name?"

"Brendan."

"Ugh, a Brendan?" Piper gags. "God, it just gets worse!"

"I know, I know," Abi sighs, turning back to me. "The point is, I've been where you are, and it breaks my heart to see you going through the same thing."

I'm almost thankful she's been through this too. It feels like it's giving me permission to be angry, but more importantly permission to not only blame myself. Like Logan said, I can understand what Roman's going through and still want to scream at him for doing it. Yet even now, as much as I've been listening to that little voice in the back of my head telling me that this is all over, I still love him.

I need to find out what's wrong.

And I need to find a way for us to fix it.

"I just wish I knew how to get through to him," I manage to choke out.

Piper gazes at me, helpless. She's a problem solver, but even she knows this is a problem we have to solve on our own.

"He'll come around, Iggy."

"How do you know?"

"Because depression doesn't mean that we stop loving people, sometimes it just tells us that we shouldn't burden people with our shit." She pulls her chair a little closer, resting a hand on my knee. "I know you're hurting, but it's gonna be okay."

There's a quick knock on the doorframe, and Logan is leaning out with an envelope clutched in his hand.

"Sorry, I don't mean to interrupt, but this came for you, Ig."

"It's probably papers from EBU," I mutter.

"No, it's from the University of Washington."

His smile is hopeful, but I'm already anticipating the worst.

Tentatively, I get to my feet and take the envelope from him, tearing it open and gingerly pulling out the letter. Silence surrounds me as I slowly unfold it, spotting the big UW logo at the top... and then my name.

I thrust it out to Piper.

"Read it. I can't."

"Oh, uh, alright. *Dear Miss Flynn...*"

I feel like I'm going to throw up, but Piper puts her hand on my shoulder, the tone of her voice suddenly bright and excited.

"Congratulations! You've been admitted to the following program—"

I don't even hear the rest of it as Logan lets out a big whooping cheer, flinging his arms around me. I should be happy, screaming along with the rest of them, but it's all I can do to hold back the tears. I was hoping I'd have more time, but my whole life is about to change again, and I'm not ready. Not yet.

I've barely thought about school since Roman went no-contact, other than checking my application status a few times here and there. I should be thinking about all the things I have to do now: emailing my new advisor, scheduling my courses, and taking a look at this brand new admissions offer. But all these things that are critical to my future are also leading me to another city, leading me away from a chance at fixing things with him.

A solution, but not to the problem I wanted to fix the most.

It feels like the definition of bittersweet.

As all the cheers and congratulations fade further into the background, I make the decision: I need to get out of town for a few days, check out Seattle and do some apartment hunting. It might help me think a little clearer, to focus on what I can control, and to just worry about me, and not us for once.

After all, if Roman can disappear, then so can I.

CHAPTER FORTY-SEVEN

tuesday's gone

ROMAN

TWO DAYS LATER

It's been nearly two weeks of missed messages, but every time I try to compose a reply, I start coming up with excuses. Long ones. And then I sound like even more of an asshole.

Eventually, you just give up.

The anxiety, the waiting, and the fallout from all of this is making me spiral. I kept telling her to be positive, but I can barely muster the same energy for myself.

When I look in the mirror, I barely recognize the person in front of me. I don't even go on runs anymore. The most I do is take Mitzy on walks around the block a few times a day, or to the grocery store. I live in hoodies and sweatpants, and other than getting up to take a piss and eat a meal, I mostly just exist in my bed.

And I haven't even washed my pillow, because it still smells like her perfume.

I'm sinking back into the person I was just after Christa died. Sleeping all day to avoid being alone with my thoughts. Dejected. Unmotivated.

Depression turns into apathy when you feed it.

I've got dozens of missed texts, emails, and voicemails from Abi,

Logan, Frankie, and even the Dean. Every time I get a notification, I want to throw my phone in the trash, but I have to check them at least once in a while. Sooner or later the axe has to fall.

> **Roman,**
> **Your disciplinary hearing is on January 15, 2024 in conference room B. You'll be subject to a question and answer period, at which time, you'll be divulging the exact nature of the relationship between you and Ms. Imogen Flynn. Please take the time to review the following materials in order to prepare.**

I'm used to most of Frankie's emails starting with, *Hey, Dickhead,* but this is so... professional. Fuck, he must hate me.

I give Mitzy's head a scratch, reading the email over again.

And again.

I have to respond within 48 hours to confirm my attendance.

I just want this to be over.

At this point, the only concrete thing I can hold onto is it's not worth keeping my job if I can't be with her. I haven't stopped scrambling for solutions, obsessively running them through my head pretty much every minute of every day, but I've been too paralyzed to pull the trigger on the one choice that may actually matter. Instead of being an active participant in my life, I'm just fucking *sitting here* letting this all break me down. I'm so goddamn tired of picking up the pieces of my broken self, only to shatter all over again.

I lean over and take a sip of my coffee, but a vigorous knock on the front door almost makes me drop the mug. Mitzy lifts her head, running off of the bed and sprinting down the hall before I can stop her. She's been my shadow for the past month, and I can't even take a piss without her pawing at the door and checking on me. So if I've learned anything, it's that she's not going to stop growling until she finds out who's come to visit.

Shutting my laptop, I climb out of bed with a sigh, making my way down the hall and giving Mitzy a little scratch behind the ears as I head to the source of the commotion.

"No bad guys today. I promise, baby girl."

I open the door, honestly a little shocked to find Abi and Logan standing in the hallway. What I'm less surprised to see are the scowls etched on their faces.

"What are you two doing here?"

Logan scoffs.

"That's all you've got? What the hell is the matter with you?"

He looks like he wants to take a swing at me, and I don't blame him.

It's been killing me that I haven't been able to text Imogen, to tell her how much I love her, tell her how much I wish I was holding her and kissing her right now.

"I... don't even know what to say."

This whole time I've been hoping to tell her about the application I filled out to a culinary school in Seattle, but haven't submitted yet. I've wanted to tell her I have a plan or a solution, to promise her that everything will be fine.

I want to, but...

"You could start by *talking* to her," Abi cuts in. "She's anxious, she's depressed, and by the sounds of it... she might be thinking you want to end things."

My heart drops into my stomach, my knees almost giving out as I take a few steps back into the apartment.

"End things?"

I definitely didn't have it together before, but suddenly my head is an absolute whirlwind of thoughts; the next thing I know it, Logan's sitting us all down on the couch. I put my head in my hands and let out a shaky breath.

I've let this go for too long. Why didn't I just say something?

"Roman, that's not all." He sighs. "She's been tentatively accepted into the University of Washington. She's starting to make plans to move to Seattle for the new year."

My throat tightens as my grief grows, threatening to swallow me up. Seattle's not that far away from Emerald Bay, sure, but maybe she's leaving to get away from me, and all the memories we've made here.

"God, don't you give a shit?" Abi exclaims, venom completely coating her words. "You need to fight for her, Roman! What the hell have you been doing for the last two weeks?! For a man in his forties, you're behaving like a fucking child."

I snap.

"What the fuck do you want me to do?!"

Normally, Abi getting upset would make me back off, but I've been swallowing so much pain and frustration over the past month that it has to go somewhere.

"I don't have any solutions for her, Abi! I have no idea what we're supposed to do!"

I can feel myself teetering on the edge between tears and rage.

"That's not the problem here, Roman." She crosses her arms over her chest. "There's nothing wrong with not having all the answers, the problem is you're doing all this alone."

Logan puts his hand on her shoulder, picking up where she left off.

"Roman, it's fine that you shut us out for a while. We all got it, we all understood that you needed your space to grieve, but..." He shakes his head, struggling to keep himself steady. "Just think back to the last few months, man. Think about how much happier you've been finally connecting with people again. I know you might think the only solution is to pull back into yourself and avoid the pain, but it's not just about you anymore; It's about Iggy too. She loves you, man, and you owe it to her to tell her–"

"Tell her what?" I ask, struggling to hold back my tears. "That I don't know what the hell's gonna happen? That every time I promised her that I could fix things I was lying? That I've just been too goddamn fucked up about it to text her back?"

"Yes," Abi replies softly. "All you need to do is talk to her."

I can feel Mitzy begin to nudge my leg as I feel the panic rush back into me.

"I will, I— I want to, just... not yet. I have to figure things out first. I'll figure out a real solution, then I can call her and we can—"

Before I can even process what's happening I'm weeping, Logan and Abi wrapping their arms around me as I'm forced to confront reality: It wasn't the school. It wasn't getting caught. I screwed this all up by doing the one thing I told myself I'd never do again. By isolating.

By shutting down.

I promised her that nothing would change if people found out.

I promised that I would love her just as hard and just as much.

She deserves better than a man who can't even text her back.

"I love her so fucking much," I sob.

I think about losing my dad five years ago, losing Christa... I've taken hit after fucking hit, but I can't take much more.

"Roman, this isn't over, but you really have to talk to her," Abi murmurs.

Mitzy headbutts my shin, whining at me with worry.

I reach out to pet her and she puts a paw on my thigh.

"I think— I think I'm gonna quit."

There's a beat of pure silence as we all let my words wash over us, and Logan's the first to break.

"You're serious?"

I nod, closing my eyes and letting the tears flow freely down my cheeks.

"I can't take my job back and just pretend like nothing happened, but it's more than that." I breathe slowly, in and out. "Without her, there's really nothing left for me there."

"Okay, but... what are you gonna do? For a job, I mean."

Logan's voice is pinched with doubt.

"I've had a lot of time to think lately, and... I really haven't been happy at EBU for a long time. I think I need to step back and figure out a new direction." I chuckle, gesturing to the bedroom where my laptop sits open on the bed. "I even filled out an application to a culinary school. Maybe I'll do that for a while and see where it takes me."

He doesn't look the least bit surprised. In fact, he looks relieved.

"Maybe you can open a restaurant."

"Yeah," I laugh. "Maybe I will."

I run my hand through my hair, letting out a long, shaky breath. It feels good to be open and honest for a change. With them and with myself.

"But you guys are right. First, I owe her an apology for cutting off contact, and I owe you one, too. I'm sorry that I shut myself off for so long, and I'm sorry I was a shitty friend, even after all the two of you have done for me."

Logan opens his mouth, struggling with his words for a moment before forcing them out.

"I... I love you, man."

I sigh, letting everything we've all said slowly sink in.

"I love you too."

It's a sentiment that's always sat unspoken between us, shared silently in gestures and laughter, and it feels freeing to finally have it said out loud.

"When I met Imogen it was like everything suddenly opened up to me after being locked away for so long, like the weight of grief was finally lifted off of my shoulders, even if just a little bit. I felt like I could figure out what it meant to be me again."

I still remember the way she looked at me when she told me she loved me, like she was handing me her heart, trusting me not to break it.

"I spent so much time thinking I could never find even the smallest spark again, but she showed up like a fucking firework."

"Then you should fight for her," Abi whispers, nudging me with her elbow.

She's right.

Of course she's right.

I know exactly what I have to do.

"I'm turning in my resignation first thing tomorrow, and then I'll explain everything to Imogen, face to face."

I can feel my heart drop as I watch the two of them wince simultaneously.

"What?"

Abi's voice is pained, like she's crushing it down in the hope it will hurt less.

"Roman, she's in Seattle for the weekend with Piper and Jay. They're helping her look for apartments."

Fuck.

Fuck! I waited too long and now it's too late.

But, no, of course it's not too late.

"Okay, it's okay, that's fine, I can figure out—"

"Never fear, Dr. Logan Flynn to the rescue!" A grin tugs at the corners of his lips. "I just so happen to have come prepared with the AirBnB address! I am her emergency contact after all."

If there was ever a time for Dr. Logan Flynn, PhD to come through in a pinch, this was it. I feel like I could kiss him.

"She likes pink roses and gummy worms, by the way. The sour kind are her favorite, so don't skimp on them."

"Pink roses and gummy worms," I chuckle. "Okay, yeah. That's something I can do."

"Alright, so how about we help you clean this place up, and then you can write that resignation letter?" Logan chuckles. "And maybe you could take a shower?"

Immediately it's like someone's flicked a light switch, and I can suddenly see exactly how bad I've let things get these last couple weeks. Empty bottles, fast food bags, candy wrappers...

"You know what?" I groan, quickly snatching up a clean shirt from the laundry hamper. "I think that might be for the best."

CHAPTER FORTY-EIGHT

ROMAN

"How many gummy worms?"

I'm standing in Sugarland Sweets getting Imogen the second half of my apology gift. I have no idea how today is going to go. I could come back to Emerald Bay with the woman I love, or drive the whole way back listening to Adele.

It's a scary thought, but at least I love Adele.

"How many do you think it takes to say sorry?" I ask with a somewhat pained expression.

"Okay, you're in the dog house. Got it," the girl laughs, pointing out a giant barrel of rainbow colored taffy. "You should probably avoid those. They hit pretty hard if someone throws them at you."

"God, it's like you read my mind."

When all is said and done, I've paid $50 for the biggest bag of candy I've ever seen, and the girl even wraps it all up with some pink ribbon. All I have to do now is turn in my resignation, then head to Seattle so that I can make things right.

Mitzy is waiting for me when I get back to the car, a bright pink bow around her neck as she sticks her head out the window. She's been a little nervous all day, probably just matching my own somewhat manic energy, and I've already gotten used to the sound of her tail excitedly thumping against the leather. Thankfully, as I round the car to the driver's seat, I can clearly see she didn't decide to ruin my day by going to town on the two dozen roses sitting up front. It's never mattered how many treats I give her, if she senses something's wrong she won't calm down until I do.

"These aren't for you," I tell her, holding up the bag of candy. "They're going in the glove box where you can't get to them."

I hop in, reaching into the back seat to give her a good scratch.

"Let's hope this goes well, huh, Mitz?"

I pull down the sun visor and take a look at myself in the mirror, just in time for her to wedge herself up between the seats and give me a big slobbering lick of encouragement. At the very least my face looks brighter and more hopeful after I shaved that depression beard. Being covered in dog drool might not be doing the most for my image, but this feels like a brand new start, however it turns out.

I start the car and head for the university, my heart immediately feeling like it's trying to climb up my throat. The resignation letter feels like it's burning a hole in my pocket, and I have no idea what I'm walking into, but at least now I know I'm making a concrete decision.

I just hope it's the right one.

I take deep breaths, keeping myself steady through winding roads until I get to the top of the mountain, looking out over Emerald Bay University for what might be the last time. I'm going to miss this place, even though I'm no longer in love with the job anymore. I had a routine, familiarity, and things to ground me— but life is about moving forward. Sometimes the things we relied on to get us through our hardest moments don't just keep us stable, they hold us back.

I have an interview set for next week with the Seattle Culinary Academy to see if I'm a good fit for the program, but more importantly, if it's a good fit for me. It feels like applying to school for the very first time, and there's an excitement to it that I haven't felt since I was in my 20s. It's a brand new industry with brand new challenges, and all I can hope is that I'm ready to meet them head on.

I get out of the car and slip the leash onto Mitzy, nuzzling her for a few heartbeats before we head out to the Sociology building. When we get inside, I breathe in the familiar scent of this place: coffee, old pastries, and stress. As I make my way to the elevator I pass by students filling up the study area, hunched over their laptops, scrolling through their phones, and napping on the couches. I can honestly say I'm going to miss seeing this every morning. No matter how right the decision is, it always hurts to walk away from something you used to love.

But I'm doing this for me.

Because I deserve to start over.

The elevator doors ding and I make my way down the hall, my bones beginning to grow heavier with each step. Instead of spiraling, I make sure to look down at my little furry companion, feeling instantly calmer as she gazes back up at me with curiosity. They say animals lower your blood pressure and I believe it. If it weren't for her by my side right now, I think I'd be a few steps away from a stroke.

I knock on Frankie's office door, lighter than I ever have before, with my heart in my throat and one of the weightiest things I've ever written in my pocket.

"Come in."

Frankie looks up at me, his eyes wide with surprise as I step inside.

"You didn't respond to the email about the hearing, and I thought..."

"I know." I motion to the chair in front of him. "Can I sit? I brought Mitz, hope that's okay."

"That's cool." I drop Mitzy's leash, and Frankie leans down as she runs to him. He scratches her behind the ear, shooting me a befuddled look. "So what's going on?"

I reach into my jacket pocket and pull out the letter, sliding it across the desk.

Frankie's head falls forward and he groans.

"Roman..."

"I have to, Frankie. That disciplinary hearing was going to put Imogen and I through the fucking wringer. You know what I'd have to tell the graduate committee when they asked me if I've ended the relationship, don't you? I'd tell 'em no, because I love that woman too much to let her go, and I'm not going to let the good things in my life pass me by anymore." I take a deep breath. "All I want is Imogen, my dog, and some goddamn peace. That's what I've been aching for since Christa died."

Frankie stares at me, but he no longer looks surprised. I think he saw this coming from a mile away.

"You're really doing this?"

"You were on my ass about finding someone? Well, I found them."

Frankie looks back down at the letter, brushing his fingertips against the sharp corners, one by one.

"The letter says everything I just said to you, except there's no cursing."

"Damn, I was hoping there'd be more, like an R-rated version," Frankie chuckles, opening it up to read it over.

I watch him for a long time as he takes in every word that's on the page. It's not the most professional resignation letter, but I thanked him for being an incredible colleague and an even better friend. I thanked him for being there for me after Christa's death, for helping me get back in the saddle after I came back from sabbatical, and exactly what that meant to me. It was surprisingly easy to write.

"Dude, I think I have to frame this."

I laugh and shrug my shoulders.

"Go nuts. It belongs to you."

"Actually, I've gotta submit something to Ian, but I'm gonna keep the original because I need proof that you've actually said nice things about me." He leans back in his chair, folding the letter back up and setting it on his desk. "So you're really walking away from all of this for your girl, huh?"

I lean back, smiling as Mitzy bumps her head against my thigh.

"I haven't really been living these last couple years, Frankie. You know that. When I met Imogen, everything changed. It was explosive, and it happened so fast— and I swear to you, this wasn't some huge orchestrated thing. But for some reason, the universe pushed us together despite all the roadblocks. Even when we tried to ignore it, and tried to fight against it, things just kept happening that would make us give in. *I* kept giving in. At first, I thought I was just weak, that I had just been alone for too long, but that's not it. Bit by bit, she was unlocking parts of me that I thought died when—"

Now that I'm finally laying the truth bare, everything else I've been holding in seems to want some air time, too.

"Look, I just realized leaving this place was always in the cards for me."

Frankie smiles, the look in his eyes confirming for certain that he knew this was coming for a while. Maybe everyone did, and I was just too stubborn to see it. I threw myself back into my work because it was all I knew; it became something that I could get lost in— so lost that it took time to find myself again.

"So, assuming I accept this very emotional and complimentary resignation letter, what's the plan?"

"Well, I have an interview at a culinary school in Seattle."

The second I say the words, his eyes light up.

"I was hoping you'd say something like that."

"I'm not sure if it'll work out, at least not right away, but I know I have to take a breather. That, and embrace as much change as I can manage."

"You know, these are all very anti-Roman ideas." He laughs. "If you weren't quitting I'd ask you to take a mandatory medical exam."

"That was the old me. I'm new and improved now."

"Knees still suck though, right?"

"Big time."

The two of us chuckle together for a moment before Frankie lets out a sigh, clasping his hands on his desk.

"For what it's worth, I think you're doing a brave thing. I'm looking forward to shooting pool and singing karaoke with this new Roman."

"I may be new and improved, but not enough for karaoke."

"Keep telling yourself that, pal. We'll get you onstage one day."

My chin trembles and I swallow to keep myself from bursting into tears. I didn't have siblings growing up, so Frankie and Logan have pretty much been like the brothers I never had.

"I really want to be a better man, Frankie, and I think this is the first big step in that direction."

"I'm happy for you, dude. If anyone deserves a fresh start, it's you."

Relief sinks into my bones, finally allowing me a bit of calm for the first time since I started writing that letter. It's quiet and gentle. It's what I've been looking for for a goddamn year.

And I know I made the right choice.

"Well, this has been an altogether pleasant HR experience. You're really working for your salary these days."

"Yeah, and it's all your fault, dickhead."

"Hey, there he is. There's the man I love."

Life won't be the same without the two of us sniping at each other, but I welcome the change of pace. Best of all, I can finally delete the school's email app on my phone.

Frankie stands and walks me to the door, pulling me in for a hug as Mitzy dances around us.

"End of an era," he mutters, squeezing me tight.

"Yeah," I manage to choke out. "But it was a good run while it lasted."

CHAPTER FORTY-NINE

IMOGEN

SEATTLE, WASHINGTON

I'm standing in the middle of an empty apartment overlooking the water. It's got floor to ceiling windows, beautiful hardwood, and brand new appliances. Practically perfect.

"So?" The landlord asks, her voice throaty like she spends all her free time trying to break cigarette-smoking records. "You want an application?"

It really is a stunning little apartment, but my mind has been elsewhere this entire trip. Seattle hasn't been as much of a reprieve from Emerald Bay as I had hoped, with the similar look to the neighborhoods and everything; it all reminds me of Roman.

I even had to hold back tears when we passed by a western-themed diner on the drive over here.

"Uh, sure. Can I take it home? I'm on a bit of a tight schedule."

"Go nuts."

She pulls a piece of paper out of the big binder she's carrying, and I thank her one last time before heading down to the lobby where Piper and Jay are waiting for me.

"So? Was it a winner?" Jay asks hopefully.

We've been looking all weekend and I know they're both getting tired.

"Yeah, if paying three grand a month counts as winning," I grumble as the next applicant gets ushered upstairs. "Not really in my price-range."

His shoulders slump a little, but he nods empathetically.

"That's criminal," Piper mutters, getting to her feet. "I think I saw a couple more places with vacancy signs out front if you want to keep looking."

My stomach growls for what has to be the fifth time in an hour, and I just know I can't put it off any longer.

"Nah. It's time to grab some food."

"Oh, good idea!" Jay chimes in. "These viewings should have a little cheese board or something to welcome you, you know? People get snacky apartment hunting."

"Do you really want to touch cheese that's been manhandled by other people?" Piper asks.

Jay rolls his eyes and I can't help but chuckle as we get into the car. He spends a couple of minutes scrolling on his phone before suggesting a little sushi place that's not far from where we've been staying.

I'm already daydreaming about what I'm going to order when my phone buzzes.

> ROMAN: You planning on coming back to your AirBnB any time soon, darlin'? Or have I lost you to the big city forever?

"Uh... holy shit."

"What is it?" Piper asks.

"It's Roman."

I have to read the message a few times over to fully process it, scanning each word for some secret hidden meaning that isn't there.

"Are we still mad at him?" Jay asks, a hint of caution in his voice, mixed with his patented excitement.

"God, I don't know anymore."

The words on the screen almost don't seem real, and more importantly there's a big part of me that's still angry with him for not trying to contact me sooner. I've spent two weeks agonizing over the fucking punctuation marks in every message I sent, wondering what I did that pushed him away; I've let his absence take up every little bit of free space in my head, and now he just pops back into my life with a text? What the hell am I supposed to do with this?

> IMOGEN: Wow. Would have been nice to hear from you earlier.

> ROMAN: I know. I've got a lot of groveling to do, if you'll let me.

"Jay, can you drive us back to the house?"

I want to know what he has to say for himself. I want to know if it's an excuse, or a genuine apology.

"You got it!"

Jay steps on the gas, weaving skillfully through traffic as Piper turns around in her seat.

"What are you gonna say to him?"

"I don't really know."

The rest of the ride is pretty much silent, with me typing out everything I want to say to Roman before deleting it over and over, all while trying not to throw up on the rental's faux-leather seats. I was really starting to think this was over, that he had decided to move on without me.

As Jay turns down the street to our place, I spot Roman leaned up against his car, in his fucking cowboy hat. I feel sick and excited and angry all at once.

"Goddamn, look at Dr. Burke!" Piper exclaims.

The worst part is I look like shit in comparison.

I smile despite my nervousness as Roman carefully places a bouquet of pink roses on the hood of his car, fiddling with the zipper on his jacket and watching intently as we pull into the driveway.

He's just as scared as I am.

I'm frozen in my seat as Jay parks the car, staring at Roman walking up the driveway with the roses in his hands. He's even got Mitzy beside him, dressed up with a little pink bow around her neck.

He really went all-out.

I don't know what to do or what to say, and my emotions keep flipping between extremes. One second I'm elated, and the next my anger begins to overpower me. Two fucking weeks. He couldn't text me back for two weeks, and the whole time I thought he was just content to let our relationship die.

But now he's here, like this.

Piper turns to me, her hand resting on the door.

"Iggy, are you okay?"

That's when I realize I'm shaking, and it's been getting progressively harder to breathe. I dig for my inhaler in my purse, taking two deep puffs as Roman stops just short of the car.

"I think so, I am now at least."

Piper climbs out, opening my own door for me and helping me to my feet. She puts her hands on my shoulders and I'm immediately drawn into the warmth of her gaze.

"Do you need me to be here while you guys talk?"

I shake my head, tears slipping down my face, but she wipes them away and flashes me an encouraging smile.

"I'm a phone call away, okay? I promise."

"Thanks, Pipes."

I hadn't even realized that I'd started to cry.

Piper hugs me tight before heading to the house with Jay, each of them briefly acknowledging Roman as they pass. It's only another moment or two before he steps toward me, the roses clutched tightly in his fist.

"Those are for me?"

"They are," he murmurs.

My head is swimming and I'm finding it hard to focus on... well, anything.

"I'm fucking pissed at you."

"I got lost, darlin', felt helpless and didn't know what I should do. I could have done better, should have done better, and I'm sorry."

The flowers in his hands are shaking as badly as I am.

"I handed in my resignation. Wasn't going to sit in a conference room with a bunch of suits and answer questions about us. Didn't seem like there'd be a point, because for every question they'd ask, you know what I'd have to tell them?"

I shake my head.

"I'd tell them that you're my future, I'd tell you're everything to me and that I was a fool for not seeing it earlier. I'd tell them that every time we're in the same room, the only person I find myself looking at is you. I love you so much it brings me to my fucking knees, and I'm going to spend every single day going forward proving that to you. If you'll let me."

I spent two weeks terrified that I'd be left to pick up the shards of my broken heart. I was so terrified that we'd have to start over, that we'd just up and vanish from each other's lives, but even though I'm still pissed at him, there's a part of me that understands. I've been too afraid to reach out in the past, left texts unanswered only to crawl back to them weeks later and suddenly realize the impact it might have had. You just don't see what you're doing in the moment. You're always too numb.

I step toward him and take the flowers from his still-shaking hands, holding them to my chest.

"You really mean that?"

"Every word." He lets out a deep, trembling breath before gesturing awkwardly at the car. "I thought we could go for a drive? Unless you want to talk here."

I look back at Piper and Jay, dutifully watching us from the front steps. The thought of having this conversation with my friends within shouting distance fills me with an even more anxious dread than was already there.

"Sure. Let's go."

Mitzy pants softly beside us and Roman smiles, glancing back to Piper and Jay.

"You guys like dogs?"

"Love 'em!" Jay calls back. "Need us to babysit?"

Piper crouches down, her hands on her knees.

"Come on, pretty girl!" She coos. "I saw a tennis ball with your name on it!"

Roman takes my hand and leads me down the driveway toward his car while Jay and Piper coax Mitzy inside the house.

"Where are we going?"

"There's a little park nearby," he tells me, sliding into the front seat. "I figured we could sit and talk. I owe you a lot more than flowers and some gummy worms."

"Gummy worms?"

"Logan said they were your favorite. Check the glove box."

Of course my brother had a hand in this.

I round the car and plop myself down into my seat, finding a bag of candy the size of my head exactly where he said it'd be.

"Jesus, Roman! This has gotta be like a month's supply!"

"Yeah, and it's not nearly enough," he mutters, starting up the car. "You ready?"

I nod, buckling my seatbelt as the engine rumbles to life and his dad rock immediately starts blaring through the speakers.

"Sorry," he chuckles, turning it all the way down.

I hold back a smile as he starts to drive, heading away from the majority of traffic and down some narrow roads. The trip is short, but even then it feels like it only took a moment or two for each of us to lose any of the nerve we'd built up, falling silent as that familiar awkwardness of the past few weeks begins to claw its way back in. Luckily the location Roman's picked is gorgeous enough to snap anyone out of their funk.

I gaze out at the secluded little area at the edge of a sunlit-lake. It's a picturesque sight, right out of a painting, with a few boats out on the water even in spite of the chill that lingers in the air.

"Imogen, I owe you a huge apology. It was wrong of me to shut you out, and there isn't a single excuse I could give you that'll make up for what I've done. But when your brother told me you thought things were over between us, I realized how much I let everything spiral out of control. I never wanted this to be over."

His eyes are wet with trepidation, and he's struggling to keep control of his voice the whole time he talks; I'm not doing much better. My anger flared a couple times, but it quickly began to dampen when I got to hear him take responsibility. For a while I was wondering if I was going crazy, and this simple validation is a massive relief.

"Roman, I didn't know if you were okay, or if *we* were okay. You said nothing would change, even after we got caught, and then you froze me out, and that fucking hurt. If we're going to be together, we need to be able to communicate. No falling off the radar when things get hard, no leaving the other person in the dark."

It feels strange to finally be saying everything that's been filling up my notes app for the past month.

"I'm willing to do whatever it takes to make things right, darlin'."

I take a moment to stare out at the water, letting everything sink in. He drove all the way here for me when he could have just as easily let me slip through his fingers. He clearly does care about us, enough to fight for what we had when it counts, it just took him some time to get there.

"Wait, so then what have you been doing for the past two weeks?"

"Sleeping," he replies, a little sheepishly. "I was so depressed, it was the only thing I could do to get through each day. When I finally made the decision to quit, it was like the fog disappeared and everything became a lot clearer."

"Was Frankie mad? When you told him, I mean."

The last thing I'd want this to do is ruin some of his friendships, just when he had started building them back up again.

"Nah, he took it well. Told me it looked like I hadn't had passion for the work in a long time, and he's right. I threw myself into my research after Christa died, looking for some kind of answer, but it was more distraction than passion. I felt like there was a chance I could find the reason why she took her life, that someone out there had cracked the code, and it would all make sense to me." He swallows, doing his best to stay calm. "So it wasn't about the work anymore, it was only about me. The past month gave me a lot of time to think about what really matters, and I know that's you, without a shadow of a doubt."

I press my forehead against his, holding myself together through shuddering breaths. This whole time I've been looking for some kind of peace, but only finding anguish in a torturous kind of anticipation.

Now, everything I've been hoping for is right here in front of me.

"I want you too, all of you."

Roman captures my lips, and I almost burst into tears when I realize just how much I've missed this.

Missed him.

Missed us.

"So please don't go," he rasps as he pulls away, an old fear present in his eyes.

"What?"

The words stun me for a moment, and I'm not quite sure what to say.

"Don't move to Seattle."

"Roman, I'm going to school here. My life is—"

"I know, I know, but— look, I've thought this all out. I could drive you, and I could pick you up, and—"

"Every day?" I chuckle.

"Why not? I applied to a culinary school here. If I get in, I'll be making the same commute. And even if I don't, who's to say I couldn't make the time?"

"Hmm... carpooling together? That's quite the commitment," I tease. "Next you'll be asking me to move in with you."

Roman's cheeks grow redder as he bites down on his lip, and I know he's about to say something equally terrifying for the both of us.

"That part's all up to you," he breathes. "Offer's on the table. I'd never force you into anything, just... Please don't leave Emerald Bay, darlin'."

It's not like I want to, that place was just starting to feel like home after all.

"To tell you the truth, I wasn't really wowed by anything we saw out here. Except maybe this view you found."

Roman takes my lead and runs with it, not wasting a single second.

"We could rent a house by the bay, with a view just like this. You can have an office, and I can have an even bigger kitchen. We'd be close to your brother and your friends, and most importantly we'd be together. So please... Just stay."

The panicked, hopeful gleam in his eyes wrenches at my heart. I don't want to have to start all over again in a brand new city, to leave Logan behind after we've just rebuilt so much of our old relationship, but most of all I don't want to go another second without this man in my life.

I stroke his cheek, watching the light off the water glisten in his eyes.

"Alright."

I can feel a massive weight fall off me the second the words begin to leave my lips, and in that moment I know there couldn't possibly be another answer.

"I'll stay."

CHAPTER FIFTY

end of beginning

IMOGEN

EMERALD BAY, WASHINGTON
FEBRUARY

I groan and stretch myself out, waking to the sound of rain pattering against the window, and lift my head to look around a still-unfamiliar bedroom, packed with boxes. Roman and I moved into a cute little rancher by the bay yesterday, and my body still aches after lugging everything from the moving van into the house. Thankfully, it wasn't just the two of us; Logan, Frankie, and Jay helped move furniture while Piper and Abi made sure that each box was labeled and went into the right places.

The house has two bedrooms and one and a half bathrooms, and we even have a porch and a hammock where I can read and write papers in the sunshine. It's admittedly a bit of a downgrade from Logan's ridiculous mini-mansion, but it's a big step up from my apartment back in New York. Even Mitzy's got a backyard and more space to nap in.

I roll over to find the dog fast asleep on Roman's pillow, a soft snore emanating from her muscular little body, and I stifle a giggle, grabbing my phone and snapping a quick picture. She's exhausted after we took her down to the bay last night to play fetch.

"You're so cute."

That's when the smell of fresh coffee hits me, truly waking me up. I can hear music playing in the kitchen, creeping its way into the hallway, only slightly muffled by the door.

Roman and his dad rock.

As much as I want to stay in bed, the urge to get to work on the new house overwhelms me. I pad into the kitchen, carefully weaving around boxes before finding him at the stove, dressed in a white tank top and a pair of sweats while flipping pancakes. I lean against the doorframe for a second, watching him as he bops around to the music blasting from his phone.

"Morning, cowboy."

He abandons his spatula, immediately turning around with a big grin.

"Morning, darlin'. How'd you sleep?"

"Really fucking good," I laugh. "And I'm ready to get this place cleaned up for the party."

"Oh! That reminds me!" Roman waves me over to a notebook he has laid out on the counter. "I planned a whole menu for tonight. Roasted duck, potatoes, brussels sprouts— would you believe it, I didn't know it was *brussels* until I Googled it?"

"I've been up for 6 minutes and already learned something new. You've still got it, professor."

He smirks and flips the page.

"And for dessert... your dad's cheesecake."

Roman's been working his ass off in culinary school. Late nights, early mornings, and he's bone tired when he comes home. But everyone says they've never seen him this full of life before. Logan even gave him a couple of my dad's recipes to try out for the party.

On my end, I took a few days off from my course work so that we could finish the move and celebrate. I'm thriving at UW, and I'm even working on my second publication for a journal. Finally, it feels like everything's worked out the way it's supposed to.

"You wanna unpack after breakfast?" He asks.

"Yeah, and I can watch you swear while you put furniture together," I giggle, rubbing my nose against his.

Roman wraps his arms around me, kissing my forehead. He's been a big help, still using all of that knowledge of theory and practice to let me bounce academic ideas off him.

When we have weekends off, we've been going to kink clubs and trying *everything*. Roman's ended up being a natural dom, perfectly balancing his intrinsic thoughtfulness with power and degradation. And the best part is, he's more than happy to switch it up even halfway through a scene.

"I have something for you," he murmurs, stepping back and reaching into his pocket.

"What is it?"

He opens his hand to reveal a small silver claddagh ring nestled in the middle of his palm. My jaw hits the floor, and he smiles at my reaction.

"I found this in a little vintage shop in Seattle and thought it would be perfect." He swallows, still a little nervous. "Now, this isn't an engagement ring, but it *is* a promise... that when we're both ready, I want us to spend the rest of our lives together."

"You know, that actually *does* sound a lot like a proposal."

He grins, giving me a little shrug.

"Maybe it's a microscopic proposal. You make me feel like I'm home no matter where I am, Imogen, and I want that to be clear every single day."

I laugh, covering my mouth with one hand as tears start to stream down my face.

"So? Will you marry me? Sooner or later?" He asks, taking my hand and linking his fingers with mine.

"Yes."

Roman beams as the word slips past my lips so effortlessly, sliding the ring onto my finger. It fits perfectly, and I let out something in between a laugh and a sob as I wrap my arms around him.

"You're my universe, darlin'."

I sniffle, giggling as I nuzzle into his neck.

"Right back atcha, cowboy."

We opted for a small party with the people closest to us, the people we've chosen as our little family here in Emerald Bay. Maybe that's why our housewarming party went from extremely classy to smoking weed on the porch in less than an hour.

I'm stuffed from dinner, curled up on the couch as a spectator while Logan, Roman, and Frankie play Twister on the floor. Mitzy's been sniffing around them the entire time, taking the opportunity to get a lick every few minutes.

"Hey, dog interference!" Logan laughs as she slobbers up his bare arm. "Why are you doing this to me, don't you want me to win?!"

"I think it's the gravy you spilled all over yourself at dinner," Roman teases.

"Okay, everyone shut up! Left foot green, Logan, and watch the knees!"

Abi's shouting instructions from the safety of her seat as my brother twists himself up like a pretzel, trying to reach the circle. Notably, with his *right* foot.

"Wrong foot, Logan, god you're useless!" Frankie shouts from his own position on the mat.

Abi snorts, rolling her eyes at the display.

"A whole PhD and he doesn't know right from left."

"Hey, when you're in the trenches, you can offer critique!" Logan barks, his beer almost tipping over in his hand. "Until then, I really don't want to hear from the audience, okay?"

Piper smacks the ground in frustration in a somewhat futile attempt to referee the chaos.

"Hey, Logan, get your foot back on that circle!"

She's crouched down next to the mat, glass of wine in hand as she watches with intensity. She made the call very early on that it'd be her job to make sure nobody cheats, and she's been taking it very seriously.

"God, why is everyone teaming up against me?" Logan whines.

He lets out a grunt of effort, finally managing to contort himself into the correct position, his ass ending up right next to Frankie's face.

"Dude, if you fart on me, I swear to god I'll fire you."

"I made sure to have *extra* brussels sprouts at dinner," Logan warns. "And, you know what? I think I can feel a pretty good one coming..."

"Don't you dare!" Frankie roars.

Abi and I howl with laughter from the sidelines as Roman collapses onto the mat, tears streaming down his face.

"Eliminated by a fart joke, Burke? You're a fuckin' amateur!" Frankie bellows.

Roman is bright red, crawling toward me with his beer somehow still in hand.

"You did pretty well for yourself."

"Yeah, tell that to my back tomorrow morning," he grumbles, plopping himself down next to me.

"I'm sure I could give you a little spinal adjustment," I purr, leaning over to nip at his earlobe.

"Hey! PDA! There are children present!"

Frankie's pointing straight at Mitzy, his face deadly serious until Piper chimes in.

"Frankie Hughs, you get your hand back on that circle or I swear to god!"

"I got ten that Frankie's gonna lose," Roman announces, slapping a bill down on our little coffee table.

"Don't make me put you in a home!" Frankie barks. "I'm the sure-thing to win this and you all know it!"

Abi cackles, spinning the little wheel with a flick of her finger.

"Left foot, blue!"

Logan and Frankie look around in a panic. There's only one blue circle close by, and they both go for it at the same time, each trying to kick the other out of the way.

"I was here first!" Logan shouts.

"No, you weren't!"

Suddenly, the door opens and Jay steps outside, hunched over as pot smoke billows behind him. He's holding his phone up, aiming it squarely at Frankie and Logan.

"Two nerds, one heated competition..." He announces, creeping toward them like a ghoul. "And there can only be one victor."

"Get that camera out of my face!" Logan shouts.

Frankie takes the moment to give Logan a shove, knocking him onto his side and quickly jumping to his feet in celebration.

"Yes! Twister champ of 2025! Right here, baby!"

"Boo!" Roman bellows. "Boo! Cheater!"

Frankie ignores him, making a big show out of kissing his biceps. "So, what do I win?"

"You win the right to clean up the game and pick the next one," Abi says with a smirk.

"What?" Frankie groans. "This sucks. I was hoping for money."

"Sometimes it sucks to win!" Jay shouts.

"Yeah, yeah." Frankie waves him off. "Make yourself useful and go get me some more board games. Take Logan with you, he knows all the good ones."

I look around, my chest warm as Roman wraps his arm around me. A couple of months ago, it felt like the world was ending and now we're here, in *our house* playing board games with our friends.

"You know what? I think this is the first party I've thrown in years," Roman chuckles.

"Yeah, I don't think I've ever seen you laugh this much," Frankie replies, looking around the backyard as he boxes up the Twister mat. "The place looks great, by the way."

"The decor is all Imogen's handiwork," Roman replies, nudging me gently with his elbow.

"And how's UW treating you? I don't have to crack any skulls, do I?"

"No, it's good," I reply. "Really good. I'm actually submitting a paper for publication next week."

It was awkward for Frankie and I to get over that one big hurdle at the beginning. He never really got to know me, and then suddenly he had to crack down hard on the both of us after we got caught. I think he was probably worried that I'd hold a grudge, but it just didn't work out like that. I see him pretty much every weekend now, either at the Hi-Dive or at my brother's for Sunday dinner, and I wouldn't have it any other way.

"That's great. I'm really happy for you." He smiles. "Both of you."

Logan and Jay emerge from the house, arms stacked full of games. As the conversation shifts into what we're going to play next, I spot Mitzy pawing at the back gate, and turn to Piper, tapping her arm.

"Time to take the dog for a stroll, you wanna come?"

"Sure! Maybe it'll help me digest all of this damn food."

I help her to her feet, grabbing the leash that's hanging near the back door.

"Mitzy's restless, I'm just gonna take her for a stroll."

"Don't be too long!" Roman calls, as I clip Mitzy's leash to her collar. "Or I'll have to get Frankie to bust out Trivial Pursuit to kill the time!"

We head out the back gate, wandering down a small path that leads right to the bay. The air is crisp and cool, and I smile at the sound of the water lapping against the shore. It was the selling point for me when Roman and I were first looking for houses.

"God, this is nice," Piper murmurs. "You guys sure picked a great spot."

I let Mitzy off her leash so she can roll in the grass, the stars twinkling above us adding even more to the atmosphere.

"Your dad would be proud of you, you know." Piper wraps an arm around me, hugging me tight. "You've made a beautiful life for yourself, Iggy."

I've never really believed in an afterlife. I always thought that the life we were given is the real gift, and what we create here and now is what matters.

"I miss him," I whisper, a tear trickling down my cheek.

She squeezes me tighter, and I rest my head on her shoulder as I take in the glittering stars and the smell of incoming rain.

"I think he would have loved it here."

Dealing with loss is a never ending process, and in some ways, it will always be a shadow in our lives. I've learned that the trick is to give it space to transform into something beautiful.

I've made peace with the fact that my dad will never walk me down the aisle, that he'll never hold his grandchildren. But he'll be here, in stardust and atoms, and in the stories that we tell about him. The people we've loved and lost become faded memories to some, but it's up to us to carry their torch.

This is the life I've always wanted to build for myself, and now that it's right in front of me, I'm not letting it slip through my fingers.

THE END

thank you

This book would not be possible without the help and support of so many people.

My husband. He's supported me through so much, helped me edit, figure out plot points, and generally just been a fucking gem. I love you so much, I love creating things with you, and thank you for making me a better writer.

My beta and alpha readers. Aubrey, Lindsay, Aly, Tiffani, Cassandra, Becs, and Jordyn. Thank you all so much for helping shape this story and for all of your support. You were the first people to read about these characters and saw very different drafts. I love you all and appreciate you so much!

My street team. Thank you for being such amazing hype people and helping me promote this book! I couldn't have done this without you.

My ARC readers. I am forever grateful to you for taking a chance on an indie author! You're fucking awesome!

My parents. No matter what I do, no matter where I go, you have always had my back. You never told me that anything was out of reach or that I couldn't do something. I know that had so much impact on the trajectory of my life. I take risks because you made it safe for me to fail and fall down. I continue to take risks because you've both taught me that life is too short not to do the things that make us happy. I love you both to the moon and back.

Ladner, British Columbia. Ladner was where I realized I wanted to be an artist. I spent a lot of late nights sitting by the Fraser River, writing and dreaming of the future. I never thought in a million years that I'd be basing a whole book series on the town I grew up in.

about the author

Thea Lawrence is a Canadian indie romance author who has been writing since she was sixteen. She started out writing Lord of the Rings fan fiction in the back of her French class and that blossomed into a lifelong passion for storytelling.

After spending nearly a decade in academia, including getting a master's degree in criminology and making it all the way to PhD candidacy, she decided to shift gears and focus on romance novels. Thea loves to write romance stories with heart, grit, darkness, and a lot of spice.

Thea's hobbies include: Criminal Minds marathons, lifting weights, drinking coffee like it's going to pay the bills, napping, and watching cult documentaries with her partner.

She currently lives in Ottawa, Ontario with her partner and editor, Ben Browning.

You can find Thea on Instagram and Threads: @thealawrenceauthor

On TikTok: @thealawrenceauthor and @thealawrencebooks

On her website: thealawrenceromanceauthor.com

You can also sign up for Thea's monthly newsletter (signup is available on her website!) featuring sneak peeks at future books, advanced links to pre-orders, deleted scenes from previously published works, life updates, author spotlights, and more:

upcoming works in the emerald bay series

BY THEA LAWRENCE

Crushing It: Emerald Bay Book II
Untitled Marriage of Convenience: Emerald Bay Book III
Untitled Rivals to Lovers: Emerald Bay Book IV

Made in United States
Troutdale, OR
04/03/2025

30314842R00217